# Richard Wright's *Native Son*

Richard Wright's *Native Son* (1940) is one of the most violent and revolutionary works in the American canon. Controversial and compelling, its account of crime and racism remains the source of profound disagreement both within African-American culture and throughout the world.

This guide to Wright's provocative novel offers:

- an accessible introduction to the text and contexts of *Native Son*;
- a critical history, surveying the many interpretations of the text from publication to the present;
- a selection of reprinted critical essays on *Native Son*, by James Baldwin, Hazel Rowley, Anthony Dawahare, Clare Eby and James Smethurst, providing a range of perspectives on the novel and extending the coverage of key critical approaches identified in the survey section;
- a chronology to help place the novel in its historical context;
- suggestions for further reading.

Part of the *Routledge Guides to Literature* series, this volume is essential reading for all those beginning detailed study of *Native Son* and seeking not only a guide to the novel, but also a way through the wealth of contextual and critical material that surrounds Wright's text.

**Andrew Warnes** is a lecturer in American literature at the University of Leeds.

# Routledge Guides to Literature*

**Editorial Advisory Board:** Richard Bradford (University of Ulster at Coleraine), Shirley Chew (University of Leeds), Mick Gidley (University of Leeds), Jan Jedrzejewski (University of Ulster at Coleraine), Ed Larrissy (University of Leeds), Duncan Wu (St. Catherine's College, University of Oxford)

**Routledge Guides to Literature** offer clear introductions to the most widely studied authors and texts. Each book engages with texts, contexts and criticism, highlighting the range of critical views and contextual factors that need to be taken into consideration in advanced studies of literary works. The series encourages informed but independent readings of texts by ranging as widely as possible across the contextual and critical issues relevant to the works examined, rather than presenting a single interpretation. Alongside general guides to texts and authors, the series includes 'Sourcebooks', which allow access to reprinted contextual and critical materials as well as annotated extracts of primary text.

**Already available:***

* Some titles in this series were first published in the Routledge Literary Sourcebooks series, edited by Duncan Wu, or the Complete Critical Guide to Literature series, edited by Jan Jedrzejewski and Richard Bradford.

# Richard Wright's
# *Native Son*

*Andrew Warnes*

## Routledge
Taylor & Francis Group

LONDON AND NEW YORK

First published 2007
by Routledge
2 Park Square, Milton Park, Abingdon, Oxon OX14 4RN

Simultaneously published in the USA and Canada
by Routledge
270 Madison Ave, New York, NY 10016

*Routledge is an imprint of the Taylor & Francis Group, an informa business*

Typeset in Sabon and Gill Sans by RefineCatch Limited, Bungay, Suffolk
Printed and bound in Great Britain by
MPG Books Ltd, Bodmin, Cornwall

*British Library Cataloguing in Publication Data*
A catalogue record for this book is available from the British Library.

*Library of Congress Cataloging in Publication Data*
Warnes, Andrew, 1974–
    Richard Wright's Native son / by Andrew Warnes.
       p. cm—(Routledge guides to literature)
    Includes index.
    1. Wright, Richard, 1908–1960. Native son.   2. Thomas, Bigger (Fictitious character).
3. African American men in literature.   4. Trials (Murder) in literature.   5. Murder in
literature.   I. Title.
    PS3545.R815N346 2006
    813'.52—dc22

                                                                   2006018932

ISBN 10: 0–415–34447–6 (hbk)
ISBN 10: 0–415–34448–4 (pbk)
ISBN 10: 0–203–49584–5 (ebk)

ISBN 13: 978–0–415–34447–0 (hbk)
ISBN 13: 978–0–415–34448–7 (pbk)
ISBN 13: 978–0–203–49584–1 (ebk)

# Contents

# 4: Further reading and Web resources        146

# Illustrations

## A note on the images

As part of President Franklin Delano Roosevelt's attempts to end the Depression and boost the American economy, numerous governmental agencies were established during the 1930s. Some of these gave employment to artists: in particular, the Federal Arts Project, a subsection of the Works Progress Administration (WPA), offered opportunities to the writers, poets, photographers and artists who had been struggling through that hard and fractious decade. Wright himself worked for the Federal Theater Project in the mid-1930s, but the WPA is probably more closely associated with the photographers it attracted: Walker Evans, Dorothea Lange, Gordon Parks, Marion Post Wolcott, Edwin Rosskam. Scattered through this critical guide are images that the last three of these five photographers shot of landscapes that Wright knew well. From scenes of the rural poverty of the Deep South to images from the Chicago ghetto from which Wright sought escape, these images hopefully help evoke the world inhabited by the author and the book *Native Son* itself. More such images can be viewed at the impressive web site of the Library of Congress, <http://memory.loc.gov/ammem>.

# Acknowledgements

Years ago, and long before I stumbled across her fascinating work on Wright, Claudia Tate set me on my present path. At George Washington University in 1993, my fellow English exchange students and I were distracted from the city and the pleasure of regular sunshine by the African-American Autobiographies module that we had casually chosen and the new worlds that it was placing before our eyes. Introducing us to Wright's coolly outraged *Black Boy (American Hunger)*, to Zora Neale Hurston's puzzling *Dust Tracks on a Road*, to Claude Brown's ghetto documentary *Manchild in the Promised Land*, and to Audre Lorde's evocative masterpiece *Zami: A New Spelling of My Name*, Professor Tate amply demonstrated that (contrary to the impression certain teachers had given me back home) none of these texts were aberrations, unlikely exceptions to the blight of slavery and its dreadful aftermath. She made it clear that these works instead belonged (but of course!) to a formidable cultural tradition – a tradition that flourished precisely because it was able to resist such racist philosophy.

I am ashamed to admit how long it took me to realize the connection between Tate's great module and my subsequent decision to write a undergraduate dissertation on *Black Boy*, an MA dissertation on Zora Neale Hurston, and *Hunger Overcome?*, my first book. Realizing just recently, though, I drafted a long-belated e-mail of thanks to her before embarking on the familiar process of surfing the Internet for her address. It was then that I came across an old and frozen bulletin reporting the news of her death. By way of inadequate thanks for an e-mail that never got sent, I would, then, like to dedicate this book to her and her important scholarly work.

For their support and friendship, I am indebted to the following: Bridget Bennett, Bob Bliss, Denis Flannery, Richard Godden, Derek Krissoff, John McLeod, Caryl Phillips, Jay Prosser, Doris Witt and my great friend Pam Rhodes. As well as producing great scholarship, the academic contributors to this work earn my heartfelt gratitude for their help, support and, above all, patience throughout this book's long germination. In addition, Polly Dodson at Routledge made useful recommendations to the manuscript, while Mick Gidley provided a typically attentive and insightful response to it. Finally, I want to thank my family (Sue, Mum, Dad, everyone) for being patient and so much else, and my students, too, for keeping things fresh. I hope this helps.

The following publishers, institutions and individuals have kindly given permission to reprint materials.

Extracts from *Native Son* by Richard Wright published by Jonathan Cape. Used by Permission of The Random House Group Limited.

Extracts from *Native Son* by Richard Wright. Copyright © 1940 by Richard Wright, renewed 1968 by Ellen Wright. Reprinted by Permission of Harper Collins Publishers Inc.

*Notes of a Native Son* by James Baldwin. Copyright © 1955, renewed 1983 by James Baldwin. Reprinted by permission of Beacon Press, Boston, Mass.

Hazel Rowley, 'The Shadow of the White Woman: Richard Wright and the Book-of-the-Month Club', Partisan Review 66:4 (1999) 625–34. From the Howard Gotlieb Archival Research Center at Boston University.

Anthony Dawahare, 'From No Man's Land to Mother-Land: Emasculation and Nationalism in Richard Wright's Depression Era Urban Novels', *African-American Review* 33:3 (fall 1999), 451–66.

Clare Eby, 'Slouching Towards Beastliness', *African-American Review* 35:3 (fall 2001), 439–58.

James Smethurst, 'Invented by Horror: The Gothic and African-American Literary Ideology in *Native Son*', *African-American Review* 35:1 (spring 2001), 29–40.

Illustrations courtesy of Library of Congress, Prints & Photographs Division, FSA-OWI Collection, [reproduction numbers: LC-USF33–005184-M4; LC-USF 34–50720-E; LC-USF33–005182-M2; LC-USF33- 005169-M4; LC-USF33–005168-M1; LC-USF33–005185-M1; LC-USF33–005169-M1; LC-USW3–030297-D] and poster from the WPA 1936–43 [reproduction number: LC-USZC2–1124 DLC].

Every effort has been made to trace and contact copyright holders. The publishers would be pleased to hear from any copyright holder not acknowledged here, so that this acknowledgement page can be amended at the earliest opportunity.

# Notes and references

## Primary text

Unless otherwise stated, all references to the primary text are taken from *Native Son*, Richard Wright (London: Vintage, 2000). The initial reference in each part will contain full bibliographic details and all subsequent references will be in parentheses in the body of the text, stating the chapter and page number, e.g (Flight, p. 273).

## Secondary text

References to any secondary material can be found in the footnotes. The first reference will contain full bibliographic details, and each subsequent reference to the same text will contain the author's surname, title and page number.

## Footnotes

All footnotes that are not by the author of this volume will identify the source in square brackets, e.g [Baldwin's note].

## Cross-referencing

Cross-referencing between sections is a feature of each volume in the Routledge Guides to Literature series, though in this volume, all cross-references refer to the chronology. Cross-references appear in brackets and include section titles as well as the relevant page numbers in bold type, e.g. (see Texts and contexts, pp. 00–00).

# Introduction

Let us begin this critical guide by revisiting a particular moment from *Native Son*. Let us revisit a part of the novel often overlooked: the closing pages of 'Flight', and their depiction of Bigger's experiences as a fugitive on the run.

Given that every police officer in Chicago seems to be out looking for him, Bigger spends a long time at large. Black neighbourhoods, it seems, do not want to give him up. Protected by their silence, Bigger peers out of the vacant tenement block that is his temporary home. He survives. Elsewhere in the segregated city, white newspapers roll off the press, their front pages salivating over the utter monstrosity of this perfect black criminal. None needs facts to write the story. Bigger is the rapist, the grotesque, the ' "black sonofabitch" ' who skulked into a white girl's bedroom.[1] And she, in turn, is the virgin, the damsel in distress, the innocent victim of what the headlines yell was a 'SEX CRIME' ('Flight', p. 273). But Bigger, huddled against the cold, feels guiltier about what he did to Bessie. Her condemnation of his crimes, his raping and killing of her black body, haunt his movements as he scans the street for a sign of his would-be captors. A song drifts up to reach him, floating free of a storefront church.

> Steal away, steal away, steal away to Jesus,
> Steal away, steal away home,
> I ain't got long to stay here.
>
> My Lord, He calls me,
> He calls me by the thunder,
> The trumpet sounds within-a my soul,
> I ain't got long to stay here.

It was a song first sung in slavery times, some think to urge those in chains to run away from the 'here' of the plantation and head for the 'home' of the free North. Hunted down in the city itself, Bigger is deaf to the song's appeal. Unlike the fugitives whose only crime was to 'steal themselves' from slavery, he is by any

---

1  Richard Wright, 'Flight' in *Native Son* (London: Vintage, 2000), p. 301. All subsequent references to this novel are given in the text itself.

*Figure 1* Storefront church and lunch wagon, Black Belt, Chicago, Illinois. Photograph: Edwin Rosskam, 1941.

reckoning guilty. Unlike them, this boy was made by Chicago; he has nowhere left to run. His only chance of freedom lies in making himself invisible.

Newspapers certainly see him that way. On one there appears a map that is so useful to Bigger as to reveal that the journalists who drew it cannot admit, even to themselves, that he might number among their readers. Their assumptions about race and intelligence lead them to show Bigger exactly where the police manhunt has searched and exactly where it will look next. Finding himself in the latter of these – finding himself surrounded by white paper rather than drowned in black ink – Bigger's mind races ahead. Full of fear, he gropes through the darkness to find the door leading to the roof. Desperate, he kicks it open. Overnight snowfall avalanches around his legs. Nature itself, which once sent thunderclaps to assist the runaway slave, now seems to want Bigger caught. Trapped, Bigger thinks about falling to his knees and praying. He thinks about stripping naked, rolling in the snow. He is feeble now, overcome. Even his spit is frozen. But still the police approach him as you would a wild animal: 'Two men stretched his arms out, as though about to crucify him; they placed a foot on each of his wrists, making them sink deep down in the snow. His eyes closed, slowly, and he was swallowed in darkness' ('Flight', p. 301).

Reading these passages for the first time, the Communist Party members who had been the first to see the value of Wright's work perhaps felt a little disappointed. Those American Communists who still saw Karl Marx's *Capital* (1867–95) as a sacred text and who remained loyal to the Kremlin despite Josef Stalin's increasingly obvious megalomania would hardly have wanted to discover Christian imagery at the heart of *Native Son*. Nor would they have wanted to find Bigger so pitiable – so full of yearning and so clearly longing less for revolution than for love. Indeed, such readers would have wanted Bigger to be a straightforward monster: a simple nightmare, let loose from Chicago's ghetto, filled with desires crime alone could appease.

Wright himself had given them reason to believe that this would be the case. As he revealed in his most important comment on *Native Son* – the rather socio-logical reflection 'How "Bigger" Was Born' (1940) – towards the end of the 1930s Wright grew disenchanted with his earlier *Uncle Tom's Children* (1937), all but disowning it for naively allowing 'bankers' daughters . . . [to] read and weep over and feel good about' the noble racial victims that it depicted. His next major work, that essay proclaimed, would 'be so hard and deep' that such bourgeois white readers 'would have to face it without the consolation of tears'.[2] His next protagonist, Wright said, would indeed be a monster, a nightmare fit to prove the Communist expectation of proletarian rage. No white liberal could cry sympathetically but make no political response to this portentous novel. It would instead force all to address their complicity, their failure to do anything about the American class system from which even the most unprejudiced benefited psychologically, culturally and economically.

This critical guide shows that Wright's failure to stick to this agenda, while bad news for diehard Communists, is good news for readers. I show that the fascination of *Native Son* lies in its shifting attitude towards Bigger Thomas. Put another way, Wright clearly wrote certain passages of this novel with his stated polemical objectives uppermost in mind. When setting up a symbolic equivalence between Bigger and the cornered rat that he kills on the first page of the book, for example, Wright is clearly doing all he can to essay a landmark novel of black Communist dissent. The same can be said of those parts of the novel that critique aspects of life in Chicago, or of the decision to make the name of Bigger's lawyer (Max) resonate with that of Marx himself. These passages, however, grow more interesting when placed alongside complicating moments such as the closing pages of 'Flight' that I have just summarized. Not only does *Native Son* become less didactic at such points; stepping off the soapbox, it also begins to play around with imagery, improvising in such a way as to remind us that Wright is a product of the same black southern culture responsible for jazz and the blues. In such freer moments, that is, Wright begins to write in something like the manner in which a jazz soloist plays. He writes freeform, moving associationally rather than ideologically and from image to image rather than precept to precept. In turn, Bigger changes. Less concerned to keep Bigger monstrous, *Native Son* now emphasizes his hunger, fear and other ordeals that Wright himself had experi-enced at first hand. Cracks of tenderness accordingly appear in Wright's official 'hard and deep' attitude towards his anti-hero. Bigger becomes human. No longer a brute or its ennobled opposite, he becomes something far more frightening: a mixture of the two, pitiable and loathsome, sad and menacing. Scandal about sex and crime perhaps explains why Wright's first published novel was so successful in its year of publication. But *Native Son*'s complicating improvisations, its inability to stick to a Communist script and its fashioning of a new left-wing politics able to accommodate the black experience explain why its myth of black

---

criminality remains, some sixty-five years later, among the most powerful in all Western literature.

I have designed the following pages to illuminate the key literary concerns and critical debates that surround Wright's debut novel. Inevitably, however, the particular tensions that I describe above spill into this design, being reflected in each of its three major parts: texts and contexts, critical history and critical readings. For example, the next part 'Texts and contexts' begins with a brief biography in which I consider the parallels between Wright and Bigger more closely, showing that the Mississippi writer's identification with his Chicago protagonist alone casts doubt upon certain widespread assumptions about race and region in America. In the parts that follow, we draw on the Soviet-era critic Mikhail Bakhtin's rich and revolutionary theories – theories that are indispensable to the study of any modern novel, but which seem particularly relevant to those belonging to the African-American tradition. Having learned, from our definitions of *heteroglossia* and *polyphony*, that Bakhtin sees the modern novel as a form that can place different voices onto an equal dramatic footing, we approach *Native Son* alert to the diverse and conflicting American tones and accents that it brings to our attention. We consider how the African-American voices in this book – from Bessie's way of talking to the spiritual that Bigger overhears while on the run – relate to the profound debt that Wright owed to nineteenth-century European literatures. In particular, we consider how the southern culture of the blues relates, in this rich and volatile text, to Fyodor Dostoevsky's *Crime and Punishment* (1866) among the other novels to which Wright (as we will soon see) was long denied access. Additional chapters consider additional 'voices', exploring *Native Son*'s representation of black vernacular speech, its reflections on Marxism and its play with notions of race and whiteness. The 'Chronology' briefly explains historical developments key to Wright's life and work.

The second and third of our three parts, Critical history and Critical readings, are self-explanatory. At the beginning of Critical history I return to the most famous critical controversy that surrounds *Native Son*, moving through the objections that Wright's former friend James Baldwin raised against it in his unsparing attack, 'Everybody's Protest Novel' (1949). Other major critical responses then concern us. I focus on the reception of feminist readers before turning to the very different impressions of those readers who encountered the work in the colonies and, later, the independent states of Africa and the Caribbean. The former of these has been broadly but not exclusively hostile to the novel, while the latter – the group that hails from the post-slavery, post-colonial world often now called the Black Atlantic – has been broadly but not exclusively enthusiastic. In these parts, however, I take pains not to pigeonhole critics, endeavouring instead to give a full account of the nuances of individual views.

The final major part of this work, Critical readings offers an example of a classic critical statement on *Native Son* as well as some of the best scholarly writing currently being published on the book. The reproduction in full of 'Many Thousands Gone' (1951) gives readers the chance to consider James Baldwin's famous condemnation of the novel for themselves. Following this is 'The Shadow of the White Woman: Richard Wright and the Book-of-the-Month Club' (1999), in which Hazel Rowley shows us exactly how the white-dominated book industry altered *Native Son*, removing its references to white female desire among other taboos before agreeing to its publication. This part then turns to three works of recent scholarship: Anthony Dawahare's 'From No Man's Land to Mother-Land: Emasculation and Nationalism in Richard Wright's Depression Era Urban Novels' (1999); Clare Eby's 'Slouching Toward Beastliness: Richard Wright's Anatomy of Thomas Dixon' (2001); and James Smethurst's 'Invented by Horror: The Gothic and African-American Literary Ideology in *Native Son*' (2001). Each of these five essays is prefaced by a brief statement in which I elucidate the argument and situate it in *Native Son*'s overall critical history. Further reading and Web resources offers suggestions for further reading into particular areas of interest.

Given that *Native Son* is such a polemical novel, it strangely declines to provide a clear political message. Reflecting Wright's uncertainties in the late 1930s, the novel offers no absolute position on Marxism or the African-American citizen's relationship to it; although Bigger's crimes clearly spring from his social oppression, their precise moral character is impossible to quantify. As this introduction has begun to suggest, such ambiguity is the source of this novel's richness, rescuing it from predictability. But it is also the source of its profound complexity. Together, the parts of the guide that follow are intended to help you navigate such difficulties. They put flesh on the bones of the questions that concerned Wright, enabling us to ask: to what extent is racial discrimination responsible for Bigger's crimes? How do we account for those in *Native Son* who live under ghetto conditions but do not turn to crime? Is Bigger right – are they simply patsies, conned by the hollow promises of Christianity? Why are our mass media so shallow, so salacious? Why does sex, in the popular American imagination, seem always shadowed by violence? Why is Chicago's press so quick to reach for the language of contagion, to make even the local violent threat that Bigger poses seem nothing short of apocalyptic? I do not answer these questions in the following critical guide. Instead, I offer analysis and introduce materials by which you can develop your own responses to them. I offer the means by which you can formulate your own answer to the bigger question: why does *Native Son* still matter?

# 1

# **Texts and contexts**

# Richard Wright: a brief biography

At first, the young writer scarcely knew that he wanted to write, only that he wanted to read. But American racism – the white supremacist ideology that reached its nadir in the southern states that Wright called home – worked to frustrate even this modest ambition. Legislation enforcing a kind of apartheid throughout this region, among other things, did all it could to deny black southerners the right to an education (see Chronology, **p. 47**). State courts withheld money from black schools, prevented black pupils from entering the professions and even went so far as to ban black readers from municipal libraries. To those who were alert to such matters, however, this vicious legislation was itself built upon a paradox. Racist ideology publicly denigrated the intellectual capacity of African-Americans. But the effect of racist laws was ironically to acknowledge this capacity and to deny it the materials that it needed if it was to flourish. As the historian of the black South Leon F. Litwack has suggested:

> Curtailing the educational opportunities of blacks, along with segregation and disfranchisement, were important mechanisms of racial control. . . . A story that would make the rounds among blacks . . . revealed . . . a marvelous insight into the workings of the white mind. As he was leaving the railroad depot with a northern visitor, a southern white man saw two Negroes, one asleep and the other reading a newspaper. He kicked the Negro reading a newspaper. 'Would you please explain that?' the Northerner asked. 'I don't understand it. I would think that if you were going to kick one you would kick the lazy one who's sleeping.' The white southerner replied, 'That's not the one we're worried about.'[1]

Wright's works would prove wonderfully alert to the paradoxes of such behaviour. More than any other American writer, he would expose the intellectual dishonesty of racism, showing that its small acts of intimidation and discrimination secretly acknowledged the potential for black equality that it officially

---

1  Leon F. Litwack, *Trouble in Mind: Black Southerners in the Age of Jim Crow* (New York: Vintage, 1999), pp. 102–3.

*Figure 2*  Negro children and old home on badly eroded land near
Wadesboro, North Carolina. Photograph: Marion Post Wolcott,
1938.

denied. No other novelist is more alive to the vicious contradictions involved in
racial segregation. And few others overcame quite so much discrimination, or had
to be quite so courageous, in order to piece together a literary career. Indeed, we
might ask ourselves: if white racists kicked other black men simply for reading
newspapers, how on earth would they respond to the atheistic Marxist Richard
Wright?

The circumstances of Wright's youth were appalling. Born in 1908 near
Natchez, Mississippi, Wright was the product of a southern culture not yet
reconciled to Abraham Lincoln's Emancipation Proclamation of 1863. Though
abolished almost fifty years previously, slavery still cast a long shadow over
this world. As Wright grew up on the same plantation on which his paternal
grandparents had worked as chattel, memories of the so-called Peculiar Institution proliferated at home as well as in the worlds beyond it. Out there, the
iconography of the Old Confederacy – the southern army defeated in the Civil
War – dominated urban space. Statues of noble southern generals, frozen in the
defence of slavery, stood outside courtrooms and political offices. Away from the

towns, 'lynching' trees ripped into the limitless horizon of the Mississippi Delta. Everywhere stood the signs of Jim Crow segregation – legal signs such as 'Whites Only' and 'For Colored Passengers', and unofficial signs such as 'Nigger, Don't Let the Sun Go Down on You Here' (see Chronology, **p. 47**).[2]

Named after a show in which a white minstrel 'blacked' up, this Jim Crow system that produced Wright was established after the American Civil War and the Reconstruction that followed it.[3] More specifically, Jim Crow resulted from the fact that even those in the South who could accept slavery's abolition felt inflamed by this subsequent Reconstruction. Reconstruction's attempt to enfranchise former slaves and generally to secure them the rights of full citizens struck many white southerners as an act of gross humiliation. The fact that most of their white compatriots in the North shared their doubts about the wisdom of enfranchising ex-slaves effectively meant that Reconstruction never had much hope of succeeding. By 1877, the national government abandoned the enterprise altogether. In the historian Kenneth Stamp's words, it renounced all responsibility for 'the Negro, and, in effect, invited southern white men to formulate their own program of political, social, and economic readjustment'.[4] Jim Crow segregation was what filled the void that this federal withdrawal left behind.

During the 1890s the national government's indifference towards such segregation turned into active consent. Entering what the historian Hugh Brogan has called 'its dimmest intellectual period', the Supreme Court concocted 'barely plausible constitutional arguments for upholding the racist legislation of the Southern states'.[5] Most notoriously, its ruling on the provision of railway carriages in the *Plessy* vs. *Ferguson* lawsuit allowed southern states to provide 'separate but equal' facilities on the basis of colour difference. Segregation, from this point forward, was thus deemed constitutional.

Wright's early years bore the brunt of racism's new constitutional respectability. The understaffing and underfunding of the black schools that he attended as a boy directly resulted from the fact that, as the Supreme Court judges well knew, racist state legislators would always cherish the 'separate' part of the *Plessy* vs. *Ferguson* ruling precisely at the expense of its 'equal' element. While some of his individual teachers had good intentions, ultimately they could do little about the chronic disadvantages such schools faced. Leaving without any qualifications to speak of, Wright entered a world of menial and underpaid labour that was in many ways even more adept at keeping books beyond his reach. The merest whiff of intellectual curiosity invited ridicule from Wright's employers and bemusement from his friends. Some whites felt that an African-American holding a book was fair game, a veritable provocation to racist attack. Others considered that such 'uppity' men or women should undergo some kind of debasement – should be sarcastically addressed as 'Professor' or 'Doctor', and generally put back in their place. To those black southerners willing to risk such treatment, moreover, the act

2   Litwack, *Trouble in Mind*, p. 410.
3   Litwack, *Trouble in Mind*, p. xiv.
4   Kenneth Stamp, *The Era of Reconstruction, 1865–1877* (New York: Vintage, 1965), pp. 186–7.
5   Hugh Brogan, *The Penguin History of the United States of American* (London: Penguin, 1985), p. 426.

of acquiring a book could itself be astonishingly dangerous. As his excellent auto-biography of 1945 recalls, Wright was one of vast numbers of black southerners forbidden from using their local libraries thanks to Jim Crow bans. Indeed, in order to read H. L. Mencken (Mencken was a satirist from Baltimore, famous for lambasting southern vulgarity and for praising the work of Fyodor Dostoevsky among others), Wright had little choice but to break the law. As his auto-biography would show, he had little choice but to address:

> myself to forging a note. Now, what were the names of books written by H. L. Mencken? I did not know any of them. I finally wrote what I thought would be a foolproof note: *Dear Madam: Will you please let this nigger boy* – I used the word 'nigger' to make the librarian feel that I could not possibly be the author of the note – *have some books by H. L. Mencken?* I forged the white man's name.
>
> I entered the library as I had always done when on errands for whites, but I felt that I would somehow slip up and betray myself. I doffed my hat, stood a respectful distance from the desk, looked as unbookish as possible, and waited for the white patrons to be taken care of . . . The white librarian looked at me.
>
> 'What do you want, boy?'[6]

This scene is pivotal to Wright's autobiography. Prior to it, the life that Wright has written has been unrelenting in its difficulties. He has been abandoned by his illiterate father. He has watched helpless as his mother fell into ill health. He has been farmed out, separated from his brother Leon and forced to spend time in an 'orphan home' that feeds him with all the grudging contempt of a Dickensian institution. Jim Crow has, in other words, crept into every corner of his life. Even after Wright has escaped the orphanage and has gone to live in his grand-mother's house, it soon becomes evident that things will get no better for him. Hunger renews itself, colonizing his stomach as his grandmother forces him to subsist on 'mush,' beating him whenever possible for the crime of 'talking at the table'.[7]

Books alone seem to offer the teenage Wright a way out. Stealing into the Memphis library, impersonating a white authority in print and a black servant in person, Wright's defiance of the library ban seems to be the only way in which he can assert his humanity under Jim Crow law. Mencken's importance con-sequently stands far in excess of the basic information that his essays offer to the young black autodidact. Although such essays constituted a priceless guide to Western literature, introducing Wright to the works of Theodore Dreiser and Fyodor Dostoevsky (which we will consider later), their value was ultimately more philosophical than practical. They opened a window onto another world: a world in which Wright's own intellectual consciousness was not routinely deni-grated, in which vulgarity was denounced and prejudice ridiculed and in which he could come to realize his superiority over his racist aggressors. His autobiography

---

6   Richard Wright, *Black Boy (American Hunger): A Record of Childhood and Youth* (New York: Harper Perennial, 1993), p. 291.
7   Wright, *Black Boy (American Hunger)*, p. 16.

could not be clearer on the point: Mencken's 'clear, clean, sweeping sentences' bring about nothing less than an epiphany in the young black writer. They make him wonder: 'How did one write like that? I pictured the man as a raging demon, . . . consumed with hate, denouncing everything American.' For some time, indeed, Wright seems unable to assimilate that 'this man', Mencken, 'was fighting, fighting with words. He was using words as a weapon, using them as one would use a club.'[8] With the shock of this encounter, it becomes inevitable that Wright will soon get on board a Chicago-bound train. His discovery of literature is a discovery of the social background behind his own dehumanization: it guarantees that he will join the Great Migration and leave Jim Crow behind (see Chronology, **p. 48**).

Not that there was anything naïve about Wright's decision, at the age of nineteen in 1927, to move north. As the many parallels between his and Bigger's childhoods reveal, Wright was never less than mindful of similarities between southern states such as Mississippi and northern cities such as Chicago. *Native Son* introduces Bigger as a 'black boy', and the fact that Wright would go on to adopt this phrase as the title of his autobiography is another sign that he identifies profoundly with the boyhood experiences of his anti-hero even though they occur in a supposed site of black freedom. That is to say, despite the fact that Bigger and Wright grow up at opposite ends of the Great Migration, both are forced to play the role of the servant. Both offer a similar interpretation of this role. Both speak meekly, in monosyllables and with deliberate stupidity. And even though Jim Crow posts no signs in the North, no warnings about sunsets and the like, the prospect of the walk back home seems if anything more terrifying to Bigger than it does to Wright. Both know they must return as quickly as possible to their side of the colour line. Both know they must keep their heads down.

*Twelve Million Black Voices* (1941), a lyrical narrative of African-American history that was Wright's next book after *Native Son*, pays close attention to this apparent reproduction of Jim Crow conditions in the North. Here, tiny 'kitchen-ettes' initially seem like 'havens from the plantations' but soon enforce their 'new form of mob violence', casting 'unhappy people into an unbearable closeness of association'.[9] Morgues remain 'crowded with our lost children'.[10] A bureaucratic labyrinth defends unofficial, de-facto segregation: the 'restrictive covenants' of 'real-estate boards' now assume 'the role of policemen in enforcing residential segregation'. Should such covenants fail, tactics escalate and soon recall the South. 'Bricks are hurled through the windows of our homes; garbage is tossed at our black children when they go to school; and finally bombs explode against our front doors.' *Twelve Million Black Voices* as such confirms that, for Wright, the Great Migration was an economic phenomenon, the main tide of which rolled 'from the farm to the factory'.[11] It was not an escape from southern racism to northern tolerance. Life was more complicated than that, and racism endemic to America overall.

---

8  Wright, *Black Boy (American Hunger)*, pp. 291–3.
9  Richard Wright, *Twelve Million Black Voices* (New York: Thunder's Mouth, 1995), pp. 105–8.
10  Wright, *Twelve Million Black Voices*, p. 117.
11  Wright, *Twelve Million Black Voices*, p. 93.

Wright's life in Chicago was a struggle. Throughout the 1920s and 1930s, universities played a crucial role in the African-American cultural and literary flowering known as the Harlem Renaissance. Institutions such as New York's Barnard College and Washington's Howard University equipped such aspiring writers as Zora Neale Hurston and Nella Larsen with the time, contacts and confidence they needed to forge literary careers. At the same time as this flowering flowered, however, Wright was feeling the sting of economic depression. Poverty was again frustrating his hopes of returning to high school to complete his education. It was again forcing him to do whatever he could to survive – to dig ditches, sell insurance, tend laboratory rats and schlep post all around a Chicago metropolis that (as his friend Margaret Walker recalled) he unsurprisingly found 'a bleak and grimy city'.[12]

Even Wright, however, tempered the scepticism that he felt about the Great Migration. Even at his hungriest and poorest – even when the city's postal service initially turned down his job application on the grounds that he was too thin – Wright knew that his decision to move north had not been mistaken and that this 'bleak and grimy' Chicago offered tangible improvements on life in Mississippi. De-facto segregation led to acute overcrowding, disease and the spread of other problems among the black migrants of the South Side. But it also drew their resources together, enabling more African-Americans than ever before to pool their time and money and to support any enterprise they considered worthwhile. Most conspicuous among these were the black restaurants and cafeterias that, as Tracy N. Poe has shown, flourished throughout the South Side.[13] Fictionalized in *Native Son*'s Ernie's Kitchen Shack – the African-American eatery in which Mary Dalton, having cast Bigger as a chauffeur and a comrade at once, indulges in a little racial tourism – these establishments served up southern food that could offset homesickness while announcing the growing black presence in the city. Yet the concentration of resources into the South Side ghetto also lent substantial backing to sundry other black-run organizations, sustaining new charities, newspapers, magazines, banks, sporting clubs.

And libraries: Wright could now browse their shelves without fear of arrest. He could even use a local branch, the George Cleveland Hall library in Bronzeville, that specifically catered to the black community. A remarkable institution, the George Cleveland Hall library was run by the city's first black librarian, Vivian G. Harsh, who among other things established a section devoted to African-American literature, slowly but surely filling it with classic slave autobiographies as well as the new works being produced by Harlem Renaissance writers. As the Kenyan novelist and academic Ngũgĩ wa Thiong'o has said in another context, the George Cleveland Hall library was thus an institution 'among the first to recognize ... that there was something worthwhile out there beyond the traditional location of the European imagination'; and although we know little other than that Wright used it often, we can surely surmise that its stock of black

12  Margaret Walker, *Richard Wright, Daemonic Genius: A Portrait of the Man: A Critical Look at His Work* (New York: Amistad, 1988), p. 54.
13  Tracy N. Poe, 'The Origins of Soul Food in Black Urban Identity: Chicago, 1915–1947' in Carole Counihan (ed.) *Food in the USA: A Reader* (New York and London: Routledge, 2002), pp. 91–107.

writing amazed him.[14] At the very least, it would have disturbed the simple binary opposition that Wright's cultural education had hitherto followed. Until this point, after all, the racial dynamic had been clear. Literature was 'white': on the other hand, the spirituals that Wright heard in church, the blues he heard in the delta bars into which he trespassed as a boy and the jazz that was everywhere around his Beale Street apartment in Memphis, were 'black'. As we will see, Wright was always ambivalent about prior African-American literature and maintained an awkward silence on the subject throughout his life. Whatever the meaning of this silence, however, Wright's discovery, in the George Cleveland Hall library, of the very existence of such seminal black texts as W. E. B. Du Bois's *Souls of Black Folk* (1903) and Jean Toomer's *Cane* (1923) cannot have seemed anything other than incredible.

The Communist Party members who Wright encountered in the first years of the 1930s similarly nourished his emerging intellect. Marxism offered him a way of explaining the systems and histories that had generated the terrible conditions of his upbringing as well as those still being endured by Chicago's black youth. The black and white street-speakers who drew crowds all around the South Side, denouncing the ghetto as capitalism's offspring, the sign of its addiction to under-paid labour and dependence on inequality, convinced Wright, as they did many members of these often hard-to-impress audiences. But such activists were also among the first to offer Wright personal intellectual support. They were the first to encourage Wright's literary interest, enabling him to see that he could profit from writing as well as reading. In particular, key comrades in the Party presented it to him that he might shape from the ordeals of his life a kind of Marxist parable – a body of work that could expose more fully than any before it the sheer hypocrisy of America's claims to democracy and freedom. Persuaded by much in the Communist analysis, Wright duly became a card-carrying member of the Party in 1934, actively working to promote revolutionary feelings among Chicago's working class.

Some American critics seem uncertain about how to respond to this period of Wright's life. Robert Bone, for example, treads carefully through it, admitting that Wright was indeed a 'dependable wheel horse in a wide variety of party activities' but insisting that 'a stubborn and incorruptible individualism kept him in constant conflict with the party bureaucracy'. Bone thus suggests that this brief Communist period was a marriage of convenience: as 'an excluded Negro and an alienated intellectual, Wright needed above all to feel . . . [a] sense of belonging'.[15] But this formulation does something of a disservice to Wright, in so far as it comes close to suggesting that he joined the Communists for nothing but personal reasons. The ideological path that led Wright, during the 1930s, from alliance to disaffection with Communism demands more serious critical attention than this and should instead be placed alongside the similar journeys undertaken by such important contemporary figures as George Orwell and the Trinidadian intellectual C. L. R. James. That is to say, Wright did not join the Communist

---

14  Ngũgĩ wa Thiong'o, *Moving the Centre: The Struggle for Cultural Freedom* (London: James Currey, 1993), p. 8.
15  Robert Bone, *The Negro Novel in America* (London and New Haven, Conn.: Yale University Press, 1973), p. 143.

Party because he was young, naïve and barely knew what he was doing. Instead, like Orwell and James, he gravitated towards Communism because he agreed with much of its diagnosis about the untenable cruelties of capitalism. Like them, too, Wright's disaffection with Communism in the time of *Native Son*'s artistic germination (he would eventually break with party in 1942) stemmed, not from some instinctive and 'incorruptible individualism', but from his own, sophisticated, political analysis. Individualism, to be sure, mattered greatly to the development of this analysis. But it mattered for reasons far more nuanced than those that Bone envisages; and indeed, as we will later see, even after his break with the Party Wright remained adamant that it was actually the *American* system – the capitalist system – that homogenized, deindividualized and controlled human behaviour. Wright lost faith with Marxism, not because he initially misunderstood it but because he felt his comrades had and because he came to feel that their professed commitment to combating racism and inequality was less than firm. This continuing concern with equality explains why Wright grew less and less active in Communist Party politics from 1937 onwards, and why his move to New York that year amounted to an attempt to distance himself from his former comrades.

Wright always seemed happier when a step ahead of his fictions, a step nearer a freedom that remained elusive. His successful books all have one thing in common: they return to places that he abandoned. All of the harrowing stories of the collection *Uncle Tom's Children*, his breakthrough work of 1937, take place in the South that he had left ten years beforehand. Similarly, in 1947, when living in Long Island, Wright began his New York novel *The Outsider* – and only managed to finish it in 1952, after he had set up a home of sorts in Catford, south-east London.

*Native Son* epitomizes this pattern. Before his move in 1937 to Brooklyn, it was almost as though Wright was too close to Chicago, too embroiled in its political intrigues, to write about it well. But after the move, it was as though Wright could suddenly view Chicago from the plane that Bigger and his friends spy early in *Native Son*, 'writing high up in the air' ('Fear', p. 46). Asking Margaret Walker to send him *Chicago Tribune* cuttings of the alleged black murderer Robert Nixon's trial, Wright plotted a kind of imaginative return to the metropolis he had left. Throughout *Native Son*'s composition, he rose at six in the morning every day. Working in Fort Greene Park and the Brooklyn Public Library, Wright's obsessive writing of *Native Son* at once took him out of and placed him back into the world, forcing him to become a kind of alert recluse. Out of this concentrated creativity, as a kind of culmination of all the libraries he had visited and all the books he had striven to read, Wright suddenly found that he had a success on his hands – a novel that would gain him financial royalties and critical acclaim. As the leading Wright scholar Keneth Kinnamon has put it:

> *Native Son* very quickly became a popular as well as critical success. Advance sales ... and first-week sales totaled 215,000 copies, an extremely large printing for a first novel. In its issue of 16 March 1940, two weeks after publication, *The Publishers' Weekly* alerted the book trade to high rates of reorders from bookstores and to Harper's heavy advertising campaign. An advertisement entitled 'Public Stampedes for

"Native Son"' that appeared in various black newspapers was only mildly hyperbolical. . . . Moreover, library copies were circulated briskly, although at least one library in a major Southern city refused to purchase the book . . . .

[I]nterest in *Native Son* . . . revived in the sixties and continues to the present. The novel has been widely translated and reviewed abroad. Along with his fourteen other books, *Native Son* brought its author global recognition and a permanent place in American literature.[16]

Some later sections of this critical guide consider subsequent developments in Wright's life: in 'Bigger: Silenced by Whiteness?' I touch on his presence at the Bandung Conference of post-colonial nations in 1955 (see Texts and contexts, **pp. 41–6**), while 'First responses: James Baldwin' considers *Native Son*'s unprecedented success and the new literary possibilities it opened (see Texts and contexts, **pp. 53–60**). Other sections centre on Wright's text *Son*: 'The Dostoevskian voice' puts flesh on our consideration of Russian culture's influence on *Native Son* (see Texts and contexts, **pp. 53–60**), while 'The transplantation of the blues' and 'Bigger's vernacular voice' place it more firmly within the more immediate context of African-American culture (see Texts and contexts, **pp. 20–6 and 26–34**). Taken overall, however, these sections will, I hope, demonstrate why and how this novel changed the face of American literature, establishing a new kind of African-American novel at the heart of the national culture.'

## The voices of *Native Son*

Much African-American literary criticism emphasizes the voice. Houston A. Baker, Jr., bell hooks, Gayl Jones, Albert Murray, Hortense Spillers and Claudia Tate have all made the argument that African-American literature is particularly attuned to its characters' speech, and unusually determined to render their conversations imaginatively. Henry Louis Gates, Jr., the leading critic on the subject, has meanwhile demonstrated that this special attention to orality ultimately results from the history of slavery.[17] In his persuasive historical analysis, oral culture helped Africans and their children to survive and to resist the institution of slavery. While the transatlantic slave trade snatched slaves from diverse West African language groups and forced them to converse not only with their masters but also with each other, the system of American slavery into which such chattel were compelled forbade their education and so made them rely on this improvised tongue. The criminalization of black literacy in many slave-holding states, in turn, required oral culture to over-perform, forcing slaves to turn their songs and

16  Keneth Kinnamon, 'How *Native Son* Was Born' in *Richard Wright: Critical Perspectives Past and Present* (New York: Amistad, 1993), eds. Henry Louis Gates, Jnr., and Kwame Anthony Appiah, pp. 110–131 (pp. 126–78).

17  Henry Louis Gates, Jr., 'Introduction: Talking Books' in Henry Louis Gates Jr. and Nellie Y. McKay (eds) *The Norton Anthology of African-American Literature* (New York and London: Norton, 2004), pp. xxxvii–xlvii.

stories into what Wright would call '[our] most indigenous and complete expression'.[18] Unlike the successful fugitives who wrote their lives for white abolitionist readers, those who remained on the plantation crafted their dissident texts in speech, reworking old West African folktales into anti-slavery parables and composing spirituals that placed the Bible firmly on the side of the slave rather than the slaveholder (see Chronology, **p. 46**).

As the library episode from Wright's autobiography revealed, attempts to prohibit African-American education continued long after the abolition of American slavery in 1863. Although most African-Americans acquired literacy in these years, their exclusion from these libraries, together with a widespread lack of leisure time and low disposable income, meant that literary culture remained the preserve of a fortunate minority. Largely written for white readers, the Harlem Renaissance of the 1920s and 1930s did much for black pride but little to reach black readers. It was an 'offshoot of W. E. B. Du Bois's idea of the "talented tenth", in which the cream of the black artistic and intellectual crop would . . . mingle with the white intellectual elite'; it silently bypassed ordinary African-Americans.[19] Oral culture – the sermons, songs and storytelling sessions that Harlem Renaissance writers often celebrated – remained far more accessible to them (see Chronology, **p. 48**).

Wright felt some disgust at this situation. He hoped instead to author what he saw as a properly black literature. This literature, he hoped, would entertain and politicize black readers even as it reversed the Renaissance's reactionary habit of addressing white readers – of carving the vernacular up into easy and manageable mouthfuls, fit for white consumption. Such objectives received their fullest expression early in Wright's career, in the left-wing manifesto of 1937 'Blueprint for Negro Writing'. Wright's predilection for knowing titles – a predilection by which the name Bigger Thomas seems to allude to Uncle Tom, Max to Marx, and Bessie to Bessie Smith (see Chronology, **p. 48**) – is already evident in this early title. By implicitly installing 'Blue' as the colour for future 'Negro' print, Wright's punning title suggests that this music among other vernacular forms will be central to *Native Son* and all subsequent fictions. This is certainly what Wright envisions in the manifesto itself:

> Blues, spirituals, and folk tales recounted from mouth to mouth; the whispered words of a black mother to her black daughter on the ways of men; . . . the swapping of sex experiences . . . from boy to boy in the deepest vernacular; work songs sung under blazing suns – all these formed the channels through which the racial wisdom flowed.
>
> One would have thought that Negro writers . . . would have continued and deepened this folk tradition. . . . But the illusion that they could escape through individual achievements the harsh lot of their race swung Negro writers away from any such path. Two separate cultures sprang up: one for the Negro masses, unwritten and unrecognized; and

18  Richard Wright, 'Blueprint for Negro Writing' in *The Norton Anthology of African-American Literature*, pp. 1380–8 (p. 1382).
19  Lisa Meyerowitz (1997) 'The Negro in Art Week: Defining the "New Negro" Through Art Exhibition', *African-American Review*, 31(1): pp. 75–89 (p. 77).

*Figure 3* Circus posters, Black Belt, Chicago, Illinois. Photograph: Edwin Rosskam, 1941.

the other for the sons and daughters of a rising Negro bourgeoisie, parasitic and mannered.[20]

Several critics have felt suspicious about Wright's attitude towards black vernacular culture. Thinking of those moments in which the vernacular appears bankrupt – thinking of how Bigger overhears an old-time spiritual but proves deaf to its appeal – these critics have often partnered their hostility towards Wright by extolling the apparently straightforward celebrations of African-American English (AAE) to be found in Zora Neale Hurston's novels of the 1930s. Since at least 1970, indeed, many have gone so far as to place Hurston's and Wright's novels into a perfect binary opposition, simplifying matters to the point of suggesting that, if Hurston's *Jonah's Gourd Vine* (1934) and *Their Eyes Were Watching God* (1937) unequivocally affirm AAE as well as vernacular culture, then *Native Son*, in a word, does not.

The above excerpt from Wright's 'Blueprint for Negro Writing' reveals that the situation is a good deal more complicated than this binary opposition suggests. It reveals that, in fact, Wright neither abandoned oral culture nor considered it the price of his ticket into the literary world. Instead, he felt that most preceding literary treatments of the vernacular, and not least those by Hurston herself, lapsed into minstrelsy, parading black exoticism to the delight of white readers. Whether or not this harsh judgement was warranted, Wright clearly wished to retain his oral influences and to do something different with them – to use them to overhaul the realist novel, to make it altogether more bluesy and accessible

---

20  Wright, 'Blueprint for Negro Writing', p. 1382.

and, by doing so, to reach the 'unrecognized' masses that the 'parasitic' Harlem Renaissance overlooked.

In his first published novel, Wright achieved some of these ambitions and disappointed others. As the 'Bigger's vernacular voice' section makes clear, oral culture exerted a powerful influence over *Native Son* (see Texts and contexts, pp. 26–34). But it is also clear that, when Henry Louis Gates, Jr., propounds his rightly famous theories, citing the history of slavery to demonstrate that African-American novelists today tend to produce 'talking books', *Native Son* is not uppermost in his mind. And although he is a great admirer of Wright's work, Gates's suggestion that 'the vernacular tradition . . . continues to nurture' black writing in a 'reciprocal relation' seems likewise more applicable to newer, less realist, works.[21] It seems more relatable to the writings of such post-1960s novelists as Charles Johnson, Toni Morrison, Gloria Naylor and others. After all, unlike *Native Son*, such writings revel in the black voice from start to finish. Preferring first- to third-person narrative, they typically delegate storytelling duties to a single black narrator, in the process allowing the rhythms of AAE to break free of the dialogue, flow over all speech marks and spill into the prose itself.

*Native Son* answers to a different description. It does not delegate its entire story to a single narrator: to use one of Jacques Derrida's favourite phrases, it does not endeavour to make the reader's 'eye listen' on its every single page.[22] Instead of focusing on an African-American narrator and making his or her speech central to proceedings, *Native Son* oscillates from voice to voice. Wright's brilliantly innovative representations of Bigger's exchanges with his friends and with Bessie, for example, are constantly confronted by conflicting voices that seem to reinstate white authority. Neither Bessie nor Bigger take control of the narrative long enough to let us forget the grip white Chicago holds over their lives. Wright's supposedly omniscient third-person narrative is itself prone to fierce fluctuations. At times it seems almost to parrot the clichés of this white city, as though it is in league with the conditions that drive Bigger to crime. At others, it penetrates this protagonist's mind, humanizing his criminalization and laying his terror bare. Other voices seem likewise able to seize control of *Native Son*. Marxists, tabloid journalists, churchgoers, Hollywood stars and gangsters come to the fore, their infiltration of the narrative and their juxtaposition with each other filling the novel with far greater complexity than Wright, at least in his official statements about the book, would ever acknowledge.

This antagonistic array of voices – *Native Son*'s movement from racist to Marxist language, from white to black points of view, from journalese to legalese, and so on – indicates that the novel is less usefully related to Henry Louis Gates's scholarship than to some of the European theories of narrative that stand behind it. The useful and illuminating theories of the Soviet-era Russian critic Mikhail Bakhtin, in particular, elucidate our reading of *Native Son*. For one thing, Bakhtin saw the modern novel as a bulwark of freedom. For him, the novel could challenge Soviet oppression; its ability to accommodate different voices, to place

21  Gates, 'Introduction: Talking Books', p. xlvii.
22  Jacques Derrida, *Dissemination* (London and New York: Continuum, 2004), p. 33.

them on the same footing, made it implicitly anti-authoritarian, implicitly democratic. For reasons that the short biography has already touched on but which the section 'The Black Atlantic and beyond' develops further (see Texts and contexts, **pp. 68–74**), Wright, in common with many African-American writers, felt an association of the novel and freedom that was, if anything, even more powerful. It is subsequently unsurprising to find that *Native Son* exemplifies the heteroglossia and polyphony of the modern novel, its array of conflicting voices fruitfully confirming Bakhtin's belief in its multi-textual and many-voiced character.

Let us clarify this point by drawing a metaphor from the field of music. Inspired by Bakhtin's view of the modern novel as a form in which different voices from different corners of society interact, many critics have come to see (or 'hear') such books less as the work of a gifted soloist and more as that of a conductor who organizes the divergent parts of an orchestra and prevents it from disintegrating into chaos. Although this theory can enrich readings of all modern literature, however, Dale E. Peterson is quite right to point out that black critics 'are culturally situated to give ... [it] an especially full hearing and creative response'.[23] In the African-American jazz orchestra, after all, the 'voices' of individual musicians grow even more democratic. A culture of improvisation allows them far greater space for individual interpretation. Their 'voices' grow even more autonomous.

The difficulty of saying where *Native Son*'s moral centre lies, or exactly what we are supposed to think about Bigger, stems from the fact that the novel's different voices belong to a heterogeneous 'orchestra' of this kind. Each of *Native Son*'s voices, in other words, possesses an autonomous status of its own. Each is able to seize control of the work and push it into new directions. Thus Bigger can be lifted out his monstrosity, made pitiful by the ordeals he undergoes when on the run. But thus this hero, too, can be made an anti-hero once more, can be delivered back to monstrosity, as *Native Son* spins away from his innermost thoughts and back to describing white journalists' views. Far more than the sum of its political diatribes, *Native Son*'s richness lies in the interplay of these divergent voices.

## The Dostoevskian voice

In the inter-war period, as they developed their ideas about literature, Mikhail Bakhtin and Richard Wright drew from the same source. The novels of the Russian writer Fyodor Dostoevsky – landmark works such as *Crime and Punishment* (1866), *The Idiot* (1868) and *The Brothers Karamazov* (1880) – struck the Russian critic and the American novelist alike as offering a new direction in Western letters. For both men, Dostoevsky seemed the first significant Western novelist who could really get into the minds of the mad and the criminal, for the first time telling their stories from their point of view.

---

23  Dale E. Peterson, 'Response and Call: The African-American Dialogue with Bakhtin and What It Signifies' in Amy Mandelker (ed.) *Bakhtin in Contexts: Across the Disciplines* (Evanston, Ill: Northwestern University Press, 1995), pp. 89–98 (p. 98).

In the estimation of both men, previous Victorian novelists had been likelier to bestow pity on the poor than to identify genuinely with their predicaments. Such novelists, in their view, braced themselves, taking deep breaths before plunging into the underworld. Dostoevsky alone could write novels from the social margin. He alone did not look down at the gutter; he alone was already in it. To put it more formally, both Bakhtin and Wright felt that Dostoevsky's novels transcended sympathy, establishing a far profounder *empathy* for those on the margin of life, and that they did so by surrendering narrative space to the poor, granting them unprecedented dramatic autonomy.

This new kind of novel – the optimized empathy of Dostoevsky's masterpieces – exerts a vital influence over *Native Son*. Throughout *Native Son*'s germination, Wright remained unwavering in his verdict that Dostoevsky was 'the greatest novelist who ever lived'.[24] Indeed, as Dale Peterson observes, 'while working on *Native Son*', Wright 'avidly pursued ... and ... reread analytically the major Dostoevsky novels'.[25] Ten years earlier, though, Bakhtin had been no less enthusiastic in his evaluation of these works. Exiled for suspected anti-Stalinist activities to the distant Soviet outpost of Kuranai, Kazakhstan, Bakhtin whiled away the time working in provincial bookstores and libraries that were as culturally distant from the metropolitan centres of Leningrad and Moscow as the George Cleveland Hall library was from downtown Chicago. In the eventual result of this enforced period of introspection, *Problems of Dostoevsky's Poetics*, Bakhtin would revise much of his earlier thinking on the novelist, producing a study that would – at least by the time of its posthumous publication in 1973 – revolutionize literary criticism.

*Native Son* is as such indebted to *Crime and Punishment*, transforming into the industrial black ghetto Dostoevsky's ground-breaking insistence on the squalor and indignities of modern life, his unflinching accounts of violence, his dense analyses of criminalization. But modern critical understandings of literature also owe much to the Russian novelist, and for the simple reason that his oeuvre was so important for Bakhtin's revolutionary theories, destroying what the latter saw as 'the established forms of the basically *monological* ... European novel', collapsing its characteristic omniscience and replacing it with a crowd of autonomous voices (*polyphony*) taken from the full spectrum of Russian society.[26]

The fact that both Bakhtin and Wright, during their respective domestic exiles in Kazakhstan and Chicago, were so exhilarated by Dostoevsky's work demands explanation. Almost everything Dostoevsky believed in, Wright rejected. Emphatically Christian, despite his lifelong weakness for gambling, the Russian novelist would have recoiled from Wright's equally forceful atheism, as he did from the Communist doctrines to which the latter was for a time committed. Dostoevsky's antipathy for left-wing politics resulted from the embarrassment he felt at his disastrous flirtation, during his youth in the 1840s, with the socialist utopianism of Charles Fourier and Saint Simon. In 1849, the reactionary

24  Walker, *Richard Wright, Daemonic Genius*, pp. 75–81.
25  Dale E. Peterson (1994) 'Richard Wright's Long Journey from Gorky to Dostoevsky', *African-American Review*, 28(3): 375–87 (p. 381).
26  Mikhail Bakhtin, *Problems of Dostoevsky's Poetics* (Ann Arbor, Mich.: Ardis, 1973), p. 5.

tsarist government, keen to avoid the revolutions that had just engulfed Europe, arrested Dostoevsky and other members of the so-called Petrashevsky Circle and sentenced them to death, a punishment reduced only on the point of execution to several years in a Siberian camp. As Susan McReynolds notes, while the punishment drove some of his fellow prisoners insane and others to suicide, Dostoevsky 'by all accounts remained composed' and instead 'initiated a revaluation of his beliefs that led to his decisive repudiation of . . . socialism and capitalism . . . as dying forms of civilization that would be succeeded by a universal Russian Christian culture'.[27] A novelist whose major fictions all end by affirming Christianity – *Crime and Punishment* concludes with the incarcerated Raskolnikov picking up a Bible – Dostoevsky thus seems an unlikely source of Wright's inspiration, a writer far removed from the latter's scathing belief that '[w]herever I found religion in my life I found strife'.[28]

Arguably, though, Dostoevsky's Christian ethos makes him an even unlikelier source for Bakhtin's revolutionary critical theories: arguably, it suggests his works were moralistic, predictable and not at all the progenitors of the slippery 'polyphonic novel' that *Problems of Dostoevsky's Poetics* acclaims them to be.[29] Moreover, Dostoevsky was decidedly risky material for a literary critic already known to Soviet authorities. Novels such as *Crime and Punishment* and *The Devils* (1871), with their parodies of revolutionary idealism and earnest Christian appeals, could only be properly read in Stalinist Russia as cautionary tales – as what more orthodox critics called an 'example by which we can see how impermissable [*sic*], how criminal it is to be inconsistent'.[30]

Questions subsequently arise. Why did Bakhtin take this risk? What was so valuable about the work of this seemingly pious novelist, whose ideological position was hazardous for Bakhtin and anathema to Wright? The appraisal of a third twentieth-century reader helps answer these questions:

> The novels of Dostoevsky are seething whirlpools, gyrating sandstorms, waterspouts which hiss and boil and suck us in. . . . [They reveal] a new panorama of the human mind. . . . The old divisions melt into each other. Men are at the same time villains and saints; their acts are at once beautiful and despicable. We love and we hate at the same time. There is none of that precise division between good and bad to which we are used. Often those for whom we feel most affection are the greatest criminals, and the most abject sinners move us to the strongest admiration as well as love.[31]

Here, Virginia Woolf's perceptive reading of Dostoevsky's novels – her emphasis on their destabilizing, intoxicating effect – directs attention away from their concluding affirmations of Christianity and towards those unrulier passages in which moral certainties disappear and anti-heroes such as Raskolnikov seem to

27  Susan McReynolds (2002) 'Dostoevsky in Europe: The Political as the Spiritual', *Partisan Review*, 69(1): 93–101 (p. 93).
28  Wright, *Black Boy (American Hunger)*, p. 159.
29  Bakhtin, *Problems of Dostoevsky's Poetics*, p. 228.
30  Theodore Dreiser, *Letters of Theodore Dreiser: A Selection, Volume 2* (Philadelphia, Pa.: University of Pennsylvania Press, 1959), ed. Robert H. Elias, p. 595.
31  Virginia Woolf, *The Common Reader* (London: Hogarth Press, 1925), pp. 226–7.

wrestle the narrative from their creator's hands. Put another way, Woolf is here more fascinated by the journey Dostoevsky's novels take than by their destination. Bakhtin assembled a similar case. 'Dostoevsky the artist always wins out over Dostoevsky the publicist', he argued, insisting that the novelistic practice from which works like *The Devils* or *The Brothers Karamazov* (1880) result is in fact so egalitarian and profoundly transformative that it makes its conductor's own Christian ideals 'completely dialogized', forcing them 'into the great dialog of the novel *on completely equal terms*' with other ideologies.[32] Bakhtin suggests that, whereas most preceding novels bestow credibility and verisimilitude only on those ideas that the 'monological' writer favours, Dostoevsky's 'dialogic' and 'polyphonic' imagination creates a far fuller, selfless drama. Even those intended as anti-heroes now respond and talk to the world around them; the narrative places their personalities no longer in stasis but in flux. In *Crime and Punishment*, Bakhtin suggests, the murderer Raskolnikov is no longer an eternal criminal like Dickens's Fagin or Hugo's Valjean – monsters who cannot imaginably be anything else. Rather, the 'unfinalized inner nucleus' of Raskolnikov is criminalized before our very eyes; we watch every step in its degeneration.[33] Bakhtin accordingly zooms in on those moments in *Crime and Punishment* when Raskolnikov converses with himself, bombarding himself with questions:

> Raskolnikov went into his closet of a room and stood in the centre of it. Why had he returned here? He looked at that yellowish, scraped wallpaper, at the dust, at his little couch . . .
>
> He felt yet again that perhaps he really did hate Sonya, and particularly now that he had made her even more unhappy. Why had he gone to her to ask her for her tears? Why was it so essential for him to make her life a misery? Oh, what vileness!
>
> 'I shall stay as I am, on my own!' he said suddenly, in a decisive tone of voice. 'And she's not going to visit me in jail, either.'
>
> About five minutes later he raised his head and gave a strange smile. He had had a strange thought. 'Life might really be better in penal servitude,' he suddenly reflected.[34]

As *Problems of Dostoevsky's Poetics* insists, in such moments Raskolnikov 'tries to convince himself, taunts, exposes and mocks himself, etc'.[35] Like *The Devils'* anti-hero Stavrogin, Raskolnikov speaks in 'a decisive tone of voice', and his 'words with their convincing accent [are] . . . addressed to himself . . . and are intended to convince the speaker himself'.[36] He is thus another example of the new kind of anti-hero that Dostoevsky is placing before us: an anti-hero full of doubt and questions, a three-dimensional figure. A figure, indeed, much like that of Bigger Thomas. For Bigger, too, talks to himself constantly, assuring

---

32 Bakhtin, *Problems of Dostoevsky's Poetics*, p. 75.
33 Bakhtin, *Problems of Dostoevsky's Poetics*, p. 69.
34 Fyodor Dostoevsky, *Crime and Punishment* (Harmondsworth: Penguin, 1991), trans. David McDuff, pp. 493–4.
35 Bakhtin, *Problems of Dostoevsky's Poetics*, pp. 199–200.
36 Bakhtin, *Problems of Dostoevsky's Poetics*, p. 221.

himself, cajoling himself, teasing himself into the role of the black gangster. He, too, seeks obsessively to convince himself of the appropriateness of his actions according to a received image of cold criminality. And he, too, bombards himself with questions:

> He should disguise his handwriting. He changed the pencil from his right to his left hand. . . . Now, what would be the best kind of note? He thought, I want you to put ten thousand . . . Naw; that would not do. Not 'I'. It would be better to say 'we'. *We got your daughter*, he printed slowly in big round letters. . . . Now, about the money. How much? Yes; make it ten thousand. *Get ten thousand in 5 and 10 bills and put it in a shoe box* . . . That's good. He had read that somewhere . . . *and tomorrow night ride your car up and down Michigan Avenue from 35th Street to 40th Street*. . . . Now, he would sign it. But how? . . . Oh yes! Sign it 'Red.' He printed, *Red*.
>
> ('Flight', pp. 206–7)

Questions proliferate here. As Bigger interrogates himself, his voice spills into Wright's third-person narrative ('Naw'), making itself palpable. Just as Raskolnikov cajoles himself into brutishness, adopting a 'tone of certainty' in order to convince no one so much as himself, so Bigger, here, no less incessantly compares his own personality with a mental image of the hoodlum that he seems to have acquired from the mass media. 'What would be the best kind' of note, he wonders, measuring his behaviour against a received gangster style; a vindication of sorts arrives when he remembers: 'He had read that somewhere.'

In this way, Bigger chases Raskolnikov's tail, offering a parallel – another character who is not a criminal so much as he is being criminalized – another character, indeed, whose ugly undergoing of brutalizing criminalization has been thrown open to the public. The experience of reading *Native Son*, as with the experience of *Crime and Punishment*, is thus to witness moral degeneration. It is to be made to consider the lessons that an important case study might hold – to inquire into the nature of the blood that covers Raskolnikov's hands and to ask why Bigger's murders are, by contrast, bloodless. What impels the first to cut, to stab, and what impels the second to suffocate and cut the body only after the life has been forced out of it? Where does this joint impulse to murder come from?

Nor is this desire to repeat Dostoevsky's novelistic innovations apparent only in *Native Son*'s characterization of Bigger. The sheer breadth of *Native Son*'s representation, its diversity of voices, confirm that Wright shared Bakhtin's appreciation of Dostoevsky's development of the polyphonic novel (even if he did not call it that) and wished to follow his example by creating a literary image of Chicago every bit as kaleidoscopic as *Crime and Punishment*'s image of St Petersburg. To Bakhtin, novels such as *Crime and Punishment* presented a kind of democracy of voices, an equality resulting from Dostoevsky's artistic desire, linked to his Christianity, to lend representation to those who he felt previous literature had overlooked: the mad, the lost, the wretched; all those whose undesirable qualities are compressed in the opening lines of *Notes from Underground* (1864): 'I am a sick man . . . I am an angry man. I am an unattractive man'.[37] Although the Communist and racist ideologies that *Native Son* dramatizes might not exist on the *'completely equal terms'* Bakhtin identifies in Dostoevsky's narratives, Wright nonetheless shared with the Russian a desire to give voice to 'criminal types, the warped, the lost, the baffled' and explore the 'tragic toll that the urban environment exacted of the black peasant'.[38] Thus was spawned the polyphony of *Native Son*, its distinctive heteroglossia of voices, its reiteration of the accents and phrases mouthed by racist journalists and policemen, by Gospel singers, legal authorities, the blues.

My commentary thus far has perhaps come close to enforcing a perfect distinction between form and content, as though Wright, when handling Dostoevsky's œuvre, effectively discarded its Christian morals like so much fat in order to gorge himself on its lean formal innovations. Radical French theorists Etienne Balibar and Pierre Macherey have persuasively described the problems in such thinking, suggesting that a binary opposition in which 'literature is sometimes perceived as content (ideology), sometimes as form ("real" literature)' is in fact a way of defusing writing, of containing its rebellious, dissenting potential.[39] Balibar and Macherey's position, as such, encourages us to acknowledge that Dostoevsky influenced Wright, not *despite* their political disagreements, but *because* this discordance on some key points was accompanied and so sharpened by their agreement on others. This more ambiguous situation needs to be addressed if we are now to develop further our understanding of *Native Son*'s relationship with its chief literary source.

For a start, the fact that Dostoevsky was an anti-Communist Christian and Wright was an atheistic socialist, while true, also tells something less than the full story. Both men in fact arrived at these conflicting ideologies because they shared a commitment to the common folk and a distrust of the ruling classes. Although he never veered from an atheistic position, Wright frequently registered the enormous power of religious rhetoric. Elsewhere, he echoed Dostoevsky's hatred of the industrialization and automation that he associated with modernity, even claiming that he would prefer 'to live under a system of feudal oppression' than under the mechanical controls of modern white supremacist law.[40]

Dostoevsky, meanwhile, indeed regarded Communism and other socialistic philosophies as bourgeois doctrines, tainted by a continuing investment in industrial progress, which the Russian intelligentsia were seeking to impose upon a peasantry more inclined to Christian worship. But even in this belief, which could not apparently be more remote from Wright's thinking, we find that Dostoevsky shared Wright's commitment to the culture of a common folk – to the 'peasant' from whom, the latter felt, urbanization and ghettoization had exacted such a dreadful price. The formal innovations that flood *Crime and Punishment* with Russian voices, and which Bakhtin would later celebrate as the invention of 'polyphony', as such did not arise from thin air but the fact that the Christian

37  Fyodor Dostoevsky, *Notes from Underground and The Double* (Harmondsworth: Penguin, 1972), trans. Jessie Coulson, p. 15.
38  Wright, *Black Boy (American Hunger)*, p. 334.
39  Etienne Balibar and Pierre Macherey, 'On Literature as an Ideological Form', in Dennis Walder (ed.) *Literature in the Modern World* (New York and Oxford: Oxford University Press, 1990), pp. 223–8 (p. 226).
40  Wright, *Black Boy (American Hunger)*, p. 313.

*Figure 4* Entrance to apartment house in the Black Belt, Chicago, Illinois. Photograph: Edwin Rosskam, 1941.

Fyodor Dostoevsky shared with the Communist Richard Wright a desire to give voice to the marginalized, criminalized, drunken rejected figures who stalked St Petersburg and the Chicago South Side.

Furthermore, while Bakhtin and Virginia Woolf's discussions are drawn more to the journey Dostoevsky's novels take than to the Christian redemption at which they arrive, the same cannot be said of Wright. The Dostoevskian narrative's characteristic movement towards a merciful conversion is not erased in *Native Son* so much as it is transformed into the reaffirmation of a secular but no less idealistic Communistic philosophy. Revolution thus replaces redemption, yet retains something of its narratorial freight. Just as Bigger drops the 'r' from many words, turning 'sir' into 'suh', so the name of the lawyer Max abbreviates Marx and presents him as a socialist mouthpiece who will perhaps find some good in all the awful things that have hitherto occurred. Many find the ending of the novel unconvincing, disliking Max's concluding appeal to revolutionary politics. Yet it must be stressed here that many have expressed similar disappointment at the Christian conclusions of *Crime and Punishment* and *The Devils* – if the conclusion to *Native Son* disappoints, it does so in a thoroughly Dostoevskian fashion.

### The transplantation of the blues

Slicing through this Dostoevskian analysis, the blues also influence *Native Son* profoundly. As the 1950s black novelist Ralph Ellison once suggested, a striking combination of high and so-called 'low' culture distinguishes all Wright's best writing, which tends to mix Dostoevsky and other 'literary guides . . . with blues-tempered echoes of railroad trains, . . . estrangements, fights and flights, deaths and disappointments, charged with physical and spiritual hungers and pain'. Wright's blues influences, indeed, inspired Ellison to produce his celebrated definition of this southern black song-writing tradition. As he famously put it, singers and songwriters working in the form of the blues share:

> an impulse to keep the painful details and episodes of a brutal experience alive in one's aching consciousness, to finger its jagged grain, and to transcend it, not by the consolation of philosophy but by squeezing from it a near-tragic, near-comic lyricism. As a form, the blues is an autobiographical chronicle of personal catastrophe expressed lyrically.[41]

In this section I argue that this blues sensibility, which Ellison here summarizes with Wright's autobiography in mind, is no less palpable in *Native Son*. Bigger's narrative, I suggest, also forces the 'black' blues into the 'white' literary domain, so disrupting the binary opposition into which these cultures are routinely placed, collapsing the distance between *Crime and Punishment* and the blues that originated on the plantations of Wright's native Mississippi.

Much of *Native Son* resonates with the 'estrangements, fights and flights, deaths and disappointments' that Ellison identifies with the blues' emotional vocabulary. But this music's distinctive temperament becomes especially conspicuous in the characterization of Bigger Thomas and Bessie Mears, who respectively evoke the forsaken belligerent men and downtrodden women whose tribulations are dramatized by a host of blues lyrics. Exchanges such as the following, in which Bessie at last realizes that Bigger is capable of killing her, resemble predicaments imagined by blues lyricists.

> 'I'm scared, Bigger,' she whimpered. . . .
> Fear sheathed him in fire. His words came in a thick whisper.
> 'Keep still, now. I ain't playing. Pretty soon they'll be after me, maybe. And I ain't going to let 'em catch me, see? I ain't going to let 'em! The first thing they'll do in looking for me is to come to you. They'll grill you about me and you, you drunk fool, you'll tell! You'll tell if you ain't in it, too. . . .'
> 'Naw; Bigger!' she whimpered tensely. . . . He stood looking down at her, waiting for her to quiet. . . . He reached under the pillow and brought out the bottle and took out the stopper and put his hand round her and tilted her head. . . .
> 'Bigger, please! Don't do this to me! *Please*! All I do is work, work like a dog! From morning till night I ain't got no happiness. I ain't never had none. I ain't got nothing and you do this to me. After how good I been to you. Now you just spoil my whole life. I've done everything for you I know how and you do this to me. *Please*, Bigger . . .' She turned her head away and stared at the floor. 'Lord, don't let this happen to me!

41  Ralph Ellison, 'Richard Wright's bluesrsquo; in *The Norton Anthology of African-American Literature*, pp. 1538–48 (p. 1539).

I ain't done nothing for this to come to me! I just work! I ain't had no happiness, no nothing. I just work. I'm black and I work and don't bother nobody . . .'

('Flight', pp. 209–10)

On one hand, this intense excerpt offers further proof of Wright's debt to European literature. The demonic aura in which Bigger is increasingly enveloped as he menaces Bessie and as his 'Fear' comes to 'sheath . . . him in fire' clearly owes something to the infernal, Dantean iconography that, in *Crime in Punishment*, surround Raskolnikov's equally brutish degeneration. The above scene, which takes place on the threshold of Bigger's flight and the novel's subsequent denouement, also recalls the similarly climactic moment when Raskolnikov's lover Sonya stumbles upon his crimes.[42] Other European sources are also apparent. Russian dramatist Anton Chekhov's famous instruction that, if a gun appears in the first scene of a play, it must be fired before the final curtain here resurfaces in Wright's decision to hand Bigger a pillow that, by reminding readers of Mary's earlier murder, illuminates the danger of Bessie's position.[43]

Yet we can also observe that these European influences pertain to the parts of the above excerpt written in a third-person narrative. And that the black voices that this narrative houses, in contrast, 'whimper' and sob, come out in a 'thick whisper' and sound a little as though they could be sung by Ma Rainey, Bessie Smith or another blueswoman famous in the 1930s. Lost in a literary universe developed from white culture, they call out a soft moan that, even as it echoes against the South Side's tenement walls, fading at last to nothingness, reanimates a previous era and the 'hollers, cries, whoops, and moans of black men and women working in fields without recompense'.[44] The hopelessness of their situation, their feeling that such dire straits are merely a logical conclusion of their troubled lives, their repetitions, low murmurs, anguished howls and last-minute calls to God: everything that Bessie and Bigger say here suggests that theirs is less an ordinary conversation than a call and response session between a bluesman and a blueswoman. Everything they say certainly corresponds to Ralph Ellison's famous definition of the blues, conveying its 'impulse to keep the painful detail and episodes of a brutal experience alive in one's aching consciousness, to finger its jagged grain and to transcend it, not by the consolation of philosophy but by squeezing from it a near-tragic, near-comic lyricism'. Theirs is another 'chronicle of personal catastrophe expressed lyrically'.[45] As the provocative African-American literary critic Houston A. Baker suggests, *Native Son* is thus part of an ongoing black 'project of achieving a blues book most excellent'.[46]

*Native Son*'s attention to the blues runs deep and is even alert to the gender nuances within the music tradition. As they conduct their fractious dialogue, the

42  Dostoevsky, *Crime and Punishment* (London: Penguin, 1991), p. 482.
43  See Pekka Tammi (1979) 'Chekhov's Shot Gun and Nabokov: A Note on Subtext, Motifs, and Meaning in the Novella "Lik"', *Notes on Contemporary Literature*, 9(5): pp. 3–5.
44  Houston A. Baker, *Blues, Ideology and Afro-American Literature: A Vernacular Theory* (Chicago, Ill. and London: University of Chicago Press, 1984), p. 8.
45  *The Collected Essays of Ralph Ellison*, p. 129.
46  Baker, *Blues, Ideology and Afro-American Literature*, p. 140.

differences in temperament and style that Bigger and Bessie's lyrical statements exhibit come to map closely onto those distinguishing classic 'male' blues from its 'female' equivalents. Replacing Bessie's sorrow for anger and her despair for intimidation, Bigger's statements are ragged and spontaneous but in other ways resemble the lyrics of those ostentatiously macho blues songs that valorize rebellion, aggression and fearlessness. Such lyrics celebrate the character type that the historian of the black South Leon F. Litwack has labelled the 'bad nigger'. Litwack suggests that this figure is exalted

> for his cunning, boldness, coolness, and wit, often in the face of over-whelming odds, and for the uncanny ability and imaginative powers he displayed in outwitting his enemies. Unlike his counterparts in white folklore, he did not rob from the rich and give to the poor. He preyed on his own people as well as white, terrorizing both ... the innocent and the guilty, the wealthy and the poor. Rather than show any remorse for his depredations, he mocked piety and expressed indifference about his fate.

> *I'm so bad, I don't ever want to be good, uh, huh;*
> *I'm going to de devil and I wouldn't go to heaven, uh, huh,*
> *No I wouldn't go to heaven if I could.*[47]

Although the 'bad nigger' that such macho blues lyrics celebrate evokes Bigger Thomas's personality, important differences remain. Bigger cannot outwit his adversaries; his attempts to sound defiant or calmly satanic never quite convince. Such shortcomings result from the fact that the so-called 'bad nigger' of macho blues music is not what Bigger Thomas *is* so much as what he aspires to be.

That is to say, many critics have approached *Native Son* as a study of criminal-ization rather than criminality – as a novel that implicitly understands individual identity as neither static nor permanent but as a fluid process constantly open to change. This fluid understanding grows evident in the blues accents of Bigger's speech; these accents indicate that Wright is more interested in the means by which Bigger comes to inhabit the 'bad nigger' stereotype than he is in the stereo-type itself. Bigger's act as a 'bad nigger' is therefore precisely that – an act – a performance which, if we are honest, is inept. When he insists to Bessie that 'Pretty soon they'll be after me, maybe', for example, Bigger's attempt to mimic a common blues trope of pursuit – his attempt to evoke the mood of classic songs such as Robert Johnson's 'Hellhound on my Trail' – is undermined by his concluding, contradictory note of doubt – that oddly incongruous 'maybe' – which accidentally reminds us he is less 'bad nigger' than scared boy.

The irony of this performance is that the more accomplished it gets the less artificial it becomes. The artifice has a purpose; the impersonation chases reality. Put another way, just as Robert Johnson lyrics like 'I'm going to beat my woman / Till I get satisfied' seem to draw him (or rather, his lyrical persona) closer to his crimes, just as they imagine these crimes and therefore make them seem more possible, so Bigger's threatening discourse with Bessie ('Keep still, now. . . . I ain't playing') at once rehearses an artificial criminal persona inherited from the blues

---

47  Litwack, *Trouble in Mind*, p. 438.

and makes this artifice more lifelike. In statements such as these, Bigger anticipates the moment when he will iron hesitancy and humanity out of his speech and
so make the pretence involved in his performance disappear. As soon as his occasional uncertainties ('maybe') vanish, Bigger will stop acting like, and will have
become, a hoodlum. By then, his objective fulfilled, his long-standing attempts to
act like the 'bad nigger' of the blues imagination will have helped turn him into
one.

The name of Bigger's girlfriend, meanwhile, raises the possibility that Wright
named her in homage to the famous blues singer Bessie Smith, who died in a
car crash in late 1937, the period of *Native Son*'s artistic germination. Mears
certainly displays the same tendency towards overt, outrageous self-pity, 'to
probe [her] . . . own grievous wound', that Ellison associates with Bessie Smith.[48]
At other times, Mears seems every inch the careworn blueswoman. Indeed, the
fact that her performance of this stereotype suffers neither the hesitancy nor the
lapses that Bigger brings to bear on his 'bad nigger' role is of great significance,
a sign, perhaps, that Wright is less alert to female than male stereotypes, less
sensitive to the patriarchal demands that force them into being.

Another victim of male violence, Bessie Mears's speech could, as the black
feminist Angela Y. Davis says of Bessie Smith's lyrics, 'be interpreted as accepting
emotional and physical abuse as attendant hazards for women involved in sexual
partnerships'. As with her namesake, however, such apparent acceptance masks
'implicit critiques of male abuse'. Simply by reminding Bigger that her life has
been as hard as his and has not made her violent, Mears highlights 'the inhuman-
ity and misogyny of male batterers'.[49] And, perhaps because she targets misogyny
in general, Mears's speech also repeats the classic blues tendency to foreswear
egotism and elevate self-pity into a category of dissent, allowing the autobiographical 'I' to stand for a maligned group – for all working-class black
women.

Moreover, whereas what Bigger says is ragged and loose, devoid of the syllabic
economy and meter characteristic of the blues lyric, what Bessie says, by contrast,
meets such conventions halfway. Exclamation marks function almost as line
breaks, partially versifying her protests: 'Bigger, please! Don't do this to me!
*Please*! All I do is work, work like a dog!' Bessie's repetition of 'please' and 'me'
subsequently acquire at least the semblance of an AAA rhyming structure, a
three-line structure that one writer suggests is 'common enough in traditional
African music' and which also recalls the Bessie Smith lyric, 'Please Help Me Get
Him off My Mind'.[50]

> I've cried and worried, all night I've laid and groaned
> I've cried and worried, all night I've laid and groaned
> I used to weigh two hundred, now I'm down to skin and bones

Nor is the symmetry between such lyrics and Bessie Mears's speech only formal.
Both Smith and Mears repeat simple phrases, respectively savouring plain speech

---

48  Ellison, 'Richard Wright's blues', p. 1539.
49  Angela Y. Davis, *Blues Legacies and Black Feminism: Gertrude 'Ma' Rainey, Bessie Smith, and
    Billie Holiday* (New York: Vintage, 1999), pp. 26–7.
50  Ronald Segal, *The Black Diaspora* (London: Faber & Faber, 1995), p. 378.

such as 'laid and groaned' and '*Please*, Bigger', and this marked formal similarity expresses an equally marked thematic parallel, whereby both universalize, and even democratize, the lament, rendering it accessible to all. Just as Bessie Smith's tribulations – her crying, worrying, groaning and weight loss – become meaningful because they parallel those of her listeners, so the same dynamic, in which the transition is again from the personal to the representative, and from the representative to the political, occurs in Mears's semi-versified speech: 'I just work. I'm black and I work and don't bother nobody'.

And yet, although it is part of *Native Son*'s radical intent, and although it champions what Houston A. Baker calls the 'resonantly energetic capability for disruptive expressive action' of black vernacular culture, this use of the blues is not without problems.[51] The fact that Bessie slips into the role of the jaded blueswoman so effortlessly, and without recourse to a hesitancy that would disturb its silhouetted, insincere, perfection, contrasts very pointedly with the prolonged process whereby Bigger corrects himself for himself and to himself in order to realize himself as a fully paid-up member of Chicago's criminal fraternity.

Put another way, if we read Bessie Mears at any level as a stereotypical manifestation of such blueswomen, it soon becomes clear that Wright's understanding of this stereotype makes much room for its tones of lamentation and outraged victimhood but none whatsoever for the righteous anger that should surely be just as prominent within it. The Bessie Smith who emerges from the opening lines of 'Please Help Me Get Him off My Mind' is imploring, sorrowful, oppressed, a Bessie Smith who indeed resembles Bessie Mears very closely. But the song soon moves into a radically alternative lyrical terrain, voicing fantasies of compensatory violence that Bessie Mears is powerless to enact:

> It's all about a man who always kicked and dogged me 'round
> It's all about a man who always kicked and dogged me 'round
> And when I try to kill him that's when my love for him comes down

The cultural affirmation intended in *Native Son*'s use of the blues is compromised by the fact that one of its principal manifestations, Bessie Mears, is deprived of the physical and psychological power that one of her likely sources famously epitomized. Writers such as Angela Y. Davis now emphasize Bessie Smith's unbowed stridency, her effective anti-racist and anti-sexist defiance, fondly retelling how she told some Klansmen bent on disrupting an outdoor concert in the South to pick up them sheets and run![52] Bessie Mears is far less commanding: though she does not exactly surrender to victim status, her resistance to it – her imploring 'Bigger, *please*' – seems doomed to failure.

One of the most remarkable aspects of Wright's use of the blues is that it updates and urbanizes a music genre that at the time remained largely associated with the South. Admittedly, the blues enjoyed enormous popularity in northern cities at this time, flourishing in the bars and music shacks of Harlem and Detroit as well as the Chicago South Side. But the music that emanated from these venues

51  Baker, *Blues, Ideology and Afro-American Literature*, p. 139.
52  Chris Albertson, *Bessie* (London and New Haven, Conn.: Yale University Press, 2003), pp. 155–7.

chiefly resonated with the part within recent migrants that still felt scarred by and strangely nostalgic for the southern world which they been forced to discard so abruptly. The repertoires of most artists, including many of those who had permanently relocated to the North, certainly remained doggedly orientated towards what we might think of as a pre-urban, southern worldview, which engaged with present conditions only in fleeting, bittersweet allusions to migration. Despite Angela Y. Davis's insistence that 'Bessie Smith's evocations of the South ... did much more than cater to a wistful yearning for home', the fact is that, like many of her contemporaries, her song lyrics engage with the urban North only obliquely and are far more explicitly embroiled in the pressures of a recognizably southern life.[53]

*Native Son*'s great accomplishment is to modernize this music, to lift it decisively from the southern plantations on which it originated and to illuminate its salience for the new field of the African-American struggle: the industrial ghetto. Over a decade before Wright's fellow southerners B. B. King, Muddy Waters and Howlin' Wolf started interspersing the rural standards they carried north with new songs responding to the Chicago cityscape, *Native Son* revealed that the music could indeed accommodate this switch in black life, adjusting its tropes of flight, sexual misadventure, oppression and violence to fit the urban terrain. Snow blizzards now replace the inundation of the Mississippi that Bessie Smith famously likened to the Old Testament flood. Order may now be enforced by policemen with Billy clubs rather than by lynch mobs and prison 'farms'. Labour, likewise, might now be industrial, performed in factories rather than plantations. But *Native Son* reveals that the blues still speak to this brave new world. And it suggests that, if the Mississippian Robert Johnson once sang of a need 'to keep moving' – to escape a 'hellhound on my trail' – then Bigger's predicament is comparable to this and, as such, is far graver, for he has been brought to this familiar fugitive plight in Chicago – a locale Robert Johnson himself associated with freedom. Bigger, in other words, is a blues outlaw with no options left, a fugitive with nowhere left to run.

## Bigger's vernacular voice

Even when not evoking the blues, Bigger's voice and those around it clearly belong to the black vernacular tradition. *Native Son*'s artful respelling of selected words from Bigger's monosyllabic speech, its depiction of signifying sessions and its references to gospel lyrics, all manifest Wright's demand in 'Blueprint for Negro Writing' that future literature pay heed to and represent the oral 'channels through which the racial wisdom flowed'. All of these textual effects, in other words, reflect Wright's desire to rectify a situation that his important early manifesto 'Blueprint for Negro Writing' outlined in the following terms:

> Not yet caught in paint or stone, and as yet but feebly depicted in the poem and novel, the Negroes' most powerful images of hope and despair still remain in the fluid state of daily speech. How many John

53 Davis, *Blues Legacies and Black Feminism*, p. 89.

*Figure 5* Untitled. Photograph: Edwin Rosskam, 1941.

Henrys have lived and died on the lips of these black people? How many mythical heroes in embryo have been allowed to perish for lack of husbanding by alert intelligence?[54]

Henry Louis Gates, Jr., author of an illuminating study of the relationship between African-American literature and its vernacular traditions, is understandably wary of the patrician tone that Wright adopts here, lamenting his decision to dismiss the 'feeble' poems and novels of the Harlem Renaissance in a single stroke.[55] Yet, although the manifesto's subsequent preference for 'Eliot, Stein, Joyce, Proust, Hemingway, and Anderson' can seem somewhat Eurocentric, this appearance is offset by the fact that Wright is pointedly designating earlier black writing as inferior, not to this dazzlingly white list, but to the vernacular creations – the satirical folk tales, coded spirituals and the countless 'John Henry' and other blues lyrics – that ordinary African-Americans created.[56] Motivating Wright's rejection of African-American culture's literary works is an enthusiastic affirmation of its oral apotheoses – of the ingenious mischief of its signifying sessions, the sublime despair of its blues lyric, even the power of its gospel song. Wright weighs literature against these vernacular accomplishments and thus finds it wanting largely on intra- rather than interracial grounds.

A similar mix of influences, in which the classic texts of the Western canon snake into the oddly 'nameless tradition of black mythology', is prominent in

54  Wright, 'Blueprint for Negro Writing', p. 1382.
55  Henry Louis Gates, Jr., *The Signifying Monkey: A Theory of African-American Literary Criticism* (New York and Oxford: Oxford University Press, 1988), p. 119.
56  Wright, 'Blueprint for Negro Writing', p. 1385.

*Native Son* itself.[57] On one level, *Native Son*'s attempt to record Bigger's voice imaginatively can be seen as another Dostoevskian influence, encouraging yet more comparisons with *Crime and Punishment* and its dramatization of what we have seen Bakhtin call 'the so-called *familiar speech of the street*'. But on another level – and as the 'Blueprint for Negro Writing' makes clear – Wright's approach to orality is governed by a racial politics quite unlike anything to be found in Dostoevsky. As this section shows, *Native Son* consistently devotes far more attention to rendering AAE than to 'standard' white talk. Almost exclusively it concentrates its stylistic innovations on AAE – on a language whose difference, to paraphrase sociolinguist Geneva Smitherman, is often mistaken for deficiency.[58] And this special attention places Wright back into the literary tradition that he sometimes dismissed, illuminating his intervention in a debate about the uses and abuses of AAE to which every major African-American writer, from the 1890s storyteller Charles W. Chestnutt to our present Nobel Laureate Toni Morrison, has contributed.

All world literature, every one of its numerous and interrelated narrative traditions, originally developed from an oral mode of storytelling in which the narrator sat amongst the audience and engaged them face to face. And all of these traditions are in turn still haunted by this oral inheritance. Through striking rhetorical flourishes, direct addresses, and the techniques by which they withhold information and create suspense, all register the abiding presence of this original storytelling mode. Readers of *Moll Flanders* (1722) cannot fail to be struck by Daniel Defoe's delight in his protagonist's earthy speech, the ribaldry of which seems sometimes audible, decisively counteracting the overweening puritanism of the novel's surface narrative. Similarly, leading Marxist theorist Fredric Jameson has suggested that Victorian literature's frequent lapses into overt omniscience – those rather jarring moments when writers such as Charles Dickens and Charlotte Brontë address readers or second-guess their emotions – 'attempt to restore the coordinates of a face-to-face storytelling institution which has been effectively disintegrated by the printed book and even more definitively by the commodification of literature and culture'.[59]

And yet the ghosts of oral culture, while marking all literary narratives, haunt the African-American novel with particular force. Details from Wright's own biography explain why this should be so. For every writer of *Native Son*, for every exceptional and (eventually) fortunate black southerner who managed to infiltrate the Jim Crow library, thousands of others remained frozen out of such institutional fortresses, forced back onto the oral means of cultural production that everyone could access. But the scene of this imprisonment turned out to be the method of its resistance. That is to say, racists during and after slavery were so busy ring-fencing literature and defending its status as an exclusively white venture that they rarely noticed or even bothered to deny that the oral sphere into which they had forced most African-American artists could in fact be moulded

57  Gates, *The Signifying Monkey*, p. 119.
58  Geneva Smitherman (1971) 'Black Idiom', *Negro American Literature Forum*, 5(3): pp. 88–91, 115–17.
59  Fredric Jameson, *The Political Unconscious: Narrative as a Socially Symbolic Act* (London and New York: Routledge, 2002), p. 141.

into a culture in its own right. Desperate to believe that educational inequalities resulted not from segregation law but from nature, and utterly convinced of the supremacy of all written over all oral culture, these Eurocentric authorities would have been horrified to discover that the Jim Crow civilization they constructed – the white supremacist fantasies they published and the segregation signs that they erected – would fade from the landscape even as the spoken, invisible, ungraspable words and songs of their erstwhile black inferiors lived on.

But they did. While the inter-war plantation novels of John Pendleton Kennedy and Catharine Ann Warfield are now read as historical curiosities if at all, while the ghastly racist fantasies that Thomas Dixon produced in the 1900s are now approached not as literature so much as the closest American culture has got to producing *Mein Kampf*, while such figureheads of Jim Crow's literary 'civilization' lapse into abeyance, those black vernacular artists who protested segregation and chronicled its abuses have become increasingly fêted, their oral archive of folk tales and song lyrics championed for being altogether more humane, altogether more heroic. Today's cultural marketplace takes little interest in those romanticizations and justifications of slavery that were wildly popular in Wright's day and which – as the article by the literary critic Clare Eby will argue later in this book (see Critical readings, **pp. 114–32**) – inform *Native Son*'s reflections of racism. Rather, this marketplace now focuses on the rebellious vernacular produced by the men and women such racism denigrated. A process of commodification that would seem remarkable had it not grown so familiar has progressively rehabilitated these marginal figures, turning the names of Lead Belly, Howlin' Wolf, Bessie Smith and others into brands of rebellion, passports by which consumer capitalism can gain entry into the new markets it associates with teenagers, thirty-somethings and other archetypal personalities of its own design. Fuelling what Paul Gilroy calls the 'planetary commerce in blackness', the old and necessary protests of the southern blues have in this way been digitally remastered and transferred to CD, furnishing a soundtrack for the very different rebellions of today.[60]

Such commodification discomfits some academics, who prefer to concentrate instead on the actual content of African-American cultural masterpieces. Others, though, follow Paul Gilroy's lead and insist that black culture's new-found position at the helm of today's spectacular global media cannot help but reposition the way in which such masterpieces are read. Gilroy himself obviously loves Wright's work, but a wider interest in the commodification of blackness makes him seem aware that the present popularity of novels such as *Native Son* and secondary studies such as the one you now hold effectively reveal, like so many Che Guevara T-shirts, that even anti-capitalist rhetoric, in this age of compulsory commodification, can be productively bought and sold. Wright's veneration of oral culture is key to this commercial success: iconoclastic in its own time, today it flows smoothly into an MTV-led culture in which the blues, soul and the new vernacular of hip hop advertise every product that we have been able to imagine.

---

60  Paul Gilroy, *Between Camps: Nations, Cultures and the Allure of Race* (London: Penguin, 2001), p. 13.

Wright is not the only African-American writer of the mid-twentieth century whose reputation has been revamped by this 'planetary commerce'. At least since 1980, the once-forgotten works of Zora Neale Hurston have enjoyed a similar restoration, her suddenly unforgettable name undergoing a process of reification not unlike that by which, in Richard Dyer's brilliant analysis in *Stars* (1979) of the American film industry, Hollywood stars such as 'Marilyn Monroe' or 'Denzel Washington' cease to refer to individuals alone but to a set of marketable associations – in Hurston's case, to a sense of racial pride and well-being and an informal rather than doctrinaire commitment to gender equality, which are in keeping with the interest in Africa and womanism prevailing among black artists and intellectuals since 1970.[61]

Indeed, in the final analysis, Richard Wright shared more with his immediate African-American predecessors than he let on. In the end, his disquiet with the major works of the Harlem Renaissance, his feeling that their attempts to capture the vernacular were 'feeble', arguably amounted to a difference of technique, which he unfortunately mistook for a difference of principle. Not only Hurston but the majority of black writers of the Harlem Renaissance of the 1920s and 1930s actually shared Wright's love of the vernacular. Many were as conscious as he was that Standard American English, for those transported to the New World, had been the language of the master, its lessons administered with the whip. And few, in turn, would have objected to Wright's assessment that 'the Negroes' most powerful images of hope and despair still remain in the fluid state of daily speech'.[62]

What was different was that this common horror at linguistic inequity inspired such important forerunners as Paul Laurence Dunbar and Sterling A. Brown to launch a wholesale renovation of official English orthography far more comprehensive than anything undertaken in *Native Son*. Throwing out the dictionary, these writers deliberately vandalized English spelling, recasting *I'll* into *Ah'll* and *last* into *las'*, finally tailoring an entirely new lexicon to suit those AAE speakers who previous literature had marginalized or erased. From such radical formal innovation there resulted new versions of what Henry Louis Gates Jr. would later call 'talking' poems and 'talking' books, texts whose unorthodox appearance drew the reader's ear as much as his eyes to the page.

> Lay me down beneaf de willers in de grass,
> Whah de branch'll go a-singin' as it pass.
>     An' w'en I's a-layin' low,
>     I kin hyeah it as it go
> Singin', 'Sleep, my honey, tek yo' res' at las''.[63]

Verses such as Paul Laurence Dunbar's 'A Death Song' (1900) disfigure Standard English orthography, pressing it into the service of a new poetry that is at once egalitarian and fictitious. Egalitarian, because, as I have argued elsewhere, these

61  Richard Dyer, *Stars* (London: BFI, 1979).
62  Wright, 'Blueprint for Negro Writing', p. 1382.
63  Paul Laurence Dunbar, 'A Death Song' in James Weldon Johnson (ed.) *The Book of American Negro Poetry* (San Diego, Calif.: Harcourt, 1931), pp. 62–3.

poems seek to delegate aesthetic agency to sharecroppers, house servants and those other black folk whose 'conversance in the vernacular amply compensated [their assumed] . . . illiteracy'.[64] And fictitious, because, to vindicate this assumption of illiteracy, these compositions must feign to be transcriptions – must impersonate facsimiles of oral performances that have never taken place.

The need to maintain this illusion, to ensure that the mask of transcription does not slip, forces Dunbar to bend official English to meet AAE's distinctive grammar and pronunciation. It encourages Dunbar to turn the standard singular usage 'I'm' into 'I's', thus reflecting the 'unique use of the verb "to be"' that Henry Louis Gates considers 'the most assaulting aspect of' AAE grammar.[65] It makes Dunbar weave into his verse the intensifying prefix a-, another AAE hallmark, which appears when his unlettered protagonist remembers 'a-layin''. And it persuades Dunbar to work his apostrophes hard, to make them indicate at least three familiar traits of AAE pronunciation: the gerund's abbreviation ('singin'', 'layin''), glottal stops ('An''), and non-rhotic pronunciation ('yo''). Crudely summarized by the anti-colonial Martinique intellectual Frantz Fanon as 'the myth of the nigger-who-eats his R's', this latter phenomenon is denoted elsewhere by the respelling of 'where' as 'whah'.[66] Dunbar, too, finds new ways of depicting AAE's alternative pronunciation of the th- suffix's hard and soft pronunciations, turning the former into the Cockneyesque 'beneaf' and the latter into that familiar d- in which 'the' becomes 'de'.

Like so many puppet strings, these innumerable apostrophes and other orthographic marks strive to make the inanimate seem animate – to make the controlled composition seem more like an oral, spontaneous event. Indeed, the sheer gusto with which Dunbar sets about his task tempts him to employ some orthographic strings that are actually surplus to requirements. His apostrophizing of the h when rendering 'w'en', for example, does not alter its pronunciation and is a clear example of what linguists call 'eye dialect' – a string the poem could have managed without.

Hurston herself employed many of these techniques. Invariably, whenever speech marks interrupt the narrative of *Their Eyes Were Watching God* (1937), Hurston discards the dictionary to clear space for a glut of vernacular formulations: double negatives, non-rhotic pronunciations, abbreviated gerunds, 'dis' and 'dat'. Apostrophes graffiti her dialogue, each one proof of a desire to deface the accepted façade of written English and to force it to register AAE's presence. Almost half of the spoken words in Hurston's most famous novel deliberately violate their official dictionary spelling.

> Janie never thought at all. . . . She rushed into the cane and about the fifth row down she found Tea Cake and Nunkie struggling. . . .
> 'Whut's de matter heah?' Janie asked in a cold rage. They sprang apart.

64  Andrew Warnes, *Hunger Overcome: Food and Resistance in Twentieth Century African-American Literature* (Athens and London: University of Georgia Press, 2004), p. 22.
65  Henry Louis Gates, Jr., *Figures in Black: Words, Signs, and the 'Racial' Self* (New York and Oxford: Oxford University Press, 1989), p. 188.
66  Frantz Fanon, *Black Skin, White Masks* (London: Pluto, 1986), trans. Charles Lam Markmann, p. 21.

'Nothin',' Tea Cake told her, standing shamefaced.

'Well, whut you doin' in heah? How come you ain't out dere wid de rest?'[67]

To Wright, the painstaking care with which Dunbar and Hurston wrote down AAE speech resulted in 'feeble' effects because they skirted too close to stereotype for comfort. Intersecting with the indecent glossary of Negro caricaturists and feeding the same white appetite for the African exotic, this radical orthography could sometimes be mistaken for that mouthed by those outright racist stereotypes who became prominent in the national literature and culture during the 1890s (see Chronology, p. 47). Wright objected to *Their Eyes Were Watching God* in particular, saying that it was 'cloaked in that facile sensuality that has dogged Negro expression', that it bordered on minstrelsy and that it was addressed 'to a white audience whose chauvinistic tastes she knows how to satisfy'.[68] And indeed, the problems Wright identified in this radical orthographic system can seem exacerbated by Hurston's tendency, illustrated above, to apply it to her characters' speech but not to her third-person narrative. Nowadays it is hard not to see this sharp technical disparity between narration and dialogue as hierarchical. Selectively remembering and forgetting that all 'alphabetic writing . . . strives to represent sounds and succeeds only in representing possibilities', Hurston's doomed attempts to rectify every single 'mismatch between sound and symbol' in her dialogue while ignoring such instances in her own prose – so that the narrator writes 'here' but Tea Cake says 'heah' – tends to normalize the former while exoticizing the latter.[69] *Native Son* assiduously avoids such linguistic stratification. It seeks to indicate AAE without fetishizing it, to depict but not exacerbate its marginality. It makes Bigger and his family talk like this:

'Suppose those rats cut our veins at night when we sleep? Naw! Nothing like that ever bothers you! All you care about is your own pleasure! . . . Bigger, honest, you the most no-countest man I ever seen in all my life!'

'You done told me that a thousand times,' he said, not looking round.

'Well, I'm telling you agin! And mark my word, some of these days you going to set down and *cry*. . . .'

'Stop prophesying about me,' he said.

'I prophesy much as I please!' . . .

'Aw, for chrissakes!' he said [.]

('Fear', p. 39)

Some puppeteers might use hundreds of strings, their determination to register even the microscopic tics or mannerisms of their puppets making them thread connections to every limb, every feature, every bone. And yet this intricate web of strings, though resulting from a desire to make the illusion complete, actually

---

67  Zora Neale Hurston, *Their Eyes Were Watching God* (London: Virago, 1986), p. 204.

68  Richard Wright, 'Between Laughter and Tears', *New Masses*, 5 October 1937, p. 25.

69  Ralph Emerson (1997) 'English Spelling and its Relation to Sound', *American Speech*, 72(2): pp. 260–88 (p. 260).

betrays it: becoming knotted together, catching the light, they, ironically, prevent the audience from losing itself in the show. Wright's criticism of *Their Eyes Were Watching God* and *Native Son*'s far less pernickety representation of AAE suggest he felt Hurston's orthographic revisions had produced a similarly ironic betrayal. Originating in a desire to perfect the depiction of AAE, these revisions likewise catch the light in so far as they, too, call attention to the artifice they are intended to sustain, advertising the fictitiousness of the fiction.

By contrast, *Native Son*'s passages of AAE dialogue do not emblazon its marginality. Generally, the novel renders AAE neither as an alien nor wholly alternative language that calls for a completely new orthography, but as a branch of English that, while different, remains connected to its historic root. This is not to say that Wright's representation of AAE denies its alterity, or that he inherits nothing from Dunbar and Hurston's experimentation. He retains some of the strings they devised, pulling them to signal not only Bigger and his mother's non-rhotic pronunciation ('naw', 'Aw') but also the AAE tendency to emphasize the first part of disyllabic words ('agin'). Other strings, though, are shorn away in *Native Son*. The eye dialect that mars Dunbar and Hurston's approach disappears, its redundant respellings and the linguistic marginalization they compound avoided altogether. Reluctant to use apostrophes, Wright now redistributes the multiple tasks by which Dunbar overworked these punctuation marks, indicating glottal stops by a more discreet respelling ('chrissakes') while retaining the unspoken gerund ('nothing', 'prophesying').

This more streamlined approach results in a written version of spoken AAE that is much closer to the spellings of Standard English, violating the dictionary far less regularly than *Their Eyes Were Watching God*. But the effect it produces still evokes black speech. This suggests not only that some of Hurston and Dunbar's techniques were indeed surplus to requirements, but that Wright here combines his orthographic restraint with an attention to the penetrating phrases, striking Christian aphorisms and improvised imagery that more broadly distinguish AAE. The emphasis now is not on respelling existing words but on showing how AAE places these words into new and striking grammatical arrangements ('You done told me', 'your own pleasure') or unforgettable images ('rats cut our veins'). Ignoring local idiosyncrasies of pronunciation, Wright's ear is tuned towards the social qualities of his characters' speech – towards its deliberate overstatement, its turns towards Christian prophecy and its proclivity to combat such prophecy with sudden blasts of blasphemy.

I mentioned at the start of this section that Wright, though sceptical of the black literary tradition, nonetheless made a significant contribution to its continuing inquiry into the best way of depicting AAE. This significance has grown clearer with time and with the accumulation of seminal black American, Caribbean and African writers whose own works incline towards *Native Son*'s less 'orthographic' approach to black speech. Writing of *Texaco* (1992), for example, Derek Walcott attributes his particular love of Chamoiseau's much-loved novel to its ability to evoke Martinique's Creole without resorting to 'orthography' and its inelegant squiggles, wild apostrophizing and oddly unsystematic respellings. Walcott deplores such 'orthography' for being 'visually crass' and because 'its aural range is limited to a concept of peasant or artisan belligerence that denies its own subtleties of pronunciation, denying its almost completely French roots.'[70] In interview, meanwhile, Toni Morrison has joined Walcott, declaring that she 'always hated with a passion when writers rewrote what black people said, in some kind of phonetic alphabet that was inapplicable to any other regional pronunciation'. Morrison continues by suggesting that, above the over-eager transformation of 'this' into 'dis' and 'that' into 'dat', and beyond the gimmicky abbreviation of the gerund, AAE's real spirit lies in 'the way words are put together, the metaphors, the rhythm, the music – that's the part of the language that is distinctly black to me when I hear it'.[71] Many reasons suggest that Richard Wright should have received the Nobel Prize for Literature that has more recently been bestowed on Morrison and Walcott. But perhaps the greatest is that his approach to black speech anticipates theirs, that *Native Son* pioneers a new method in Black Atlantic literature, which has lately acquired massive canonical acceptance.

## Social determinism: an anti-American accent?

In early 1941, still swept up in *Native Son*'s immediate success, Richard Wright was visited by Robert E. Park, the octogenarian sociologist who had pioneered the Chicago School's focus on the survey of new and industrial urban landscapes. Though somewhat conservative, Park rose with the help of a walking stick to honour the revolutionary novelist. Inspecting Wright, scrutinizing him carefully, Park demanded of the novelist: 'How in the hell did you happen?'[72]

Park's enquiry, the impatient manner in which he insists that the source of his disorientation explain his disorientation away, suggests that Wright is upsetting his assumption that certain social conditions produce certain human person-alities. Park seems to feel that the success of this young, gifted and black artist violates some invisible but vital anthropological code. This feeling, however, forces a problem to the surface. Tactless as it is, Park's question envisions a relationship between the individual and society not so distant from that which *Native Son* offers. Park's deterministic world view – his feeling that certain contexts make certain personalities 'happen' – was obviously confounded by Wright's illustrious career, but it was just as obviously supported by the work that this unclassifiable novelist produced. At the very least, *Native Son* intimates that Bigger does not choose his crimes so much as they choose him. An atmosphere of inevitability pervades his every move.

> It was all over. He had to save himself. But it was familiar, this running away. All his life he had been knowing that sooner or later something like this would come to him. And now, here it was. He had always felt outside of this white world, and now it was true. It made things simple. He felt in his shirt. Yes; the gun was still there. He might have to use it.
>
> ('Flight', p. 251)

---

70  Derek Walcott, 'A Letter to Chamoiseau' in *What the Twilight Says: Essays* (London: Faber & Faber, 1998), pp. 213–32 (pp. 228–9).
71  Toni Morrison, *Conversations with Toni Morrison* (Jackson, Miss.: University Press of Mississippi, 1994), p. 96.
72  Hazel Rowley, *Richard Wright: The Life and Times* (New York: Henry Holt, 2001), p. 250.

*Figure 6* Street urchin, Black Belt, Chicago, Illinois. Photograph: Edwin Rosskam, 1941.

Passages such as these present Bigger's predicament as little more than the culmination of a set of forces beyond his control. Lost on the white rooftops, aware that the police are closing in on him, Bigger here realizes that he is helpless. As clearly as those readers who know that *Native Son* wants to deny us the 'consolation of tears', he realizes that his fate is preordained. Such passages reinforce the unmistakable implication of the novel overall, confirming that, in this harsh and brutal ghetto environment, Bigger's criminality is likely – and perhaps even guaranteed – to occur.

At the same time, though, the passage implies the corollary of this deterministic ethos. Its insistence on the likelihood of Bigger's criminality amounts to a complementary insistence on the unlikelihood that this unpromising ghetto could allow air to reach an autodidact such as Wright. Put another way, Ralph Ellison's famous observation that 'Bigger could not possibly imagine Richard Wright', although intended as an attack of the novel, actually calls attention to one of its most important and deliberate effects: the fact that its anti-hero's imaginative scope is narrowed, not by Wright, but by American society itself.[73] Effectively, then, *Native Son* takes Robert Park's question and turns it full circle. It asks: how in the hell *couldn't* Bigger happen?

*Native Son*'s determinism, its decision to deprive Bigger of agency, results from Wright's close reading of the key texts not only of American sociology but also of literary realism and Marxism. What these intellectual traditions of the late nineteenth and early twentieth centuries shared was a broad belief that social

73  Ralph Ellison, 'The World and the Jug', in *The Norton Anthology of African-American Literature*, pp. 1578–99 (p. 1583).

or economic hierarchies work to limit free will and to produce certain types of individuals. In literary realism, the narratives that this belief spawned tend to contextualize the moral degeneration of a given protagonist and to attribute it to broad social forces. Though Dostoevsky himself repeatedly dramatized the desensitization and corruption of the individual by industrial society, this invest-ment in social or economic causality is even clearer in the work of Émile Zola, Stephen Crane, Theodore Dreiser and those other novelists who practised the more systematic and apparently scientific form of realism that Zola, for one, called naturalism. Often casting human beings as cogs in a social machine that lies beyond their comprehension or control, naturalism's classic texts such as Crane's *Maggie: A Girl of the Streets* (1896) and Dreiser's *Sister Carrie* (1900) exhibit a more forceful determinism in which objects and commodities – machines, goods, property, even cities – make choices on behalf of human beings. In the early 1930s, according to Hazel Rowley, such works were already making Wright wonder how 'would Zola, Dreiser and Crane write about the South Side? He wanted to apply their seemingly impartial naturalistic techniques to depict the daily lives of black people. But he was serving a bewildering apprenticeship, without a guide or fellow writer in sight.'[74]

Isolation was not the only thing that made Wright's apprenticeship bewilder-ing. Its sheer expansiveness, the astonishing impetus that led Wright into as many intellectual spheres as possible, presented other challenges. In the years leading up to *Native Son*, even as he read the major works of literary realism, Wright some-how found time to digest the major writings of the Marxist-Leninist tradition. In this revolutionary canon he encountered the more doctrinaire and far simpler determinism that Friedrich Engels' *Socialism: Utopian and Scientific* (1880) called historical materialism and defined as an insistence that 'the ultimate causes of all social changes . . . are to be sought, not in men's brains, . . . but in changes in the modes of production and exchange. They are to be sought, not in the *philosophy*, but in the *economics* of each particular epoch.'[75] Defining individuals entirely by their relationship to the economy – or, in the Marxist vocabulary, to the means of production – such materialism installs class as the overriding factor. Not only does it insist that one's membership to the proletariat, bourgeoisie or aristocracy completely cancels out the power of individual 'free will'; it actively discredits this latter concept altogether, recasting it as a convenient myth by which the privileged insist that they deserve their privilege.

Wright's apprenticeship ran further. On the shelves of the several dour South Side apartments he rented in the 1930s, such leftist tracts as Karl Marx's *Capital* (1867–83), John Strachey's *The Coming Struggle for Power* (1939) and even Joseph Stalin's *The National and Colonial Question* (1936) variously pressed against studies produced by the Chicago School of Sociology. If anything, the latter influenced the young writer more profoundly. As he later recalled:

> The huge mountains of fact piled up by the Department of Sociology at
> the University of Chicago gave me my first concrete vision of the forces

74  Rowley, *Richard Wright: The Life and Times*, p. 250.
75  Friedrich Engels, *Socialism: Utopian and Scientific* (London: Bookmarks, 1993), p. 87.

that molded the urban Negro's body and soul. (I was never a student at the university; it is doubtful if I could have passed the entrance examination.) . . .

[The] men most responsible for this . . . were not afraid to urge their students to trust their feelings for a situation or an event, were not afraid to stress the role of insight . . . Scientific volumes brilliantly characterized by insight . . . Louis Wirth's *The Ghetto* [1928], Everett Stonequist's *The Marginal Man* [1937], . . . [and Robert] Park's and [Ernest] Burgess's *The City* [1925].[76]

Here and elsewhere, Wright punctuates his appreciation of such sociological research with the verb 'to mould'. The effect of this repetition, as it choruses through Wright's prose, casts society as a kind of sculptor and the individual as his clay. Some form of determinism accordingly comes to seem integral to the 'truth' that this sociological canon revealed to Wright. And indeed, while many of this canon's authors revised or rejected the historical materialism of orthodox Marxism, it is true that the three major intellectual traditions exposed to Wright in these years – literary realism, Marxism and sociology – overlapped with each other considerably. Sociology originated in the Marxist concept of 'human reality', according to the leading theorist of our own time Zygmunt Bauman; literary realism constitutes 'the central model of Marxist aesthetics', according to Fredric Jameson; and *Native Son*, in turn, mouths the causality common to all, presenting Bigger, in Robert Bone's words, as 'a human being whose environment has made him incapable of relating meaningfully to other human beings except through murder'.[77] *Native Son* in this way digests these distinct but interrelated intellectual traditions, all three of which originated in Europe, and applies their common determinism to the altered sphere of the black ghetto. It affirms that, here, no less than in the Lancashire factories Engels studied or the French mines Zola depicted, people are made more than they make themselves.

Wright was aided in this endeavour by a handful of sociological works that, as his autobiography puts it, directly 'bore upon the causes of my conduct and the conduct of my family'.[78] Black academics' studies, and chiefly E. Franklin Frazier's *The Negro Family in the United States* (1939) and Horace Cayton and St Clair Drake's *Black Metropolis* (1946), concentrated on milieux very like that of *Native Son*. They, too, address the problems ghettoization made endemic: family breakdown, delinquency, unemployment, poverty, addiction, violence. Wright was particularly enthusiastic about the second of these texts, the *Black Metropolis* title of which was Cayton and Drake's way of referring to the Chicago South Side, that ghettoized 'city within a city' whose kitchenettes, factories, bars, cafeterias and libraries Wright knew so well.[79] In an admiring introduction to the landmark text, Wright noted:

76  Richard Wright, 'Introduction' in Horace R. Cayton and St Clair Drake, *Black Metropolis* (London: Jonathan Cape, 1946), pp. xvii–xxxiv (pp. xviii–xix).
77  References are respectively to Zygmunt Bauman, *Society under Siege* (Cambridge: Polity, 2002), p. 1; Jameson, *The Political Unconscious*, p. 90; and Bone, *The Negro Novel in America*, p. 151.
78  Wright, *Black Boy (American Hunger)*, p. 327.
79  Cayton and Drake, *Black Metropolis*, p. 12.

> *Black Metropolis* pictures the environment out of which the Bigger
> Thomases of our nation come.... If, in reading my novel, *Native
> Son*, you doubted the reality of Bigger Thomas, then examine the
> delinquency rates cited in this book; if, in reading my autobiography,
> *Black Boy*, you doubted the picture of family life shown there, then
> study the figures on family disorganization given here. *Black Metropolis*
> describes the processes that mold Negro life as we know it today, pro-
> cesses that make the majority of Negroes on Chicago's South Side sixth-
> graders, processes that make 65 percent of all Negroes on Chicago's
> South Side earn their living by manual labor.[80]

Again, here, Wright's appraisal calls attention to the underlying determinism
of sociological methodology, repeats the verb 'to mould' and its implied
inevitability, and so envisions a city where omnipotent social forces swamp
human will. *Black Metropolis* is thus presented as a post-facto vindication
of *Native Son*; the considerable generic divergence between the two, Wright
suggests, masks an affinity of intellectual purpose.

Wright's other commentaries on *Native Son* sustain this approach. They, too,
often protect his incendiary novel against attack by cloaking its fictional qualities
in the camouflage of verifiable fact: sociological statistics, direct observation,
empirical insights. Thus, just as *Black Metropolis* intersperses its statistical
analyses with illustrative case studies of individual South Side residents, 'How
"Bigger" Was Born' lists a number of men Wright knew who, labelled as 'Bigger
No. 1' and '2', etc., corroborate his anti-hero's brutish nihilism and pre-empt the

*Figure 7* Untitled. Photograph: Edwin Rosskam, 1941.

80  Wright, 'Introduction' in *Black Metropolis*, pp. xviii–xx.

charge of sensationalism. As Wright's exploration of this composite personality unfolds, Bigger comes to seem a figure lifted from the pages of classic Chicago sociology – to seem the product, indeed, of another 'mould':

> But why did Bigger revolt? No explanation based upon a hard and fast rule of conduct can be given. But there were always two factors psychologically dominant in his personality. First, through some quirk of circumstance, he had become estranged from the religion and the folk culture of his race. Second, he was trying to react to and answer the call of the dominant civilization whose glitter came to him through the newspapers, magazines, radios, movies, and the mere imposing sight and sound of daily American life. In many respects his emergence as a distinct type was inevitable.[81]

On one level, this essay's title, 'How "Bigger" Was Born', confirms Wright's continuing commitment to the social determinism of his intellectual sources. Far removed from a romantic paradigm in which characters are dreamt or spring unfettered from the authorial unconscious, Bigger is here the product of a rational, explicable process, his 'birth' remaining in this sense 'inevitable'. But on another level, the more digressive path by which Wright's rhetoric inches towards this restatement of the 'inevitable' occasions an attempt to modify determinism and to force it to accommodate the complex varieties of experience that the 'dominant civilization' produces. What Fredric Jameson would later call the 'billiard-ball causality' by which Engels straightforwardly explained class consciousness and by which Crane straightforwardly depicted Maggie's moral descent, having thus fallen into Wright's hands, now gets bent and distorted into a less linear and less elegant but much more lifelike system.[82]

For what these modifications do is present Bigger no longer as the automatic product of the ghetto per se but of the fact that, for him, its characteristic conditions have fallen into a particularly bad configuration. Qualifications and notes of uncertainty, the opening dismissal of easy 'explanation' and the later admission of 'quirk[s] of circumstance', are as such readable as signs of Wright's growing disenchantment with orthodox historical materialism and of his retrospective desire to emphasize those moments when *Native Son*, though written under the sign of Marxism, departs from the oversimplified linearity of its deterministic model. Put another way, Ellison was right to grasp that 'Wright could imagine Bigger, but Bigger could not possibly imagine Richard Wright. Wright saw to that.'[83] To Wright's mind, however, this famous critical statement is more of an observation than an attack. For the American ghetto in *Native Son*'s formulation, clearly, can imagine both: can push one frustrated young man through the doors of the George Cleveland Hall, and another into a drunk white woman's bedroom.

For all these modifications, however, for all Wright's eventual repudiation of a simplistic Marxist analysis that 'gyrates and squirms to make the Negro problem

---

81  Wright, 'How "Bigger" Was Born', pp. 5–8.
82  Jameson, *The Political Unconscious*, p. 10.
83  Ralph Ellison, 'The World and the Jug', in *The Norton Anthology of African-American Literature*, pp. 1578–99 (p. 1583).

fit rigidly into a class-war frame of reference', this clearly remains a form of social determinism.[84] It is one thing to exercise free will. It is quite another to succumb to the multifarious 'quirk[s] of circumstance' that push Bigger into this lethal bedroom and from it into the electric chair. For all that this passage from 'How "Bigger" Was Born' complicates traditional Marxist determinism, its conclusion remains that keyword, 'inevitable'. Its equation, at root, still suggests that Bigger's ghetto life will in time equal criminality.

This beautifully simple equation, in turn, still repels many American and Americanized readers. It still offends those committed to an American interpretation of democracy in which capitalism and Christianity intertwine to create the impression that anyone can rise from rags to riches, that even Bigger could transcend his unpromising circumstances to make himself anew. Many men and women who have otherwise felt dazzled by *Native Son*'s outraged brilliance have found it hard to countenance its un-American, even anti-American, permutations. Paul Green, the white southerner who adapted *Native Son* for the stage, voiced the classic objection:

> Bigger Thomas . . . was practically completely a product of his environment; and I wouldn't subscribe to that. A human being has got some responsibility for his career; and I don't care what Freud says or what whining people say, you can't put [the blame] on somebody else. . . . Bigger Thomas must, in my version, become conscious of the fact that he himself was partly responsible for his own character and what that character did.[85]

Today, Green's insistence on individual responsibility attracts widespread consensus throughout the Americanized world. The belief in social determinism that Green found so repellent and subsequently erased from his theatrical version of the novel is likewise spurned nationally and internationally. One example of this consensus is the disdain that the War on Terror's leading strategists express for the kind of 'nation-building' pioneered by an earlier generation of American politicians; their rhetoric focuses much more on the need to restore individual responsibility to such war-torn states as Afghanistan and Iraq. Another example is that present historians of slavery often seem far more comfortable when chronicling instances of slave resistance than when attending to those who, institutionalized and deprived of agency by the slave-holding system, internalized racial inferiority and submitted to the whims of their masters. Whatever the rights and wrongs of this consensus – and whatever the merits of Wright's countervailing determinism – *Native Son* clearly cuts against the grain of twenty-first-century American culture. Where Wright emphasizes social pressures and 'moulds', this culture emphasizes free will. Where he places responsibility in the society as a whole, it places responsibility in the individual. And where he sees inevitability, it sees guilt.

---

84  Wright, 'Introduction' in *Black Metropolis*, p. xxix.
85  Quoted in Judith Giblin Brazinsky (1984) 'The Demands of Conscience and the Imperatives of Form: The Dramatization of *Native Son*', *Black American Literature Forum*, 18(3): pp. 106–9 (pp. 106–7).

But against all this – and here the nuances multiply further, and paradoxes proliferate – Wright hardly intended *Native Son* to be anti-democratic. Paul Green's criticism of the novel effectively blames its denial of individual responsibility on Wright himself and so sidesteps Wright's clear belief that such determinism actually resulted from American ghetto conditions. Green, in Wright's terms, thus blames the messenger, blames *Native Son* for the very oppression it critiques. For in the final analysis what the sociological, Marxist and literary realist traditions share is not only a desire to prove the existence of a deterministic social dynamic but also the secretly democratic and libertarian hope that by doing so they will begin to dismantle it. Crane no more welcomed Maggie's descent into prostitution and eventual suicide than Engels lauded the bourgeois infatuation with profit or Cayton and Drake hailed the family's disintegration in *Black Metropolis*. Implicit in their critiques, in fact, is a quintessentially American belief in individual freedom and horror at its curtailment by social inequity. The rebellious offspring of such divergent traditions, *Native Son* is equally appalled by the lack of choice that it concentrates into Bigger's melodramatic cry: 'What I killed for, I *am*!' ('Fate', p. 453). *Native Son* is horrified by the erosion of individual freedom; it not only identifies but also decries a determinism nowadays more often disparaged than understood.

## Bigger: silenced by whiteness?

Racism goes to great lengths to simplify humanity. It is an ideology that seeks to pigeonhole the world – to place humankind into neat and orderly compartments. But this is also an ideology vexed by humanity's refusal to sit neatly within such compartments. It is an ideology confused by the evidence placed before it. The prospect of someone in whom the 'races mix', the discovery of affinities between us – such ordinary incidents spell crisis to racist thought. They force it in on itself, compelling it to deride those of 'mixed' identity, to deny interracial empathy and, generally, to come up with ever-more complicated justifications for its simple view of the world.

Ku Klux Klansmen's robes are a good example of this ideology's tendency towards paradox. Bleached to perfection, the whiteness of these robes after all illustrates nothing so much as the 'flaws' of human skin. Flagging up the pinkness of the Klansmen's skin, revealing their tragic inability to achieve their perfect hue, it illustrates that white people are not really white. Not only extremists, however, but general Western cultures remain prone to this kind of paradox. As Richard Dyer points out in his extremely readable *White* (1997), the agreed language by which we talk about race today likewise forgets that particular racial groupings are not 'really of one hue'; it, too, obscures the fact that whiteness is 'a matter of ascription – white people are who white people say are white'.[86]

Richard Wright seems to have anticipated some of the findings of Dyer's important study. For example, in 1955 he travelled to Indonesia, there attending the Bandung Conference of the African, American and Asian countries that had

---

86  Richard Dyer, *White* (London and New York: Routledge, 1997), p. 48.

recently won their independence from European empires. His subsequent *The Color Curtain* (1956) features much in the way of intercultural incomprehension, taking particular delight in recalling how delegates from around the world came to realize that racial identities that they had assumed to be biological were in fact cultural creations. Thus, Wright recalls talking to an Indonesian who, unnerved by this strange big American with his penetrating questions and odd interest in the conference proceedings, visibly relaxed upon being assured that he was a 'Negro'.[87] And thus, too, Wright savours Adam Clayton Powell's predicament at Bandung, mischievously noting that the conference's African and Asian delegates saw the 'Negro Congressman . . . [as] a white man' and so required him to explain that 'he was "colored," that his grandfather had been a branded slave'.[88] Such situations, it seems, made Wright laugh because they exposed the fictitiousness of the white–black division, reminding him that, if white people were really white and black people were really black, their offspring would be grey.

Let us illustrate this simple point with a suitably simple experiment. Think of the colour of black skin – your own or that of others. Compare it to any black objects that come to mind: stereos, shoes, tar, new tyres, funeral robes, even the ink of these words. Think in the same way of white skin. Compare it to white objects: fridges, radiators, toilets, snow, death shrouds, wedding dresses, the paper on which this black ink is printed. While we could add to these contrasts by considering other racial groups, the disparities between white paper and white skin and between black ink and black skin alone substantiate Wright and Dyer's point. For they reveal that, although the palette of human skin colour and the palette of the world around us are often taken to be identical, the first is narrower than the second and lacks its perfect oppositions. Blackening blackness and whitening whiteness, the tendency to blur skin colour into our surrounding environment and to force the former towards the more conspicuous polarities of the latter, thus makes differences of degree seem like differences of kind. And in this way our familiar confusion performs a racializing process: in America, it creates what Wright called 'a fatal division of being', which lent an 'an air of unreality' to America's 'actions, . . . rendering ineffectual the good deeds she feels compelled to do in the world'.[89]

*Native Son* duly presents America as a nation of 'riven consciousness', a nation divided by another 'color curtain'. Key moments in the novel seem preoccupied, mesmerized by fields of black and white colour. The Gothic and terrifying scene in which Bigger finds himself trapped in Mary Dalton's bedroom is classic in this regard. Here Bigger seems to grow terrified, not so much by the prospect of touching Mary's white skin, but, more uncannily, by materials perfect in their whiteness. In these moments, as hemlines or other boundaries grow porous and white material leaks into white skin, erasing its blemishes and making it blood-less, Bigger is suddenly paralysed, unable to master the racial mountain before his eyes:

87  Richard Wright, *The Color Curtain: A Report on the Bandung Conference* (Jackson, Mich.: Banner Books, 1994), p. 78.
88  Wright, *The Color Curtain*, p. 177.
89  Wright, 'Introduction' in *Black Metropolis*, p. xxi.

At the far end of the room he made out the shadowy form of a white bed. . . . he saw the furtive glints of her white teeth. . . . A white blur was standing by the door, silent, ghostlike. It filled his eyes and gripped his body. It was Mrs Dalton. . . . Frenzy dominated him. . . . He clenched his teeth and held his breath, intimidated to the core by the awesome white blur floating toward him. . . . *She's dead.*

('Fear', pp. 115–19)

The Gothic imagery that James Smethurst's essay 'Invented by Horror' will later show is characteristic of Wright's fiction (see Critical readings, **pp. 133–46**) here grows overt, forced to the surface by the glowing white materials that infiltrate Mrs Dalton and Mary's skin and make their respectively feeble and comatose bodies seem ghostly, dangerous, blessed with a power beyond physical strength. Even as it reawakens a known Gothic symbolism of death, however, the women's spectral whiteness places a more rational menace before Bigger: those who the emergency will alert, the seething white Chicago mob who consider themselves racially alike and who share a resolve to annihilate the black rapist. The sexual allure of the woman whose face sinks as though without trace into the wonderfully white pillow in this way calls a wider authoritarian world into action: her promise of satisfaction is a promise of death, which is why it transforms the fear that is Bigger's default emotion into terror. 'The reality of the room fell from him; the vast city of white people that sprawled outside took its place. She was dead and he had killed her. He was a murderer, a Negro murderer, a black murderer. He had killed a white woman' ('Fear', p. 119). Like the infamous 1994 *Time* magazine cover that darkened O. J. Simpson's features, *Native Son*'s bedroom scene drains colour from the world, widening the gulf between blackness and whiteness.[90] Empowered, the second of these polarized colours now grows imperialistic: its leakage through the nightdress and pillow's hems and subsequent lightening of Mary and Mrs Dalton's skin stand revealed as the opening stages of a conquest whose object is Chicago itself. Yet this expanding whiteness can only grow into the city by calling upon the opposite polarity constituted in Bigger's hands, the expectant fingers of which, as they dangle before the pillow and before Mary's prone alabaster neck, darken into an achieved blackness and thus further whiten its putative racial opposite. Indeed, as this terrifying scene inexorably whitens whiteness and blackens blackness, drawing both towards their ubiquitous misnomers, it seems almost to parody the opening sequence from *The Wizard of Oz* (1939) – by far the most successful film to be released when Wright was writing *Native Son* – and turn a Technicolor world monochrome. At the very least, such moments make it seem important that *Native Son* nowhere specifies the actual hue of Bigger's 'black' skin, make this absence in characterization seem a way of confirming that (as Adam Clayton Powell's predicament would suggest) such 'blackening' could occur to anyone on the wrong side of America's racial partition.

Whiteness and the deep anxieties gathered under its sign have had a long career

---

90 See *Time*. Online. Available online at <http://www.time.com/time/covers/0,16641,19940627,00. html> (accessed 2 July 2006).

in American letters. The icebergs that jut above the sea in Edgar Allen Poe's *Narrative of Arthur Gordon Pym of Nantucket* (1837–8), the colourless whale at the heart of Herman Melville's *Moby Dick* (1851) and the pallid Valley of Ashes in F. Scott Fitzgerald's *The Great Gatsby* (1925) all attest to American literature's abiding fascination with whiteness and its connotations in American society. Yet these are also famously enigmatic images (the whiteness of Melville's whale is deliberately, notoriously, indefinable), and their status remains the subject of debate. Long recognized as proof that American literature is far more pessimistic than the nation it represents, these white images have been connected by Harry Levin among others with the distinctive shrouds and pallor of death.[91] Only after Ralph Ellison and Toni Morrison's post-war interventions were such critics forced to recognize that their interpretations remained incomplete and that these white images could also indicate the colour binary splitting America in two. Morrison's *Playing in the Dark* (1993) convinced many to accept that whiteness haunted American literature, not only because the democratic republic found it hard to assimilate death into its vigorous narratives of progress and possibility, but also because death itself had become surcharged with unbearable racial guilt. As Morrison argued, Poe's icebergs and Melville's whale present images of 'impenetrable whiteness ... [that] appear almost always in conjunction with representations of black or Africanist people who are dead, impotent, or under complete control'. Though accepting that these images dramatize America's difficulties with death, Morrison emphasizes their political 'function as both anti-dote for and meditation on the shadow that is companion to this whiteness – a dark and abiding presence that moves the hearts and texts of American literature with fear and longing'.[92]

The white and black images that adorn *Native Son*'s description of Mary's murder map closely onto this critical discourse. In its opening sentences, the Gothic, ghostly, aura enshrouding Mrs Dalton vividly evokes the readings of classic American literature prevalent in Wright's own lifetime: it, too, associates whiteness with death, flagging up an area of life that contemporary American culture arguably preferred to sensationalize, infantilize or suppress. By the scene's conclusion, however, Bigger's apprehension of a baying lynch mob, not to mention the overwhelming whiteness of Chicago itself, make this colour's racial resonance explicit in a manner that anticipates Morrison's *Playing in the Dark*. Proof of Wright's close readings of the major American novelists, this sensitivity to black–white power relations is sustained throughout *Native Son*.

> He looked at the paper and saw a black-and-white map of the South Side. . . . He was trapped. . . . Empty buildings would serve only as long as he stayed within the white portion of the map, and the white portion was shrinking rapidly. He remembered that the newspaper had been printed last night. That meant that the white portion was now much smaller than was shown here. . . .

91  Harry Levin, *The Power of Blackness: Hawthorne, Poe, Melville* (London: Faber & Faber, 1958).
92  Toni Morrison, *Playing in the Dark: Whiteness and the Literary Imagination* (New York: Vintage, 1992), p. 33.

Before him was a maze of white, sundrenched roof-tops.... The memory of the bottle of milk Bessie had heated for him last night came back so strongly that he could almost taste it. . . He felt like dropping to his knees and lifting his face to the sky and saying: 'I'm hungry!' He wanted to pull off his clothes and roll in the snow until something nourishing seeped into his body through the pores of his skin. . . . He felt something hard at the corners of his lips and touched it with his fingers; it was frozen saliva.

('Flight', pp. 276–8)

The polarization of whiteness and blackness that Toni Morrison considers characteristic of nineteenth-century American fiction is terrifying because it relegates African-Americans to the level of metaphor and places their humanity at the service of the white imagination. Agency evaporates the moment the black subject is forced into this polarized realm: as Morrison puts it, the 'Africanist character' is divorced from the actual black people to whom it supposedly refers and is turned into a mere 'surrogate and enabler' of white expression. Even narratives as well intentioned as Harriet Beecher Stowe's *Uncle Tom's Cabin* (1852, see Chronology, **p. 46**), precisely because their benevolence objectifies African-Americans and turns them into the source of mere pity, fall into this trap; they, too, create an impossible milieu in which black characters 'can be evil *and* protective, rebellious *and* forgiving, fearful *and* desirable', but not human.[93]

The subject of the summary that opened the Introduction, the above scene comprises another moment when *Native Son* appears to reverse *The Wizard of Oz* and to drain all colour from the world. But this scene can also be read as a prophetic application of *Playing in the Dark*'s thesis, in the sense that it effectively forces Bigger into a Manichaean realm in which blackness and whiteness are no less polarized from each other than they are in such earlier American fictions as *The Narrative of Arthur Gordon Pym of Nantucket* or *Moby Dick*. In other words, it is as though Wright was here mindful of Poe's wonderfully white icebergs or Melville's wonderfully white whale and wished to fill *Native Son* with materials whose respective blackness or whiteness similarly surpasses that of skin: snow, milk, ink, paper. Yet Wright then diverges from his literary sources in that, where they place 'Africanist' or otherwise stereotypical figures into their polarized realms, he places Bigger – a more realized, humanized figure – and waits to see what happens.

And what happens is that this monochromatic realm suffocates Bigger. What happens is that, even as the unexplored white of the newspaper map dwindles to the vanishing point, the snow coils around Bigger's neck, it reduces his 'urge to breathe', depriving his lungs of air. Whiter than white skin, the snow grows lethal as it blackens Bigger proportionately; it takes the few vestiges of humanity that this anti-hero possesses, crushes them together and reduces them to the debased simplification of caricature. This figurative dehumanization is consolidated: the milk languishing inside Bigger's belly acquires a kind of uncanny magnetism, which draws it inexorably towards the snow. Bigger's later statement that white

93 Morrison, *Playing in the Dark*, pp. 51–8.

people 'choke you off the face of the earth' ('Fate', p. 382) is in this way enacted: worming its way up Bigger's throat, the milk grows intent on obliterating all nuances of colour that stand between it and the snow outside its black host. Hallucinating wildly, fantasizing about rolling 'in the snow until something nourishing seeped into his body', Bigger at last allows the whiteness to perforate his own skin – to annihilate his difference the way it drained pigmentation from Mary Dalton's asphyxiated face ('Fate', p. 375).

# Chronology

Bullet points are used to denote events in Wright's life and literary career, and asterisks to denote historical and cultural events.

1776
* Thomas Jefferson's Declaration of Independence; during the early years of the new republic, northern US states abolish the institution of slavery one by one; slavery is increasingly seen as a phenomenon of the American South

1834
* Britain abolishes slavery from its empire

1845
* Frederick Douglass publishes his *Narrative of the Life of Frederick Douglass, Written by Himself*; the autobiography would cause a sensation, and its status as the most renowned of all slave narratives remains to this day

1848
* Karl Marx and Frederick Engels, *The Communist Manifesto*

1852
* Harriet Beecher Stowe, *Uncle Tom's Cabin*; the novel does much to foster abolitionist feeling; at the same time, the sheer saintliness of its hero strikes many as unrealistic

1861–65
* American Civil War between the northern Union and the southern Confederacy states; the conflict, fought over the future of slavery, claims more American lives than all other US wars put together

1863
* The Emancipation Proclamation freeing all slaves, issued by President Abraham Lincoln in the previous year, becomes effective

1865–77
* Reconstruction: northern liberals seek to ensure that freed slaves are granted full voting rights throughout the South

1865
*     Ku Klux Klan is founded

1866
*     Fyodor Dostoevsky, *Crime and Punishment*; in *The Idiot* (1868), *The Brothers Karamazov* (1880) and other landmark fictions, Dostoevsky offers further psychological studies of extreme or criminal states of mind

1867–95
*     Karl Marx, *Capital*; published in three volumes, this study depicted the gulf between rich and power in Victorian society as the inevitable result of the capitalist economic system; only the revolution of the proletariat, or working class, could overthrow this bourgeois, or middle-class, domination

1877
*     Reconstruction officially ends with the withdrawal of federal troops from the South; from this point forward, southern states institute a battery of laws designed to keep the races apart, and to deprive African-Americans of their new right to vote; in this period these come to be known as Jim Crow laws, the name curiously referring to a black minstrel who reputedly toured the region

1889
*     Aunt Jemima pancake mix is launched, part of a white cultural Zeitgeist utterly obsessed with black racist stereotype; from images of African savagery to black rapists, many of these stereotypes are explicitly violent; no less offensive, Aunt Jemima is typical of the alternative myth of the loyal and endlessly forgiving black maid; her male equivalent is Uncle Remus, who, the creation of Joel Chandler Harris's phenomenally popular books of the time, remains on the plantation and with his master despite the abolition of slavery; such myths were, if anything, more popular among white readers in the North than the South

1900–50
*     The Great Migration: waves of black southerners leave home to make a new life in Chicago, New York and other northern metropolises

1902
*     Thomas Dixon, *The Leopard's Spots*

1905
*     Thomas Dixon, *The Clansman*

1908
•     Wright born on a plantation near Natchez, Mississippi

1915
*     Based on the *The Clansman*, D. W. Griffiths' blockbuster film *The Birth of a Nation* is released

1917
- Wright's uncle Silas Hoskins is murdered by whites who covet his successful liquor business
* Russian Revolution leads to the establishment of the world's first Communist state

1919
* The so-called 'Red Summer' follows the First World War armistice; numerous lynchings and other acts of racist violence are committed; many of these lynchings involve mass audiences and castration among other mutilations; some involve the selling of tickets

1922–33
* Affluent white audiences flock to Harlem and other black cultural hubs; their love of jazz and black folk culture supports the Harlem Renaissance, a flowering of literature inspired by the vernacular tradition

1924
* Josef Stalin becomes premier of the Soviet Union; in the West, though some individual socialists already blame Stalin for the Soviet Union's increasing authoritarianism, official Communist Parties remain steadfast in their support

1925
- Wright leaves Mississippi for Memphis, Tennessee

1927
- Wright joins the Great Migration north and moves to the Chicago South Side

1933–37
* Franklin D. Roosevelt presides over the New Deal, creating an array of new agencies, such as the Works Progress Administration (WPA); the New Deal aimed to provide relief to the poor and jobless while stimulating the national economy

1933
* Hitler becomes German chancellor, his rise to power providing another sign of the growing allure of extremist politics in modern Western culture

1934
- Already involved in its literary activities, Wright joins the Communist Party

1935
- With little success, Wright submits a manuscript entitled *Cesspool* to various publishers; it is eventually published posthumously in 1963 as *Lawd Today!*

1936–9
* The Spanish Civil War, a prelude to the coming world war, pits a loose republican coalition of liberals, trade unionists and Communists against

General Franco's fascist movement. Numerous African-Americans volunteer to fight for the republicans

**1937**
- Wright moves to New York, and publishes 'Blueprint for Negro Writing' in left-wing periodical *New Challenge*
* Blueswoman Bessie Smith dies in car crash

**1938**
- Wright publishes short-story collection, *Uncle Tom's Children*

**1940**
- *Native Son* causes a sensation across the country, selling by the thousand; sales are boosted further as the Book-of-the-Month Club makes the novel one of its nominations; copies of the book are banned from libraries in Birmingham, Alabama

**1941**
- *Twelve Million Black Voices: A Folk History of the Negro in the United States* is published

**1942**
- Wright formalizes his dissatisfaction with Communism, finally breaking with the Party

**1945**
- Wright's autobiography *Black Boy*, originally entitled *American Hunger*, appears, scooping another Book-of-the-Month Club nomination

**1946**
- Wright emigrates to Paris, intrigued both by French existentialist philosophy and the pan-African movement focused in the city

**1949**
* James Baldwin, 'Everybody's Protest Novel'

**1950–4**
* McCarthyism, named after the obsessively anti-Communist Senator Joseph McCarthy, calls numerous black and white intellectuals, entertainers, authors and actors before the House of Un-American Activities Committee

**1951**
* James Baldwin, 'Many Thousands Gone'

**1953**
- *The Outsider*, a novel about serial killer Cross Damon that reveals Wright's growing interest in the theories of Jean-Paul Sartre, Albert Camus and other French existentialists, is published to mixed reviews

**1954**
- Wright publishes *Black Power: A Record of Reactions in a Land of Pathos*,

an ambivalent account of his travels among anti-colonial intellectuals and leaders in West Africa in the previous year; Wright also publishes *Savage Holiday*; the novel echoes the plot lines of *Native Son* and *The Outsider*, but gives them a new twist: his latest serial killer, Erskine Fowler, is white; the book garners favourable reviews in France but, like other works by black writers focusing on white protagonists, receives hostile treatment back in America

* In the first major government response to the nascent Civil Rights movement, the Supreme Court issues its famous ruling on the *Brown* v. *Board of Education* case; it overthrows the 1896 *Plessy* vs. *Ferguson* ruling which had sanctioned Jim Crow segregation, making the provision of 'separate but equal' facilities unconstitutional

### 1956

- Having attended the Asian-African Conference at Bandung, Indonesia in the previous year, Wright publishes his report of the proceeding as *The Color Curtain*; the book includes much analysis of the political and religious outlook of the leaders and peoples of the new independent nations of Africa and Asia

### 1957

- Wright publishes two works: *Pagan Spain*, his fascinating account of life under Franco's regime, and *White Man, Listen!*, a collection of lectures that several African-American journalists greet as a welcome return to form

### 1958

- Increasingly convinced that he is the subject of CIA surveillance – there is some evidence to support his anxiety – Wright publishes his latest novel, *The Long Dream*, to the poorest reviews and sales yet

### 1960

- Having suffered ill health throughout 1959, Wright dies of a heart attack towards the close of the year; his ashes are interred at Père Lachaise cemetery, Paris

### 1961

- *Eight Men*, a short-story collection featuring Wright's brilliant Dostoevskian experiment 'The Man who Lived Underground', is published posthumously

### 1963

* Frantz Fanon, a close reader of Wright, echoes *Black Boy*'s epigraphic citation with the title of his landmark post-colonial study, *The Wretched of the Earth*; Martin Luther King, Jr., organizes the march on Washington; hundreds of thousands descend on the nation's capital; some wear badges on which 'Free in '63' is printed, thereby implying that Lincoln's Emancipation Proclamation had yet to be fully implemented; on the steps of the Lincoln Memorial, King delivers his famous speech, 'I Have a Dream'

# 2

## Critical history

# First responses: James Baldwin

The next generation of African-American writers drew great strength from *Native Son*. The commercial success of the novel alone meant much to those hoping to follow in Wright's footsteps. *Native Son*'s nomination by the popular Book-of-the-Month Club came at some cost, as the writer Hazel Rowley's essay 'The Shadow of the White Woman' will show us (see Critical readings, pp. 88–97), it led to some very regrettable changes being made to Wright's original manuscript. But it also meant that the book secured an astonishingly wide readership, finding favour among ordinary Americans as well as among the country's literary intelligentsia. In the same way, few could fail to be impressed by talk of a film adaptation of the book and even after it had transpired that the film was appalling and best forgotten, the precedent thus set remained indisputably welcome.

These warm feelings about *Native Son* grew warmer with Wright's many acts of generosity. Himself an autodidact, almost entirely without schooling, he used his new-found literary influence to offer new and young writers the support that he had lacked. Collaring some publishers and whispering in the ears of others, he lent support to many among the talented African-American generation of the 1950s, creating opportunities for the novelist and poet Margaret Walker, the former prisoner Chester Himes, and the NAACP (National Association for the Advancement of Colored People) activist Gwendolyn Brooks, who would go on to become the first African-American to win the Pulitzer Prize.

Behind the widespread appreciation of Wright's achievements, however, lurked deeper feelings of ambivalence. As Rowley puts it:

> Black critics were mostly positive. The poet and Howard University professor Sterling Brown thought *Native Son* would stir the national conscience if any book could. Ralph Ellison chimed bells in the *New Masses* . . . Wright was the first best-selling black writer in American literary history. Nobody wanted to appear sour-faced. At first, it was only in private conversations that the deep ambivalence about the book surface. . . . Some thought the novel an admirable portrayal of conditions in black ghettoes; others dreaded the conclusions white

*Figure 8* Portrait of Richard Wright, poet. Photograph: Gordon Parks, 1943.

readers would draw. . . . The controversy about *Native Son* would never die.[1]

No writer received more support from Wright or used it more wisely than James Baldwin. But nor would any writer so well encapsulate the controversy about *Native Son*, or so savagely turn against his one-time mentor in critical attack. Baldwin's responses to *Native Son* still stand as the most important critical statements on the novel, and they are unrelentingly hostile. These facts alone – the fact that Wright helped Baldwin considerably and the fact that the latter turned ferociously against his mentor – reveal that the two possessed a close, perhaps too close, relationship. There was certainly an affinity between them. Although they occurred at opposite ends of the Great Migration, Wright's upbringing in the 'fire' of Jim Crow Mississippi bore a striking resemblance to Baldwin's boyhood in what Claude Brown would later call the 'frying pan'

1    Hazel Rowley, *Richard Wright: The Life and Times* (New York: Henry Holt, 2001), pp. 192–3.

of Harlem, New York.[2] Both novelists disliked the men they thought of as their fathers and, at times, disliked themselves for such feelings of antipathy. As adulterous as they are devout, as violent as they are remote, Nathan Wright in *Black Boy* and David Baldwin in writings such as 'Notes of a Native Son' (1955) inspire guilt and anger in equal measure: the figures they cut are not just repugnant but also strangely insidious, strangely powerful, as though they alone know the truth about their sons and are able, thanks to this secret knowledge, to exert a hold on them – to blackmail them from beyond the grave. And in such writings this friction – these irresolvable feelings of guilt and anger – contaminate Christianity itself. Knowledge of the fathers' hypocrisy, for Wright and Baldwin alike, spills out into the theological and leads both to reject a gospel whose emotional power they cannot help but hear. Hunger, fistfights, canings, knives, arrests, drunkenness and discord all constitute biographical connections further to the mesmerizing, narcotic, obsolete beauty both men heard in the black gospel voice. Spurning the church even as they recoiled from the dangers in the home and on the street, both Wright and Baldwin turned instead to literature, reading, not only for succour, but also for some way to avoid the traps that society set for black men. Thus, just as Wright smuggled books from Memphis's segregated library, so Baldwin virtually moved in to Harlem's two main libraries, claiming to have read everything their shelves held by the time he reached thirteen.

In May 1945, and when he was still only twenty years old, James Baldwin was taken by the journalist Esther Carlson to meet Wright. Wright had read a semi-autobiographical manuscript that Baldwin was working on and, seemingly stirred by its parallels with his own upbringing, was keen to do all he could to get it published.[3] As Hazel Rowley records, Wright suggested that Baldwin apply for the Eugene F. Saxton Trust Fund, which the publishers Harper & Brothers had recently established to help promising writers. Wright 'put in a good word' and, by the end of the year, Harper's judging committee returned a 'unanimous' decision.[4] Baldwin got the money.

As it happened, Baldwin would have to wait eight more years before the manuscript he had asked Wright to read was published as *Go Tell It on the Mountain* in 1953. But this delay had to do with matters beyond Wright's control, and it is clear that his interventions were what first placed the young Harlem novelist on the path of a literary career. Admittedly, the brilliance of this novel's prose – the way in which its sentences so beautifully mix jazz rhythms with a Jamesian intelligence, embellishing both with biblical allusion – indicate that Baldwin was talented enough not to need Wright's help to get published. But Wright guaranteed that he got published when he did, ensuring that he could devote the 1950s to the production of the superb essay collections *Notes of a Native Son* (1955) and *Nobody Knows My Name* (1961). Every bit as impressive as *Go Tell It on the Mountain*, these essays pivot on an enquiry into the nature of American democracy and of the black citizen's ambiguous role within it. In the course of this

---

2   Claude Brown, *Manchild in the Promised Land* (New York: Simon and Schuster, 1990), p. 8.
3   Lesley Conger (1995) 'Jimmy on East 15th Street', *African-American Review*, 29 (4): pp. 557–66 (pp. 557–9).
4   Rowley, *Richard Wright: The Life and Times*, p. 316.

political and philosophical enquiry, Baldwin casts his eye over some of the more intriguing phenomena of the decade. He wonders how the white Mississippian William Faulkner, having produced the most riveting explorations of race and the South in American literature, could now call upon Civil Rights activists to silence their protests against Jim Crow. He worries about the bullish white journalist Norman Mailer's controversial essay 'The White Negro' (1958),[5] instantly grasping the racial stereotypes astir in its celebration of the 'blackness' of the decade's hipster and beatnik style. And he lambastes Hollywood for its undiminished appetite for the African exotic, disparaging films such as the 1955 production *Carmen Jones* for what he saw as their reactionary racial politics.

Another of these essays – one of the first – interrogated American political literature. Initially published alongside Wright's own short story 'The Man who Killed a Shadow' in the opening edition of the Paris journal *Zero* (1949), most of 'Everybody's Protest Novel' is devoted to a critique of one of the most famous of all such political works, Harriet Beecher Stowe's *Uncle Tom Cabin* (1852). For Baldwin, Stowe's anti-slavery novel epitomized the genre's terminal weakness for 'the ostentatious parading of excessive and spurious emotion'.[6] It was hardly a difficult target. Ever since its publication prior to the outbreak of the American Civil War, *Uncle Tom's Cabin* had been the source of a great deal of contempt. Within the black community and sometimes outside it, the name of Stowe's prot-agonist soon entered popular parlance, a byword for any African-American man seen to be childish or deferential.

It is tempting to speculate on what Wright did upon collecting that opening edition of *Zero*. It is tempting to imagine him, nervously scanning the typescript of 'The Man who Killed a Shadow' for errors, before delving into 'Everybody's Protest Novel', the latest effort by his friend Baldwin. Puzzled, perhaps, by the essay's opening references to an unspecified African-American novel, Wright could well have felt increasingly convinced by Baldwin's eloquent denunciation of Stowe's 'theological terror', agreeing that she possessed a weakness for racial caricature, a tendency to reduce all human life to a 'conundrum to be explained by Science'.[7] Tempting as such speculation is, though, it is nigh on impossible not to picture the horror soon to sweep across Wright's face.

> Bigger is Uncle Tom's descendant, flesh of his flesh, so exactly opposite a portrait that, when the books are placed together, it seems that the con-temporary Negro novelist and the dead New England woman are locked together in a deadly, timeless battle; the one uttering merciless exhort-ations, the other shouting curses. And, indeed, within this web of lust and fury, black and white can only thrust and counter-thrust, long for each other's slow, exquisite death; death by torture, acid, knives and burning; the thrust, the counter-thrust, the longing making the heavier

5   Norman Mailer, 'The White Negro', in *Advertisements for Myself* (London: Flamingo, 1994), pp. 290–310.
6   James Baldwin, *Notes of a Native Son* (London: Penguin, 1995), p. 20.
7   Baldwin, *Notes of a Native Son*, p. 21.

that cloud which blinds and suffocates them both, so that they go down into the pit together.[8]

Such fiery passages effectively accuse Wright of failing to practise what he preached in his 'Blueprint for Negro Writing' of 1937. In that blueprint, after all, Wright accused the writers of the Harlem Renaissance of acting a little like Uncle Tom: they entered the 'Court of American Opinion dressed in the knee-pants of servility' when what they should have done is ignore it altogether, concentrate on black audiences and produce for their benefit a truly new and independent literature.[9] Baldwin is surely right to say that Wright fails to follow his own advice. Clearly, the last thing *Native Son* does is ignore the 'Court of American Opinion'. On the contrary, throughout the novel, Wright does all he can to offend it. And in itself, this deliberate provocation – the urgency with which *Native Son* sets about disconcerting, affronting and horrifying its readers – evidences Wright's assumption that most of these readers will be white. Indeed, the irony of *Native Son* is that, the more radical it becomes – and the more avidly black nationalistic – the further it drifts from a properly independent African-American literature of the kind Wright had demanded three years beforehand.

For Baldwin, Bigger Thomas is the walking sign of this failure, his every step illuminating *Native Son*'s continuing bondage in stereotype. Everything Bigger is, Uncle Tom is not. Rapacious rather than chaste, restive rather than content and violent rather than conciliatory, Bigger is indeed not just a 'larger' Uncle Tom but the precise and systematic opposite of this ennobled, stupid, merciful slave. And yet, whereas Wright hopes that the characterization of his protagonist will help to discredit and even perhaps to annihilate Tom and all other such cretinous stereotypes, for Baldwin this process – this development of Bigger's personality through the accumulation of antitheses – seems risky, counterproductive and a strategy that suggests nothing more than that the epistemological fetters of white supremacy still maintain their hold.

Baldwin accordingly views the distance between Stowe and Wright's characterizations as proof of an alarming and hitherto-unremarked intimacy, as proof that both spring from a common source. That is to say, Baldwin's potent critical intervention effectively suggests that, just as bullying intimidates some and makes others aggressive, so Bigger's brutality and Tom's ridiculously overdeveloped capacity to forgive simply manifest variations on the response that the powerless may make to their condition. Neither is likely to succeed; both, it seems, are compromised by an anticipated inadequacy.

And yet the evangelical fervour of 'Everybody's Protest Novel' – that fire-and-brimstone temper which leads it to pair Wright with Stowe and then to despatch both into the flames together – suggests that Baldwin's concerns ran even deeper than this. Indeed, the essay is so apocalyptic, so sadistic and so clearly indebted to the Book of Revelations, one eventually comes to feel that Baldwin regards *Native Son* as something more than an artistic failure, that he regards it, in fact, as a personal outrage. Zealously insisting upon *Native Son*'s involvement in the very practices of racial marginalization that it is meant to denounce, 'Everybody's

8    Baldwin, *Notes of a Native Son*, p. 27.
9    Wright, 'Blueprint for Negro Writing', p. 1382.

Protest Novel' eventually comes to seem like nothing so much as a new version of the old argument between the aesthete and the literary realist – a version far uglier, harder and more personally embittered than any that came before it.

Earlier versions of this argument had typically taken place between those who regarded literature and ideology as inseparable and those who felt such a viewpoint to be utilitarian, doctrinaire and corrosive to the integrity of art. Known as aestheticism and sometimes encapsulated in the slogan 'art for art's sake', this latter sensibility frequently presented an apolitical face to the world. Indeed, although the versions of aestheticism that they forward are in other ways very different, Henry James's urbane 'The Art of Fiction' (1884) and Walter Pater's overheated *Studies in the History of the Renaissance* (1873) both imply that politics is something other people do; true art, for both, must keep its distance from such a humdrum world.[10]

Henry James's influence is everywhere in Baldwin's work – in the title *Notes of a Native Son*, which glances over Wright's shoulder and toward the earlier transatlanticist's *Notes of a Son and Brother* (1914),[11] and in the labyrinthine sentences of his meditative, introspective, essays. And this Jamesian heritage flows further, seeping into the criticisms that 'Everybody's Protest Novel' makes of *Native Son*, many of which closely match those 'The Art of Fiction' makes of literary naturalism in general and of Émile Zola's œuvre in particular. Neither James's juvenile enthusiasm for Zola nor Baldwin's similar feelings about *Native Son* faded away so much as they burned with undiminishing ferocity into a negative just as strong. 'The Art of Fiction' duly berates Zola's fictions of mining life for organizing plot to suit dogma, for offering an all too 'narrow' vision and for radiating 'an air of working in the dark' appropriate to their subject but inappropriate to their form.[12] And 'Everybody's Protest Novel' bears similarly cruel witness to Baldwin's dramatic turn against his former friend Wright, denouncing *Native Son* for a similar narrowness that seemingly warped the Chicago South Side, erasing its libraries, its schools and, indeed, of anything able to keep Bigger from the electric chair.

The closeness of this structural symmetry at the same time draws attention to those moments when 'Everybody's Protest Novel' departs from this Jamesian script. In particular, it draws attention to the fact that the opposition between the *political* and the *apolitical*, which helps to organize 'The Art of Fiction' and most of James's other writings about writing is nowhere to be found in Baldwin's essay. Perhaps this was inevitable. The formidable reputation that Baldwin acquired during the 1950s owed much to the way his essays turned a sharp eye on the binary oppositions of American culture. Having unpacked the psychological terrors fermented by the division of the American people into black and white or by the organization of the earth itself into Communist and capitalist zones of influence, Baldwin could hardly then move on to an unquestioning reinscription

---

10  Henry James, 'The Art of Fiction' in Vincent B. Leitch (ed.) *The Norton Anthology of Theory and Criticism* (New York and London: Norton, 2001), pp. 851–70. Walter Pater, 'Excerpt from *Studies in the History of the Renaissance*' in *The Norton Anthology of Theory and Criticism*, pp. 833–41.
11  Henry James, *Notes of a Son and Brother* (London: Macmillan, 1914).
12  Henry James, 'The Art of Fiction' in *The Norton Anthology of Theory and Criticism*, pp. 855–70 (p. 869).

of James's aforementioned tendency to view politics as other people's business. There again, perhaps the firm objectivity cultivated by the Victorian aesthete would always have been unavailable to Baldwin. Baldwin was, after all, as close to the ghettoized cast of *Native Son* as Henry James was remote from the hard world of Zola's tough proletarian characters. The human consequences of aesthetic shortcomings were always going to seem far more conspicuous to the young black writer. After all, a novel that erased libraries from Harlem also erased Baldwin from his native landscape, sucking the air out of his lungs.

Many have since read 'Everybody's Protest Novel' psychoanalytically, the essay's violence encouraging them to see it as an obituary to a friendship that only sporadically and opportunistically analyses *Native Son*. The clutter of a thousand claims and counterclaims have since confirmed this impression, drawing attention away from the literary conflict at the heart of the controversy and towards the unseemly public rows that followed it. Indeed, critics wishing to concentrate on the personal terms of this debate have a veritable smorgasbord of documentation at their disposal. They can quote from Baldwin's 'Alas, Poor Richard' (1961),[13] a barbed homage which presents Wright as a egomaniac with whom few could get along. They can allude to an unpublished lecture Wright delivered to Paris's American Church in 1953, in which he seemingly painted 'Everybody's Protest Novel' as the work of a rampant egomaniac liable to get himself hurt.[14] Such critics could venture further, perhaps to endorse the passionate disgust of Houston A. Baker, an advocate of politicized literature and of Wright's œuvre in particular, who sees Baldwin's critical disdain for his one-time mentor as being 'extraordinarily derogatory'.[15] If taking sides is not their game, meanwhile, these critics could well turn with relief to Chester Himes's more objective account of the arguments between the men, which suggests that, although Baldwin indeed bellowed certain inane slogans ('the sons must slay their fathers') in Wright's direction, he did so only after some provocation.[16]

Although they are so obviously at variance with each other, these viewpoints share an important, and regrettable, tendency in common: they start us talking about Baldwin and Wright's personal relations and stop us talking (or worse still, *reading*) their work. Baldwin's biographer James Campbell observes:

> The old charge of slaying the father is sometimes cited by critics as if it explained *everything* about the relationship between these two highly complex men. It contains a certain amount of truth, but it is, in fact, no more than a proverbial crime, a supposition. Their quarrel, at the nitty-gritty, was actually over something more tangible – the social and artistic responsibilities of the writer.[17]

13  James Baldwin, 'Alas, Poor Richard', in *Nobody Knows My Name: More Notes of a Native Son* (New York: Dell, 1961), pp. 146–70.
14  James Campbell, *Talking at the Gates: A Life of James Baldwin* (Boston, Mass. and London Faber & Faber, 1991), p. 65.
15  Houston A. Baker, *Long Black Song: Essays in Black American Literature and Culture* (Charlottesville, Va. and London: University Press of Virginia, 1972), p. 140.
16  Chester Himes, *The Quality of Hurt: The Autobiography of Chester Himes* (New York: Doubleday, 1972), p. 200.
17  Campbell, *Talking at the Gates*, p. 69.

What Campbell characterises here is the way in which critics have repeatedly been swept up in Wright and Baldwin's personal conflagration and dragged away from their far more important, more meaningful, literary differences. It is precisely to avoid such a fate that the example of Baldwin's criticism reproduced in this book is 'Many Thousands Gone' (see Critical readings, **pp. 76–87**). The second of Baldwin's three essays on Richard Wright, 'Many Thousands Gone' sits between the denunciatory 'Everybody's Protest Novel' and the elegiac 'Alas, Poor Richard', and is blessedly free of the emotional heat of both. Neither dispatching Wright to Hell nor posthumously seeking his forgiveness, 'Many Thousands Gone' thus sets out most closely the argument I outline above: that Native Son, to Baldwin's mind, remained trapped in the logic it descried, inadvertently regurgitating racist stereotypes it sought to destroy. And this was an argument to which, as we will now see, many have returned.

## First responses: Ralph Ellison and Irving Howe

Immediately upon its publication, then, Native Son was hailed in America and beyond as the definitive 'black' novel. Critics far and wide lauded its social realism, some suggesting even as others insisted that its sustained political engagement – its attritional, unrelenting didacticism – illuminated the way forward for all black art. Baldwin was not the only successor of Wright's to feel overwhelmed by the 'definitive', canonical status of Native Son. The author of the landmark novel Invisible Man (1952), Ralph Ellison, also objected to the configuration of a post-war, post-Native Son literary landscape in which African-American novelists could only hope to sell their manuscripts if they consented to try 'out-Wrighting Richard'.[18] As his double-edged tribute 'Remembering Richard Wright' (1971) put it:

> [I]n my terms, Wright failed to grasp the function of artistically induced catharsis – which suggests that he failed also to understand the Afro-American custom of shouting in church (a form of ritual catharsis), or its power to cleanse the mind and redeem and rededicate the individual to forms of ideal action. . . . Yet it is for such moments of inspired communication that the artist lives. The irony here is that Wright could evoke them, but felt, for ideological reasons, that tears were a betrayal of the struggle for freedom.[19]

Ellison's doubts about Native Son's impact overlap with many of those that Baldwin expresses in 'Everybody's Protest Novel' and 'Many Thousands Gone'. In particular, the two writers shared a determination to escape what they saw as the mandatory politicization of the black writer. Just as Baldwin would lament

---

18  Ralph Ellison, The Collected Essays of Ralph Ellison (New York: the Modern Library, 1995), ed. John F. Callahan, p. 161.
19  Ralph Ellison, 'Remembering Richard Wright' in Going to the Territory (New York: Vintage, 1995), pp. 198–216 (pp. 211–12).

the polemicism of *Native Son*, so Ellison cautioned time and again against any attempt to straitjacket the black writer, noting, in 1955, that if 'the Negro, or any other writer, is going to do what is expected of him, he's lost the battle'.[20]

Ellison's most emotive statement of this belief was prompted by the 1963 publication in *Dissent* magazine of 'Black Boys and Native Sons', the influential Marxist critic Irving Howe's rebuttal of James Baldwin's attacks on *Native Son*. The substance of Howe's argument was that *Native Son*'s implied definition of the novel as a political tool was far preferable to Baldwin's (and by extension Ellison's) sentimental faith in its capacities for individual reinvention, expression and determination. Baldwin's and Ellison's naïve faith in the 'assertion of self-liberation', for Howe, was merely 'a favorite strategy among American literary people in the fifties'. It was 'also vapid and insubstantial. It violates the reality of social life, the interplay between external conditions and personal will.' *Native Son*, for Howe, made no such mistake and acknowledged that literature by black writers was duty bound to protest. The novel seemed implicitly to ask:

> What, then, was the experience of a man with a black skin, what *could* it be here in this country? How could a Negro put pen to paper, how could he so much as think or breathe, without some impulsion to protest, be it harsh or mild, political or private, released or buried?[21]

Ellison's answers to these questions echoed the objections 'Everybody's Protest Novel' raised: the problem with *Native Son*, as Ellison saw it, was that 'Wright could imagine Bigger, but Bigger could not possibly imagine Richard Wright. Wright saw to that'. Howe's problem, meanwhile, was that he 'seems to see segregation as an opaque steel jug with the Negroes inside waiting for some black messiah to come along and blow the cork. Wright is his hero and he sticks with him loyally'.[22] *Native Son*, Ellison suggests, for all its power, is a novel and thus neither equipped nor meant to be equipped with the messianic powers of the political saviour. Reading the novel as though through the prism of Howe's positive appraisal of it, Ellison comments:

> One unfamiliar with what Howe stands for would get the impression that when he looks at a Negro he sees not a human being but an abstract embodiment of living hell. He seems never to have considered that American Negro life (and here he is encouraged by certain Negro 'spokesmen') is, for the Negro who must live it, not only a burden (and not always that) but also a *discipline* – just as any human life which has endured so long is a discipline teaching its own insights into the human condition, its own strategies of survival. There is a fullness, even a richness here; and here *despite* the realities of politics, perhaps, but nevertheless here and real. Because it is *human* life. And Wright, for

20  Ellison, *The Collected Essays of Ralph Ellison*, pp. 212–3.
21  Irving Howe, 'Black Boys and Native Sons', available online, at the American Studies web site of the University of Virginia, <http://xroads.virginia.edu/~DRBR/howe-bla.html> (accessed 17 February 2005).
22  Ellison, *The Collected Essays of Ralph Ellison*, pp. 162–3.

all of his indictments, was no less its product than that other talented
Mississippian, [the opera singer] Leontyne Price.[23]

Although Ellison's analysis is always far more tempered than Baldwin's, at such
moments the two correspond, agreeing that *Native Son* is a failure because it
remains trapped in the very vortex of stereotype that it seeks to resolve. Indeed,
Baldwin and Ellison's clear belief that Bigger Thomas reinforces stereotype contrasts markedly with the fact that, as The Black Atlantic and beyond Section
shows (see Critical history, **pp. 68–74**). The post-colonial theorist Frantz
Fanon, reading *Native Son* from the then French territory of Algeria and amid its
constant racial violence, found the work so useful to his analysis of racism and
stereotype. Though Baldwin and Ellison agree on the role of stereotype in *Native
Son*, however, they differ in tone, and it is important to remark here that Ellison
(both here and elsewhere) characterizes Wright as a kind of unrealized novelist,
a novelist who never quite grasped just how good he was. In particular, all of
Ellison's references to Wright's handling of the black oral culture that we have
encountered in these pages strike a note of disappointment. Ellison seems consistently upset that his erstwhile mentor did not make fuller use of his palpable
ability to stir the senses with the imaginative reconstruction of vernacular performance, with a fuller description of spirituals and their effect, a fuller account of
the blues, of the stories Bigger tells with his friends. For what novels would
Wright have written, Ellison asks, if he had only allowed his readers to cry?

## Feminist readings

Feminist responses to *Native Son* have always centred on the way in which Bigger's feelings of frustration and outrage translate into violence against women. As
Hazel Rowley's research has shown, this concern arose from the moment of the
novel's publication. While most African-American critics kept their doubts about
*Native Son* to themselves, Lillian Johnson broke ranks to lament its failure to
provide 'one intelligent person', and to deplore the fact that Bigger desired 'the
white girl, even though he did not like her'.[24] As we will see, by the 1970s similar
concerns encouraged the production of several full-blown condemnations of
*Native Son*. In this section, I show that these full-blown condemnations are today
too easily swept aside, too easily repudiated as evidence of the embarrassing
excessiveness of 1970s feminism. In particular, I show that the common objection
that (as Johnson had been quick to grasp) *Native Son* offers no strong or positive
female characters is today too easily derided as a sign of the 1970s feminist
tendency to read literature literally and in the belief that it should convey a clear
anti-sexist message. For while this tendency was indeed regrettable, the critics
who dismiss it today tend in the process to dismiss the feelings that lie behind it, in
a stroke rebutting all feminist concerns about the book. I have written this section
to correct this too hasty and sweeping rebuttal. Though of use to all readers, the

23  Ellison, *The Collected Essays of Ralph Ellison*, p. 165.
24  Rowley, *Richard Wright: The Life and Times*, p. 193.

following pages are thus especially beneficial for those who, while not wishing to censor *Native Son*, remain appalled by its misogynistic savagery.

In the course of its 1970s activism, which secured women an unprecedented degree of equality throughout the Western world, feminism often cast literature as a field of political struggle. 'Woman must write her self', Hélène Cixous declared in 'The Laugh of the Medusa' (1975); she 'must write about women and bring women to writing, from which they have been driven away as violently as from their bodies. . . . Woman must put herself into the text – as into the world and into history – by her own movement.'[25] Reading the French theorist from the other side of the Atlantic, American feminists wholeheartedly agreed. Even those unacquainted with Cixous's theoretical works could intuit the necessity of her central thesis, grasping that gender equality, much like racial equality, required literature to give voice to those it once maligned. In *On Lies, Secrets, and Silences* (1978) and other essays, the American poet Adrienne Rich lodged a particularly eloquent call to undo the 'maleness' of the canon, to return to forgotten female writers of the past and to follow them in producing a new, woman-centred literature equal to Cixous's vision.[26]

Arising in the 1970s, black feminist criticism always set itself apart from feminism and black nationalism at the same time as it continued to fight patriarchy and racism. Nothing united this emergent movement so much as the need for new priorities – the need to signal that feminism's focus on getting women out of the home and into the professions, for example, meant little to those black and working-class constituents who already went to work. In spite of such important differences, however, black still paralleled white feminist discourse to some extent. Counterparts to Adrienne Rich existed within black feminist quarters, its discourse likewise seeking 'to define a feminist usable past, a legacy of writing by women offering a viable alternative to the male-dominated canon'.[27] Indeed, just as Adrienne Rich salvaged the poems of Elizabeth Bishop, returning them from the margin to the centre of the American canon, so Alice Walker at once applauded her action and recovered a forgotten writer of her own, in the form of Zora Neale Hurston.[28] But such parallels possessed a critical as well as a productive aspect. For just as feminist critics now scrutinized the male canon, condemning the machismo of Ernest Hemingway among other established writers, so black feminist readers in particular now seemed to compress their ire at sexist literature into a single target: *Native Son*.

This was hardly surprising. As we have seen, *Native Son* offers no representation of female agency or strength. Whereas African-American culture between the wars boasted many impressive, formidable and talented women, even Wright's characterization of Bessie Mears seems to strip her of the wit and courage often associated with her namesake Bessie Smith. In place of acknowledging any such female empowerment, *Native Son* offers violence. It offers rape, dismemberment,

25 Hélène Cixous, 'The Laugh of the Medusa' in Vincent B. Leitch (ed.) *The Norton Anthology of Theory and Criticism* (London and New York: Norton, 2001), pp. 2039–56 (p. 2039).
26 Adrienne Rich, *On Lies, Secret and Silence: Selected Prose 1966–1978* (London: Virago, 1980).
27 Malcolm Bradbury and Richard Ruland, *From Puritanism to Postmodernism: A History of American Literature* (Harmondsworth: Penguin, 1992), p. 403.
28 Alice Walker, 'Looking for Zora' in *In Search of Our Mothers' Gardens* (London: The Women's Press, 1984), pp. 93–118.

death. Even worse, it seems oblivious to this distortion that it is committing, oblivious to this violence that it is perpetrating upon female bodies. Taken as a whole, *Native Son* moreover radiates the impression that it is not meant for female readers. Like Eldridge Cleaver and the other black nationalists whom it would inspire, this novel seems to think of the racial struggle as a business for men and men alone. No wonder that black feminist critics disliked the book. No wonder that one of chief architects of this movement, Barbara Smith, implicated Wright's œuvre in black women's overall absence from American culture.[29] And no wonder, too, that the leading African-American literary journals of the 1970s, being home to early black feminist writings, also came to seem home to anti-*Native Son* vitriol.

> Most of Wright's female characters are . . . frequently described as being childlike, whimpering, and stupid. Wright did not attribute characteristics of a mature human mentality to them. Frequently his male characters lack the ability to rationalize, but the female characters are at the bottom of the scale of human intelligence. . . . Bessie in *Native Son* and Lil in *Lawd Today* are equally dull and mindless, and drown what little mind they have in either liquor or religion. Both function as road blocks to the actions and pursuits of the male characters. Neither Jake nor Bigger is an intelligent, rationalizing man. However, they are shown as active, whereas the women are portrayed as passive and acted upon.[30]

Appearing in the pages of the *Black American Literature Forum* in 1976, Sylvia H. Keady's 'Richard Wright's Women Characters and Inequality' typifies the black feminist response to *Native Son* and other works. In particular, it typifies the black feminist emphasis on the passivity of *Native Son*'s women. If Keady calls Wright's women 'road blocks', then most other black feminist critics broadly agree that these are unrealized figures whose principal purpose is to facilitate an epic and exclusively male narrative. This is certainly the position of another prominent black feminist critic, Barbara Christian, who notes that in Wright's novels 'black women are seldom seen except in the role of a slightly outlined mama or as a victim'.[31] As Miriam DeCosta-Willis puts it, feminist readers have generally agreed that Wright's 'female characters are flat, one-dimensional characters, portrayed primarily in terms of their relationships to the male characters'.[32]

Key commentators today feel comfortable in dismissing the logic of this argument. They are quick to grasp that at the heart of this common black feminist objection lies a desire to police literature, to force literature to temper its

29  Barbara Smith, 'Toward a Black Feminist Criticism' in *The Norton Anthology of Theory and Criticism*, pp. 2302–16 (pp. 2305–6).
30  Sylvia H. Keady (1976) 'Richard Wright's Women Characters and Inequality', *Black American Literature Forum*, 10(4): pp. 124–8 (pp. 124–5).
31  Barbara Christian, *Black Feminist Criticism: Perspectives on Black Women Writers* (New York: Teachers College, 1997), p. 15.
32  Miriam DeCosta-Willis (1986) 'Avenging Angels and Mute Mothers: Black Southern Women in Wright's Fictional World', *Callaloo*, 28: pp. 540–51 (p. 540).

treatment of misogyny by depicting 'positive' or otherwise redemptive characters on whom such prejudice seems to take no toll. Behind 1970s black feminist attacks on Wright, many critics today agree, is an untenable regret that his novels do not remain at least partly aloof from the sexism that they must nonetheless lay bare.

Paul Gilroy, whose path-finding work on the African diaspora and identity is revisited in our next section 'The Black Atlantic and beyond' (see Critical history, **pp. 68–74**), has provided the best examples of this powerful counterargument. He grasps that 1970s feminist condemnations of *Native Son* fundamentally misconceive the relationship between fact and fiction, overhastily implicating Wright in the misogynistic violence of his stories. In Gilroy's own words, those who thus attribute the 'brute machismo and uncomplicated misogyny' of *Native Son* to Wright himself are working on a 'simplistic basis'; they are crudely identifying his 'own attitudes and responses with those of his murderous and antisocial male characters'.[33] Elsewhere, in his landmark study *The Black Atlantic: Modernity and Double Consciousness* (1993), Gilroy puts flesh on his contention. He charges that the

> crude and inadequate account of Wright's misogyny . . . sees him dismissed repeatedly as the purveyor of a crude, protest-oriented fiction that not only refuses to validate the dynamic, vital qualities of black culture but denies artistic and political legitimacy to the affirmative literary enterprises which are today endowed with feminine qualities. Wright is then positioned at one wing of the great family of African-American letters while Zora Neale Hurston, the woman identified as his cultural and political opposite, is placed at the other. . . . Her conservatism answers his misguided bolshevism, her exaggerated respect for the authentic voice of the rural black folk is interpreted as a welcome antidote to his contemptuous presentation of the bestial, desperate experiences involved in being black in some metropolitan hovel. . . . However, the intellectual justification for identifying Wright personally with the woman-slaying exploits of the protagonists of *Native Son* and *Savage Holiday* has simply not been provided.[34]

Much in this analysis is persuasive. For one thing, Gilroy rightly condemns the counterproductive critical attitude that has long placed Hurston's and Wright's novels into a perfect opposition, a rigid dichotomy responsible (among much else) for encouraging people to think that, because it is so unlike *Their Eyes Were Watching God*, *Native Son* somehow mistrusts black vernacular culture. For another, Gilroy helps us understand why feminist critics were in error, showing that their plea for redemptive or positive characters amounted to a demand that Wright switch genres and abandon a realist fiction dedicated to confronting social misery. That is to say, what Gilroy sees here is that Wright's realist aesthetic requires him to stare the so-called 'metropolitan hovel' straight on and that to

33  Paul Gilroy, 'Introduction' in Richard Wright, *Eight Men* (New York: HarperPerennial, 1996), pp. xi–xxi (p. xiv).
34  Paul Gilroy, *The Black Atlantic: Modernity and Double Consciousness* (London and New York: Verso, 1993) pp. 176–7.

flinch away, or to moderate this perspective by the admission of a redemptive figure of any kind, would be to violate all that he had learned from Dostoevsky among others.

At the same time, however, Gilroy here seems to grow just a little excited by his own eloquence. He seems to overreach himself, to come close to suggesting that there is no case to answer. At the very least, as his analysis builds to its rhetorical climax, it begs an obvious riposte: for while 'the intellectual justification for identifying Wright' with Bigger has indeed 'not been provided', nor has any evidence for why we should so utterly divorce this author from his monster.

It is difficult to negotiate this profound disagreement. Gilroy not only has eloquence but also a great deal of truth on his side. He is right to expose the anti-literary impulse at the heart of black feminism's attacks against *Native Son*. At the same time, however, he is perhaps too quick to dismiss the sentiments motivating such admittedly simplistic attacks. He is perhaps too dismissive of the sense of disappointment and dismay that *Native Son* caused among its black female audiences.

The choice, then, is less than enticing. On one side stand Sylvia H. Keady and Barbara Christian, critics who seem to weigh the worth of Wright's work by the extent to which its fictional landscapes correspond to their own world view. On the other, Gilroy seems just a little too keen to draw a line under such feminist objections, to declare the matter closed and so to return to those weightier questions that interest him more. How, then, should we proceed? What course should we plot between these polarized positions?

Though it predates Gilroy's scholarship on Wright, Barbara Johnson's essay 'The Re(a)d and the Black: Richard Wright's Blueprint' (1987) offers one of the most intellectually cogent and satisfying responses to this problem. In the process, Johnson's essay also offers indispensable assistance to those wishing to piece together a sophisticated feminist critique of *Native Son*. For this work skilfully resists extremes, steering a path between anti-feminist counter-argument and that simplistic and polemical feminism which, as Jane Gaines puts it, 'insists on change *at the level of language*'.[35] No sooner does it note that 'racism' hardly 'explain[s] away the novel's careless misogyny' than it points out that, on the other hand, it would be a little too easy 'to read the novel as itself an act of violence against black women'.[36] With these negotiations, it becomes evident that Johnson wants at all costs to avoid the impression that she is putting *Native Son* on trial. Though sharing other feminist critics' focus on how Bigger's fears and frustrations lead to misogynistic violence, it becomes evident that, for Johnson, this focus should not be subject to a courtroom dialectic, should not lead us to find *Native Son* guilty or innocent, but should more simply be explored as its central problematic.

This shift is fruitful. It enables Johnson to approach *Native Son* as a novel that, far from offering a clear window into Wright's soul, plays around with existing

35 Jane Gaines, 'White Privilege and Looking Relations: Race and Gender in Feminist Film Theory' in Joanne Hollows, Peter Hutchings and Mark Jancovich (eds) *The Film Studies Reader* (London: Arnold, 2000), pp. 322–8 (p. 328).

36 Barbara Johnson, 'The Re(a)d and the Black' in Henry Louis Gates, Jr., and Kwame Anthony Appiah (eds) *Richard Wright: Critical Perspectives Past and Present* (New York: Amistad, 1993), pp. 149–56 (p. 153).

cultural myth and stereotype. This new view in turn allows her to point out that what lies in wait for Bigger in Mary Dalton's bedroom is a cultural myth that will lead inexorably towards his death. That is to say, Johnson's references to what she calls the 'overdetermination' or stereotyping of the black rapist myth remind us that it is not only the women of *Native Son* who are subject to gender stereo-type. Bigger is too. Immediately upon stumbling into its white walls, the bedroom casts him as a sexual monster, ensuring that almost regardless of his response, the 'unavailability of new plots' will prove 'deadly', ushering him towards the electric chair. Moreover, the fact that Bigger then almost inevitably slips into this monstrous stereotype, for Johnson, is intimately connected to the problem of *Native Son*'s under-representation of black women. As she argues, it 'is because the "rape" plot about white women . . . [is] so overdetermined that the plot about black women remains muffled beyond recognition'.[37] And it is because Bessie sees this – it is because she alone in the novel grasps that Bigger's crime has been to surrender to a racist stereotype that has lain in wait for him – that her 'reading' becomes so powerful.

> As Bigger completes the ransom note, he lifts his eyes and sees Bessie standing behind him. She has read the note over his shoulder and guessed the truth. 'She looked straight into his eyes and whispered, "Bigger, did you kill that girl?"' Bigger denies that she has interpreted his writing correctly, but he formulates a plan to kill her to prevent her from saying what she knows. The black woman, then, is a reader – a reader whose reading is both accurate and threatening.[38]

Establishing this scene as seminal to Wright's work, Johnson's essay concludes:

> In a surprising and fascinating passage in Wright's essay 'How "Bigger" Was Born,' we encounter the announcement of a novel that was never to reach completion: 'I am launching out upon another novel, this time about the status of women in American society.' The desire to tell a woman's story seems to infuse Wright's writing from the beginning. Yet however aborted the plots of his women protagonists, the figure of the black woman as *reader* in his work is fundamental. Silent, baffled, or filled with a dangerous insight, Wright consistently sees the black woman as the reader his writing must face. *Native Son*, indeed, is dedicated to Wright's own paralyzed mother.[39]

Johnson's essay is itself not unproblematic. As Claudia Tate has suggested, it fails to marshal sufficient evidence for these concluding assertions, leaving 'unexplored the tragic consequences of this recurring confrontation to black women in Wright's fiction'.[40] An acute disjunction moreover arises here: whereas Johnson

---

37 Johnson, 'The Re(a)d and the Black', p. 154.
38 Johnson, 'The Re(a)d and the Black', p. 153.
39 Johnson, 'The Re(a)d and the Black', p. 155.
40 Claudia Tate (2000) 'Review of Barbara Johnson, *The Feminist Difference: Literature, Psycho-analysis, Race, and Gender*', *African-American Review*, 34(1): pp. 159–62 (p. 160).

feels that 'Wright consistently sees the black woman as the reader his writing must face', numerous black female readers feel utterly bypassed by his work.

Despite this, however, it remains clear that Johnson's essay is offering us a way out of the tangled political claims and counterclaims that have long muddied critical debate. It remains clear that she is showing us that all manner of complexities and contradictions are masked by the grand pronouncements that continue to circulate around *Native Son*'s gender politics. She is showing us, for example, that the common complaint that women like Bessie are too passive, while entirely true, has also discouraged critics from fully exploring the character and meaning of this passivity. And she is showing us that, despite efforts to reorient debate about *Native Son*, questions of gender remain central to any full consideration of the novel. Any full consideration must, clearly, still grapple with the questions that once vexed feminists seeking to counter the insults and assaults perpetrated by patriarchal culture. It must still ask: why does *Native Son* pause over the bodies of these women? Why does Wright linger over the details of their pain? What larger narrative purpose is served by the misogynistic character of Bigger's crimes? Why does Wright remain preoccupied with the myth of the black rapist?

# The Black Atlantic and beyond

By insisting that Africans were unintelligent, by endeavouring to criminalize black literacy and by keeping books under lock and key, the system of American slavery effectively revealed to slaves that the route to freedom lay in literature. Although it sought to keep African-Americans and literature apart, what Ralph Ellison famously called the 'segregation ... of the Word' inadvertently made books seem all the more important, establishing education as the path out of slavery and, later, Jim Crow segregation.[41] In the minds of many African-Americans, indeed, literature and freedom walked hand in hand. As Wright said of H. L. Mencken and a government poster said of the Harlem's Schomburg Library (see Figure 9), books could be weapons – and perhaps they could even destroy racism itself.

Ellison's 'segregation of the Word', however, was not the exclusive preserve of America's white supremacist authorities. Up to the 1960s at least, European colonies throughout the world were still caught in the grip of like-minded elites, and even those imperial subjects who received excellent educations – such as the Trinidadian intellectual C. L. R. James – were made to understand that literature remained a white affair.[42] If all books were weapons, however – if all books could explode this kind of segregation – then *Native Son* was especially intimidating. As this section shows, from its publication and throughout the 1950s and 1960s, Wright's novel played a surprisingly prominent role in the formation around the world of new political movements dedicated to the overthrow of imperial control. Indeed, James Baldwin's suspicion that Wright got arrogant in later life is perhaps contradicted by the fact that the latter's many writings on these emergent

---

41  Ralph Ellison, 'Twentieth-Century Fiction and the Black Mask of Humanity' in *Shadow and Act* (New York: Vintage, 1972), pp. 24–44 (p. 24).
42  C. L. R. James, *Beyond a Boundary* (Durham, NC: Duke University Press, 1993), p. 52.

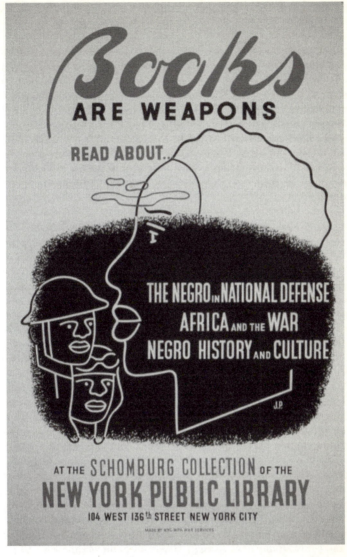

*Figure 9* WPA poster publicizing the Schomburg Collection of the New
York Public Library, 1941–3.

movements nowhere mention the importance its leaders frequently attached to
*Native Son* and *Black Boy*. In print at least, Wright retains a modest silence about
the fact that many readers outside America experienced *Native Son* as vindication
– as literary confirmation that their local battles were part of a global anti-racist
struggle. For all this unremarked modesty, however, the fact remains that Wright
is key to Black Atlantic culture, his work resonating with readers throughout the

scattered and international cultures of the African diaspora. As Paul Gilroy – author of *The Black Atlantic* and originator of the term – puts it:

> Richard Wright was the first black writer to be put forward as a major figure in world literature. . . . His work enjoyed a global reading public of an unprecedented size for a black author. It was translated into numerous languages and took the experience of racial subordination . . . to a mass black readership inside and outside America.
>
> Wright's understanding of the forms of black consciousness that grew unseen *within* the western world developed alongside a gradual change in his thinking whereby a sense of the urgency of anti-colonial political struggle displaced an earlier exclusive interest in the liberation of African-Americans from their particular economic exploitation and political oppression.[43]

Gilroy here describes an opening out – a movement from the local to the global. In the years after *Native Son*'s publication, Wright grew increasingly aware of its global resonance and increasingly keen to identify the similarities between Bigger's predicament and oppressive colonial regimes in Africa, Asia and the Caribbean. Moreover, as Wright reached beyond American borders, black audiences in these old colonies as well as new independent states responded enthusiastically. If anything, these new audiences, reading *Native* Son and *Black Boy* in Kenya, Nigeria, Jamaica and elsewhere were even more positive than Wright's compatriots had been. To them, his work confirmed that black Americans endured similar humiliations and discriminations as their brethren elsewhere in the African diaspora. Colonial oppression, the dreadful acts British and French authorities committed in the name of restoring 'order', resurfaced in *Native Son* and *Black Boy*, producing unexpected American echoes that in turn confirmed that racism was global in its compass and required a global response. Thus, these works nurtured Mĩcere Gĩthae Mũgo's pan-African political consciousness, the Kenyan poet lauding them for speaking 'clearly and passionately through [the] . . . loneliness' of life under a British colonial culture that belittled her race. Wright's faraway but resonant stories enabled her to '[defy] the isolation and . . . [feel] proud, every inch, for being an African'.[44] Even now, in a political moment that lacks pan-Africanism's clear objectives and is wary of its statements of race pride, Wright's work resonates, inspiring writers throughout Gilroy's Black Atlantic. Indeed, Caribbean and British writer Caryl Phillips is far from alone in suggesting that his response to *Native Son* was every bit as violent as Wright's had been to H. L. Mencken. Reading the book for the first time on a Californian beach in 1978, at the end of an American road trip, *Native Son* made him feel:

> as if an explosion had taken place inside my head. If I had to point to any one moment that seemed crucial in my desire to be a writer, it was then, as the Pacific surf began to wash up around the deck chair. The

43  Gilroy, *Black Atlantic*, pp. 146–8.
44  Jane Wilkinson (ed.) *Talking with African Poets, Playwrights and Novelists* (Portsmouth, NH: Heinemann, 1992), pp. 111–22 (p. 119).

emotional anguish of the hero, Bigger Thomas, the uncompromising prosodic muscle of Wright, his deeply felt sense of social indignation, provided not so much a model but a possibility of how I might be able to express the conundrum of my own existence. I had decided that I wanted to become a writer.[45]

Reading Wright's work in 1940s Paris, the Martinican anti-colonial intellectual Frantz Fanon seems to have experienced similar feelings of identification. Indeed, Fanon, the leading post-colonial theorist of his lifetime, read Wright long before he met him, devouring the French translation of *Native Son* upon its appearance in 1947. In the words of his biographer David Macey, the novel would be the Martinican's 'main – if not sole – source of information about race relations in the United States'.[46]

*Native Son*'s Dostoevskian aspect – its exhaustive detailing of the inner workings of Bigger's mind – perhaps held particular interest to Fanon. Much of Fanon's anti-colonial theory, after all, grew out of his experience working as a psychiatrist during the Algerian war of national liberation, which he called 'a favourable breeding-ground for mental disorders'.[47] During this time, Fanon treated far many more native Algerians than French settlers, and in the process came to acquire a first-hand familiarity with the likely psychological disorders that beset the colonized personality. Fanon grew particularly alert to the fact that those who had been forced onto the wrong side of the colonial partition and who received daily or even hourly reminders of this misfortune would likely develop an anger that faced two ways – within and without. The 'aggressiveness' of the colonized man, Fanon said, is 'deposited in his bones against his own people'; but the overarching privilege of the settler – the 'paradise close at hand which is guarded by terrible watchdogs' – creates other neuroses, ensuring that he feels ever envious and afraid, ever 'on the alert'. Fanon continues:

> Confronted with a world ruled by the settler, the native is always pre-sumed guilty. But the native's guilt is never a guilt which he accepts; it is rather a kind of curse, a sort of sword of Damocles, for, in his innermost spirit, the native admits no accusation. He is overpowered but not tamed; he is treated as an inferior but he is not convinced of his inferiority.... The native's muscles are always tensed.... The native is an oppressed person whose permanent dream is to become the persecutor.[48]

The native, in other words, presents a personality very like that we discover in *Native Son*. Nor are such links accidental. As Fanon rhetorically asked of Bigger Thomas in *Black Skin, White Masks* (1952):

45  Caryl Phillips, *A New World Order* (London: Vintage, 2001), pp. 18–19.
46  David Macey, *Frantz Fanon: A Life* (London: Granta, 2000), p. 127.
47  Frantz Fanon, *The Wretched of the Earth* (Harmondsworth: Penguin, 1990), trans. Constance Farrington, p. 201.
48  Fanon, *The Wretched of the Earth*, pp. 40–1.

A feeling of inferiority? No, a feeling of non-existence. Sin is Negro as virtue is white. All these white men in a group, guns in their hands, cannot be wrong. I am guilty. . . . It is Bigger Thomas – he is afraid, he is terribly afraid. He is afraid, but of what is he afraid? Of himself. No one knows yet who he is, but he knows that fear will fill the world when the world finds out. . . . In the end, Bigger Thomas acts. To put an end to his tension, he acts, he responds to the world's anticipation.[49]

In this key moment from *Black Skin, White Masks*, Fanon comes close to anticipating those aforementioned feminist or Black Atlantic readings that approach Bigger Thomas not as an endorsement of racial stereotype but as an exploration of how such stereotype influences the black sense of self under racist conditions. Fear is here presented as Bigger Thomas's default emotion; his actions, however violent they become, remain at root attributable to his upbringing in an American world that has systematically cornered him. All Bigger does, in Fanon's provocative reading, is what his surrounding society has long predicted he will do; his crime is merely to fulfil expectations, to slip too comfortably into a pre-existing caricature.

*Native Son* did not just lend shape to isolated moments from *The Wretched of the Earth* and *Black Skin, White Masks*. Instead, the novel occupied the centre of Fanon's thoughts, pervading every moment in each book. Hence, Wright's insights into the interdependence of black and white America and into the psychological pressures that it created resurface in *Black Skin, White Masks*, shaping its theorizations about the colonial 'juxtaposition of the white and black races [that] has created a massive psychoexistential complex'.[50] Arguably, too, the sensationalism which Baldwin found so troubling becomes for Fanon *Native Son*'s chief asset, reinforcing his belief that such a 'massive psychoexistential complex' could only have one outcome: violence.

But *Native Son*, even while reinforcing Fanon's own theories, broadened them. For it showed that the complexes he was identifying were not limited to Empire, were in no way the preserve of an old style of government now falling into decline, but were even central in the new world, in the heart of America. As such, *Native Son* revealed to Fanon that the colonial complexes that he was analysing were a condition of modernity. In return, Fanon's reading of *Native Son* in effect took a very particular and culturally situated American myth and made it global. The implication of Fanon's reading, after all, was that Chicago's status as a modernistic and over-industrialized metropolitan centre was interdependent on its arrangement of the races into enclaves whose proximity and stark inequality resembled the social organization of European colonies in Africa, the Caribbean and Asia. An intrinsically colonial regime thus presided within America itself, suggesting that this country's fabled progressivism and technological supremacy, not to mention its democracy, in fact relied on the same mechanisms of power that had made openly imperial centres such as Paris and London rich. Sucking America back into an imperial context that it liked to consider itself above, seeing

---

49 Fanon, *Black Skin, White Masks*, p. 139.
50 Fanon, *Black Skin, White Masks*, p. 14.

*Native Son* as classically anti-colonial, Fanon's explicit and implicit references to the novel thus rode roughshod over the democratic claims of the republic.

If Fanon's attempt to use *Native Son* as a blueprint for the anti-imperialist movement suggests the relevance of Wright's novel to students of post-colonial literatures, then a series of related observations further illustrates the point. *Native Son* remained banned by South Africa's last apartheid government, for example.[51] To varying degrees of success, critics have identified *Native Son's* legacy in the novels of Peter Abrahams, Chinua Achebe, Camara Laye, Alan Paton and Amos Tutuola.[52] Ezekiel Mphahlele, meanwhile, felt that comparisons between *Native Son* and Alan Paton's *Cry, the Beloved Country* (1948) flattered the latter, noting that: 'Wright gives us an almost minute-by-minute account of how . . . fear started and grew into something far larger than Bigger, and how he lived the fear. Bigger Thomas is not a mere vehicle of a message such as Alan Paton puts across.'[53] Similarly, Barbadian novelist and intellectual George Lamming repeatedly advertises the debt his writings owe to *Native Son*, splitting his 1958 narrative *Of Age and Innocence* into three evocatively-entitled sections ('Flight', 'San Cristobal' and 'On Trial') and dedicating his powerful historical novel of slavery *Natives of My Person* (1972) to Wright's memory.

This is a catalogue from which a new canon has been spun. Each entry is evidence that *Native Son* played a central role in the emergence of what Gilroy calls Black Atlantic culture. However, this catalogue of writers and intellectuals also embraces radically divergent and conflicting notions of what this concept of Black Atlantic cultural unity actually involves. For rationalists such as Fanon as well as Gilroy himself, this concept refers to a diaspora based on affinities of political circumstance – based on the similar social and psychological predicaments facing colonized Africans and ghettoized Americans. For others, however, this concept of Black Atlantic unity possesses a far more mystical foundation. For them, Bigger Thomas's story embodies an American version of an inherited African myth; the similarities between *Native Son* and Chinua Achebe's *Things Fall Apart*, for example, prove a common ancestral root.[54]

It is important to be clear that, whatever one's response to this second and more ancestral conceptualization of the diaspora, Wright himself subscribed to the first. For him, no mystical racial essence dwelt within his soul. No biological divisions permanently separated black from white intelligence. Racial differentiation was rather a question of degree than of kind. Indeed, Wright's clear view of identity as fluid and negotiable is perhaps what drew Gilroy to his work. For just as Gilroy suggests that American Afrocentrism can be too preoccupied with ancestry, too much concerned with Africa's past and too little with its future, so Wright's later writings concentrate squarely on the various and interconnected forms of inequality that he discovers around the present world. Moreover, although *Native*

51  See Charles R. Larson, *The Ordeal of the African Writer* (London and New York: Zed, 2001), p. 124.
52  To take one example, Fritz H. Panker, 'Laye, Lamming and Wright: Mother and Son', in Eldred Durosimi Jones, (ed.) *African Literature Today: 14: Insiders and Outsiders* (London: Heinemann, 1984) pp. 19–33.
53  Ezekiel Mphahlele, *The African Image* (London: Faber & Faber, 1974), p. 159.
54  See Bonnie J. Barthold, *Black Time: Fiction of Africa, the Caribbean and the United States* (London and New Haven, Conn.: Yale University Press, 1981), p. 116.

*Son* was written before Wright had fully developed this political identification with colonized and oppressed people around the world, its story of Bigger Thomas nonetheless held impressive global resonance. Indeed, it bears repetition that Fanon grew fascinated by *Native Son*, not because it seemed to convey some common racial essence but because it revealed to him that his own predicament as a colonial subject was, astonishingly enough, reproduced in the heart of democratic America. While the diaspora of Afrocentrism dwells in a world of myth and history, that of Wright, Gilroy and Fanon results from present conditions – from the fact that, in their lifetime as well as our own, not only Chicago but also São Paulo, Lagos and London can produce Bigger Thomases of their own.

# 3

# Critical readings

# James Baldwin, 'Many Thousands Gone'

Here reproduced in full, with Harper Perennial's permission, 'Many Thousands Gone' can be seen as a coda to 'Everybody's Protest Novel', James Baldwin's earlier, incendiary attack on *Native Son*. Appearing only eighteenth months later, in the December 1951 issue of *Partisan Review*, the essay sustains a less antagonistic tone towards Wright's novel. For one thing, while this more tempered essay still accuses *Native Son* of peddling stereotypes, it no longer blames these on Wright so much as on the regrettable power that American racial attitudes continue to hold over his imagination. And indeed, the *Native Son* that emerges here turns out to be a most enabling failure, the spark to Baldwin's brilliant disquisition on a 'race problem' that, he ultimately concludes, lies at the heart of white rather than black America.

Baldwin's movement towards this conclusion relies on a daring rhetorical conceit. On the one hand, the title of his essay is taken from one of the most directly political of all black spirituals ('No More Auction Block'); it refers to the untold masses of Africans killed by the slave trade and under slavery. On the other hand, however, the essay itself is written from a 'white' position that, throughout, Baldwin knowingly conflates with what 'Americans' think. The implication of this conceit is that white American identity has only come to know itself as natural – and as naturally superior – because it has continually compared itself with a racial Other who Baldwin summons, in the parlance of the time, by the dread word 'Negro'. The sheer fact that Baldwin has done this – has written the essay from a racial position different to his own – clearly places some distance between his work and the close identification of Wright and Bigger that we encounter in *Native Son*. Just as clearly, Baldwin's conceit is planned to subvert the idea that racial differences are essential to our identities and what keep us forever separate from each other. It is an outright defiance of Ellison's 'segregation . . . of the word'.[1] Thus Baldwin's disagreement with *Native*

---

1   Ralph Ellison, 'Twentieth-Century Fiction and the Black Mask of Humanity' in *Shadow and Act* (London: Secker & Warburg, 1967), pp. 24–44 (p. 24).

*Son* leads him to draw conclusions that, in turn, form a kind of literary anticipation of the political desegregation successfully brought about by the Civil Rights movement. Baldwin's disagreement, that is, leads him to insist that 'Negroes are Americans and their destiny is the country's destiny'; it leads him to anticipate the demand for full equality in time achieved by Martin Luther King, Jr. Indeed, in its biblical tone, its insistence on the need to recognize universal humanity and its concern with the destiny of America, 'Many Thousands Gone' bears comparison with the zenith of the Civil Rights movement: the 'I Have a Dream' speech that King delivered on the steps of the Lincoln Memorial in 1963. It is indispensable to anyone researching the history of *Native Son*'s critical reception.

In its original incarnation, 'Many Thousands Gone' contained no footnotes. The few such references given here are mine, offered to clarify Baldwin's less familiar allusions.

## From James Baldwin, *Notes of a Native Son* (Boston, Mass.: Beacon Press, 1955), pp. 29–47

It is only in his music, which Americans are able to admire because a protective sentimentality limits their understanding of it, that the Negro in America has been able to tell his story. It is a story which otherwise has yet to be told and which no American is prepared to hear. As is the inevitable result of things unsaid, we find ourselves until today oppressed with a dangerous and reverberating silence; and the story is told, compulsively, in symbols and signs, in hieroglyphics; it is revealed in Negro speech and in that of the white majority and in their different frames of reference. The ways in which the Negro has affected the American psychology are betrayed in our popular culture and in our morality; in our estrangement from him is the depth of our estrangement from ourselves. We cannot ask: what do we *really* feel about him – such a question merely opens the gates on chaos. What we really feel about him is involved with all that we feel about everything, about everyone, about ourselves.

The story of the Negro in America is the story of America – or, more precisely, it is the story of Americans. It is not a very pretty story: the story of a people is never very pretty. The Negro in America, gloomily referred to as that shadow which lies athwart our national life, is far more than that. He is a series of shadows, self-created, intertwining, which now we helplessly battle. One may say that the Negro in America does not really exist except in the darkness of our minds.

This is why his history and his progress, his relationship to all other Americans, has been kept in the social arena. He is a social and not a personal or a human problem; to think of him is to think of statistics, slums, rapes, injustices, remote violence; it is to be confronted with an endless cataloguing of losses, gains, skirmishes; it is to feel virtuous, outraged, helpless, as though his continuing status among us were somehow analogous to disease – cancer, perhaps, or tuberculosis – which must be checked, even though it cannot be cured. In this arena the black man acquires quite another aspect from that which he has in life. We do not know what to do with him in life; if he breaks our sociological and sentimental image of him we are panic-stricken and we feel ourselves betrayed. When he violates this image, therefore, he stands in the greatest danger (sensing which, we uneasily suspect that he is often playing a part for our benefit); and, what is not always so apparent but is equally true, we are then in some danger ourselves – hence our retreat or our blind and immediate retaliation.

Our dehumanisation of the Negro then is indivisible from our dehumanisation of ourselves: the loss of our own identity is the price we pay for our annulment of his. Time and our own force act as our allies, creating an impossible, a fruitless tension between the traditional master and slave. Impossible and fruitless because, literal and visible as this tension has become, it has nothing to do with reality.

Time has made some changes in the Negro face. Nothing has succeeded in making it exactly like our own, though the general desire seems to be to make it blank if one cannot make it white. When it has become blank, the past as thoroughly washed from the black face as it has been from ours, our guilt will be finished – at least it will have ceased to be visible, which we imagine to be much the same thing. But, paradoxically, it is we who prevent this from happening; since it is we, who, every hour that we live, reinvest the black face with our guilt; and we do this – by a further paradox, no less ferocious – helplessly, passionately, out of an unrealised need to suffer absolution.

Today, to be sure, we know that the Negro is not biologically or mentally inferior; there is no truth in those rumours of his body odour or his incorrigible sexuality; or no more truth than can be easily explained or even defended by the social sciences. Yet, in our most recent war, his blood was segregated as was, for the most part, his person. Up to today we are set at a division, so that he may not marry our daughters or our sisters, nor may he – for the most part – eat at our tables or live in our houses. Moreover, those who do, do so at the grave expense of a double alienation: from their own people, whose fabled attributes they must either deny or, worse, cheapen and bring to market; from us, for we require of them, when we accept them, that they at once cease to be Negroes and yet not fail to remember what being a Negro means – to remember, that is, what it means to us. The threshold of insult is higher or lower, according to the people involved, from the boot-black in Atlanta to the celebrity in New York. One must travel very far, among saints with nothing to gain or outcasts with nothing to lose, to find a place where it does not matter – and perhaps a word or a gesture or simply a silence will testify that it matters even there.

For it means something to be a Negro, after all, as it means something to have been born in Ireland or in China, to live where one sees space and sky or to live where one sees nothing but rubble or nothing but high buildings. We cannot escape our origins, however hard we try, those origins which contain the key – could we but find it – to all that we later become. What it means to be a Negro is a good deal more than this essay can discover; what it means to be a Negro in American can perhaps be suggested by an examination of the myths we perpetuate about him.

Aunt Jemima and Uncle Tom are dead,[2] their places taken by a group of

---

2   See Chronology, p. 47.

amazingly well-adjusted young men and women, almost as dark, but ferociously literate, well-dressed and scrubbed, who are never laughed at, who are not likely ever to set foot in a cotton or tobacco field or in any but the most modern of kitchens. There are others who remain, in our odd idiom, 'underprivileged'; some are bitter and those come to grief; some are unhappy, but, continually presented with the evidence of a better day soon to come, are speedily becoming less so. Most of them care nothing whatever about race. They want only their proper place in the sun and the right to be left alone, like any other citizen of the republic. We may all breathe more easily. Before, however, our joy at the demise of Aunt Jemima and Uncle Tom approaches the indecent, we had better ask whence they sprang, how they lived? Into what limbo have they vanished?

However inaccurate our portraits of them were, these portraits do suggest, not only the conditions, but the quality of their lives and the impact of this spectacle on our consciences. There was no one more forbearing than Aunt Jemima, no one stronger or more pious or more loyal or more wise; there was, at the same time, no one weaker or more faithless or more vicious and certainly no one more immoral. Uncle Tom, trustworthy and sexless, needed only to drop the title 'Uncle' to become violent, crafty, and sullen, a menace to any white woman who passed by. They prepared our feast tables and our burial clothes; and, if we could boast that we understood them, it was far more to the point and far more true that they understood us. They were, moreover, the only people in the world who did; and not only did they know us better than we knew ourselves, but they knew us better than we knew them. This was the piquant flavouring to the national joy, it lay behind our uneasiness as it lay behind our benevolence: Aunt Jemima and Uncle Tom, our creations, at the last evaded us; they had a life – their own, perhaps a better life than ours – and they would never tell us what it was. At the point where we were driven most privately and painfully to conjecture what depths of contempt, what heights of indifference, what prodigies of resilience, what untamable superiority allowed them so vividly to endure, neither perishing nor rising up in a body to wipe us from the earth, the image perpetually shattered and the word failed. The black man in our midst carried murder in his heart, he wanted vengeance. We carried murder too, we wanted peace.

In our image of the Negro breathes the past we deny, not dead but living yet and powerful, the beast in our jungle of statistics. It is this which defeats us, which continues to defeat us, which lends to inter-racial cocktail parties their rattling, genteel, nervously smiling air: in any drawing room at such a gathering the beast may spring, filling the air with flying things and an unenlightened wailing. Wherever the problem touches there is confusion, there is danger. Wherever the Negro face appears a tension is created, the tension of a silence filled with things unutterable. It is a sentimental error, therefore, to believe that the past is dead; it means nothing to say that it is all forgotten, that the Negro himself has forgotten it. It is not a question of memory. Oedipus did not remember the thongs that bound his feet; nevertheless the marks they left testified to that doom towards which his feet were leading him. The man does not remember the hand that struck him, the darkness that frightened him, as a child; nevertheless, the hand and the darkness remain with him, indivisible from himself forever, part of the passion that drives him wherever he thinks to take flight.

The making of an American begins at that point where he himself rejects all other ties, any other history, and himself adopts the vesture of his adopted land. This problem has been faced by all Americans throughout our history – in a way it *is* our history – and it baffles the immigrant and sets on edge the second generation until today. In the case of the Negro the past was taken from him whether he would or no; yet to forswear it was meaningless and availed him nothing, since his shameful history was carried, quite literally, on his brow. Shameful; for he was heathen as well as black and would never have discovered the healing blood of Christ had not we braved the jungles to bring him these glad tidings. Shameful; for, since our role as missionary had not been wholly disinterested, it was necessary to recall the shame from which we had delivered him in order more easily to escape our own. As he accepted the alabaster Christ and the bloody cross – in the bearing of which he would find his redemption, as, indeed, to our outraged astonishment, he sometimes did – he must, henceforth, accept that image we then gave him or himself: having no other and standing, moreover, in danger of death should he fail to accept the dazzling light thus brought into such darkness. It is this quite simple dilemma that must be borne in mind if we wish to comprehend his psychology.

However we shift the light which beats so fiercely on his head, or *prove*, by victorious social analysis, how his lot has changed, how we have both improved, our uneasiness refuses to be exorcised. And nowhere is this more apparent than in our literature on the subject – 'problem' literature when written by whites, 'protest' literature when written by Negroes – and nothing is more striking than the tremendous disparity of tone between the two creations. *Kingsblood Royal* bears, for example, almost no kinship to *If He Hollers Let Him Go*, though the same reviewers praised them both for what were, at bottom, very much the same reasons. These reasons may be suggested, far too briefly but not at all unjustly, by observing that the presupposition is in both novels exactly the same: black is a terrible colour with which to be born into the world.

Now the most powerful and celebrated statement we have yet had of what it means to be a Negro in America is unquestionably Richard Wright's *Native Son*. The feeling which prevailed at the time of its publication was that such a novel, bitter, uncompromising, shocking, gave proof, by its very existence, of what strides might be taken in a free democracy; and its indisputable success, proof that Americans were now able to look full in the face without flinching the dreadful facts. Americans, unhappily, have the most remarkable ability to alchemise all bitter truths into an innocuous but piquant confection and to transform their moral contradictions, or public discussion of such contradictions, into a proud decoration, such as are given for heroism on the field of battle. Such a book, we felt with pride, could never have been written before – which was true. Nor could it be written today. It bears already the aspect of a landmark: for Bigger and his brothers have undergone yet another metamorphosis; they have been accepted in baseball leagues and by colleges hitherto exclusive; and they have made a most favourable appearance on the national screen. We have yet to encounter, nevertheless, a report so indisputably authentic, or one that can begin to challenge this most significant novel.

It is, in a certain American tradition, the story of an unremarkable youth in battle with the force of circumstance; that force of circumstance which plays and which has played so important a part in the national fables of success or failure. In this case the force of circumstance is not poverty merely but colour, a circumstance which cannot be overcome, against which the protagonist battles for his life and loses. It is, on the surface, remarkable that this book should have enjoyed among Americans the favour it did enjoy; no more remarkable, however, than that it should have been compared, exuberantly, to Dostoevsky, though placed a shade below Dos Passos, Dreiser, and Steinbeck; and when the book is examined, its impact does not seem remarkable at all, but becomes, on the contrary, perfectly logical and inevitable.

We cannot, to begin with, divorce this book from the specific social climate of that time: it was one of the last of those angry productions, encountered in the late twenties and all through the thirties, dealing with the inequities of the social structure of America. It was published one year before our entry into the last world war – which is to say, very few years after the dissolution of the WPA and the end of the New Deal and at a time when bread lines and soup kitchens and bloody industrial battles were bright in everybody's memory.[3] The rigours of that unexpected time filled us not only with a genuinely bewildered and despairing idealism – so that, because there at least was *something* to fight for, young men went off to die in Spain – but also with a genuinely bewildered self-consciousness. The Negro, who had been during the magnificent twenties a passionate and delightful primitive, now became, as one of the things we were most self-conscious about, our most oppressed minority. In the thirties, swallowing Marx whole, we discovered the Worker and realised – I should think with some relief – that the aims of the Worker and the aims of the Negro were one. This theorem – to which we shall return – seems now to leave rather too much out of account; it became, nevertheless, one of the slogans of the 'class struggle' and the gospel of the New Negro.

As for this New Negro, it was Wright who became his most eloquent spokesman; and his work, from its beginning, is most clearly committed to the social struggle. Leaving aside the considerable question of what relationship precisely the artist bears to the revolutionary, the reality of man as a social being is not his only reality and that artist is strangled who is forced to deal with human beings solely in social terms; and who has, moreover, as Wright had, the necessity thrust on him of being the representative of some thirteen million people. It is a false responsibility (since writers are not congressmen) and impossible, by its nature, of fulfilment. The unlucky shepherd soon finds that, so far from being able to feed the hungry sheep, he has lost the wherewithal for his own nourishment: having not been allowed – so fearful was his burden, so present his audience! – to re-create his own experience. Further, the militant men and women of the thirties were not, upon examination, significantly emancipated from their antecedents, however bitterly they might consider themselves estranged or however gallantly they struggled to build a better world. However they might extol Russia, their concept of a better world was quite helplessly American and betrayed a certain thinness of imagination, a suspect reliance on suspect and badly digested formulae, and a positively fretful romantic haste. Finally, the relationship of the Negro to the Worker can not be summed up, nor even greatly illuminated, by saying that their aims are one. It is true only in so far as they both desire better working conditions and useful only in so far as they unite their strength as workers to achieve these ends. Further than this we cannot in honesty go.

In this climate Wright's voice first was heard and the struggle which promised for a time to shape his work and give it purpose also fixed it in an ever more unrewarding rage. Recording his days of anger he has also nevertheless recorded as no Negro before him had ever done, that fantasy Americans hold in their minds when they speak of the Negro: that fantastic and fearful image which we have lived with since the first slave fell beneath the lash. This is the significance of *Native Son* and also, unhappily, its overwhelming limitation.

*Native Son* begins with the *Brring!* of an alarm clock in the squalid Chicago tenement where Bigger and his family live. Rats live there too, feeding off the garbage, and we first encounter Bigger in the act of killing one. One may consider that the entire book, from that harsh *Brring!* to Bigger's weak 'Good-bye' as the lawyer, Max, leaves him in the death cell, is an extension, with the roles inverted, of this chilling metaphor. Bigger's situation and Bigger himself exert on the mind the same sort of fascination. The premise of the book is, as I take it, clearly conveyed in these first pages: we are confronting a monster created by the American republic and we are, through being made to share his experience, to receive illumination as regards the manner of his life and to feel both pity and horror at his awful and inevitable doom. This is an arresting and potentially rich idea and we would be discussing a very different novel if Wright's execution had been more perceptive and if he had not attempted to redeem a symbolical monster in social terms.

One may object that it was precisely Wright's intention to create in Bigger a social symbol, revelatory of social disease and prophetic of disaster. I think, however, that it is this assumption which we ought to examine more carefully. Bigger has no discernible relationship to himself, to his own life, to his own people, nor to any other people – in this respect, perhaps, he is most American – and his force comes, not from his significance as a social (or anti-social) unit, but from his significance as the incarnation of a myth. It is remarkable that, though we follow him step by step from the tenement room to the death cell, we know as little about him when this journey is ended as we did when it began; and, what is even more remarkable, we know almost as little about the social dynamic which we are to believe created him. Despite the details of slum life which we are given, I doubt that anyone who has thought about it, disengaging himself from sentimentality, can accept this most essential premise of the novel for a moment. Those Negroes who surround him, on the other hand, his hard-working mother, his ambitious sister, his pool-room cronies, Bessie, might be considered as far richer and far more subtle and accurate illustrations of the ways in which Negroes are controlled in our society and the complex techniques they have evolved for their survival. We are limited, however, to Bigger's view of them, part of a deliberate plan which might not have been disastrous if we were not also limited to Bigger's perceptions. What this means for the novel is that a necessary dimension has been cut away; this dimension being the relationship that Negroes bear to one another, that depth of involvement and unspoken recognition of shared experience which creates a way of life. What the novel reflects – and at no point interprets – is the isolation of the Negro within his own group and the resulting fury of impatient scorn. It is this which creates its climate of anarchy and unmotivated and unapprehended disaster; and it is this climate, common to most Negro protest novels, which has led us all to believe that in Negro life there exists no tradition, no field of manners, no possibility of ritual or intercourse, such as may, for example, sustain the Jew even after he has left his father's house. But the fact is not that the Negro has no tradition but that there has as yet arrived no sensibility sufficiently profound and tough to make this tradition articulate. For a tradition expresses, after all, nothing more than the long and painful experience of a people; it comes out of the battle waged to maintain their integrity or, to put it more simply, out of their struggle to survive. When we speak of the Jewish tradition we are speaking of centuries of exile and persecution, of the strength which endured and the sensibility which discovered in it the high possibility of the moral victory.

This sense of how Negroes live and how they have so long endured is hidden from us in part by the very speed of the Negro's public progress, a progress so heavy with complexity, so bewildering and kaleidoscopic, that he dare not pause to conjecture on the darkness which lies behind him; and by the nature of the American psychology which, in order to apprehend or be made able to accept it, must undergo a metamorphosis so profound as to be literally unthinkable and which there is no doubt we will resist until we are compelled to achieve our own identity by the rigours of a time that has yet to come. Bigger, in the meanwhile, and all his furious kin, serve only to whet the notorious national taste for the sensational and to reinforce all that we now find it necessary to believe. It is not Bigger whom we fear, since his appearance among us makes our victory certain. It is the others, who smile, who go to church, who give no cause for complaint, whom we sometimes consider with amusement, with pity, even with affection – and in whose faces we sometimes surprise the merest arrogant hint of hatred, the faintest, withdrawn, speculative shadow of contempt – who make us uneasy; whom we cajole, threaten, flatter, fear; who to us remain unknown, though we are not (we feel with both relief and hostility and with bottomless confusion) unknown to them. It is out of our reaction to these hewers of wood and drawers of water that our image of Bigger was created.

It is this image, living yet, which we perpetually seek to evade with goods works; and this image which makes of all our good works an intolerable mockery. The 'nigger', black, benighted, brutal, consumed with hatred as we are consumed with guilt, cannot be thus blotted out. He stands at our shoulders when we give our maid her wages, it is his hand which we fear we are taking when struggling to communicate with the current 'intelligent' Negro, his stench, as it were, which fills our mouths with salt as the monument is unveiled in honour of the latest Negro leader. Each generation had shouted behind him, *Nigger!* as he walked our streets; it is he whom we would rather our sisters did not marry; he is banished into the vast and wailing outer darkness whenever we speak of the 'purity' of our women, of the 'sanctity' of our homes, of 'American' ideals. What is more, he knows it. He is indeed the 'native son': he is the 'nigger'. Let us refrain from inquiring at the moment whether or not he actually exists; for we *believe* that he exists. Whenever we encounter him amongst us in the flesh, our faith is made perfect and his necessary and bloody end is executed with a mystical ferocity of joy.

But there is a complementary faith among the damned which involves their gathering of the stones with which those who walk in the light shall stone them; or there exists among the intolerably degraded the perverse and powerful desire to force into the arena of the actual those fantastic crimes of which they have been accused, achieving their vengeance and their own destruction through making the nightmare real. The American image of the Negro lives also in the Negro's heart; and when he has surrendered to this image life has no other possible reality. Then he, like the white enemy with whom he will be locked one day in mortal struggle, has no means save this of asserting his identity. This is why Bigger's murder of Mary can be referred to as an 'act of creation' and why, once this murder has been committed, he can feel for the first time that he is living fully and deeply as a man was meant to live. And there is, I should think, no Negro living in America who has not felt, briefly or for long periods, with anguish sharp or dull, in varying degrees and to varying effect, simple, naked and unanswerable hatred; who has not wanted to smash any white face he may encounter in a day, to violate, out of motives of the cruellest vengeance, their women, to break the bodies of all white people and bring them low, as low as that dust into which he himself has been and is being trampled; no Negro, finally who has not had to make his own precarious adjustment to the 'nigger' who surrounds him and the 'nigger' in himself.

Yet the adjustment must be made – rather, it must be attempted, the tension perpetually sustained – for without this he has surrendered his birthright as a man no less than his birthright as a black man. The entire universe is then peopled only with his enemies, who are not only white men armed with rope and rifle, but his own far-flung and contemptible kinsmen. Their blackness is his degradation and it is their stupid and passive endurance which makes his end inevitable.

Bigger dreams of some black man who will weld all blacks together into a mighty fist, and feels, in relation to his family, that perhaps they had to live as they did precisely because none of them had ever done anything, right or wrong, which mattered very much. It is only he who, by an act of murder, has burst the dungeon cell. He has made it manifest that *he* lives and that his despised blood nourishes the passions of a man. He has forced his oppressors to see the fruit of that oppression: and he feels, when his family and his friends come to visit him in the death cell, that they should not be weeping or frightened, that they should be happy, *proud* that he has dared, through murder and now through his own imminent destruction, to redeem their anger and humiliation, that he has hurled into the spiritless obscurity of their lives the lamp of his passionate life and death. Henceforth, they may remember Bigger – who has died, as we may conclude, for them. But they do not feel this; they only know that he has murdered two women and precipitated a reign of terror; and that now he is to die in the electric chair. They therefore weep and are honestly frightened – for which Bigger despises them and wishes to 'blot' them out. What is missing in his situation and in the representation of his psychology – which makes his situation false and his psychology incapable of development – is any revelatory apprehension of Bigger as one of the Negro's realities or as one of the Negro's roles. This failure is part of the previously noted failure to convey any sense of Negro life as a continuing and complex group reality. Bigger, who cannot function therefore as a reflection of the social illness, having, as it were, no society to reflect, likewise refuses to function on the loftier level of the Christ-symbol. His kinsmen are quite right to weep and be frightened, even to be appalled: for it is not his love for them or for himself which causes him to die, but his hatred and his self-hatred; he does not redeem the pains of a despised people, but reveals, on the contrary, nothing more than his own fierce bitterness at having been born one of them. In this also he is the 'native son', his progress determinable by the speed with which the distance increases between himself and the auction-block and all that the auction-block implies. To have penetrated this phenomenon, this inward contention of love and hatred, blackness and whiteness, would have given him a stature more nearly human and an end more nearly tragic; and would have given us a document more profoundly and genuinely bitter and less harsh with an anger which is, on the one hand, exhibited and, on the other hand, denied.

*Native Son* finds itself at length so trapped by the American image of Negro life and by the American necessity to find the ray of hope that it cannot pursue its own implications. This is why Bigger must be at the last redeemed, to be received, if only by rhetoric, into that community of phantoms which is our tenaciously held ideal of the happy social life. It is the socially conscious whites who receive him – the Negroes being capable of no such objectivity – and we have, by way of illustration, that lamentable scene in which Jan, Mary's lover, forgives him for her murder; and, carrying the explicit burden of the novel, Max's long speech to the jury. This speech, which really ends the book, is one of the most desperate performances in American fiction. It is the question of Bigger's humanity which is at stake, the relationship in which he stands to all other Americans – and, by implication, to all people – and it is precisely this question which it cannot clarify, with which it cannot, in fact, come to any coherent terms. He is the moment created by the American republic, the present awful sum of generations of oppression; but to say that he is a monster is to fall into the trap of making him sub-human and he must, therefore, be made representative of a way of life which is real and human in precise ratio to the degree to which it seems to us monstrous and strange. It seems to me that this idea carries, implicitly, a most remarkable confession: that is, that Negro life is in fact as debased and impoverished as our theology claims; and, further, that the use to which Wright puts this idea can only proceed from the assumption – not entirely unsound – that Americans, who evade, so far as possible, all genuine experience, have therefore no way of assessing the experience of others and no way of establishing themselves in relation to any way of life which is not their own. The privacy or obscurity of Negro life makes that life capable, in our imaginations, of producing anything at all; and thus the idea of Bigger's monstrosity can be presented without fear of contradiction, since no American has the knowledge or authority to contest it and no Negro has the voice. It is an idea, which, in the framework of the novel, is dignified by the possibility it promptly affords of presenting Bigger as the herald of disaster, the danger signal of a more bitter time to come when not Bigger alone but all his kindred will rise, in the name of the many thousands who have perished in fire and flood and by rope and torture, to demand their rightful vengeance.

But it is not quite fair, it seems to me, to exploit the national innocence in this way. The idea of Bigger as a warning boomerangs not only because it is quite beyond the limit of probability that Negroes in America will ever achieve the means of wreaking vengeance upon the state but also because it cannot be said that they have any desire to do so. *Native Son* does not convey the altogether savage paradox of the American Negro's situation, of which the social reality which we prefer with such hopeful superficiality to study is but, as it were, the shadow. It is not simply the relationship of oppressed to oppressor, of master to slave, nor is it motivated merely by hatred; it is also literally and morally, a *blood* relationship, perhaps the most profound reality of the American experience, and we cannot begin to unlock it until we accept how very much it contains of the force and anguish and terror of love.

Negroes are Americans and their destiny is the country's destiny. They have no other experience besides their experience on this continent and it is an experience which cannot be rejected, which yet remains to be embraced. If, as I believe, no American Negro exists who does not have his private Bigger Thomas living in the skull, then what most significantly fails to be illuminated here is the paradoxical adjustment which is perpetually made, the Negro being compelled to accept the fact that this dark and dangerous and unloved stranger is part of himself forever. Only this recognition sets him in any wise free and it is this, this necessary ability to contain and even, in the most honourable sense of the word, to *exploit* the 'nigger', which lends to Negro life its high element of the ironic and which causes the most well-meaning of their American critics to make such exhilarating errors when attempting to understand them. To present Bigger as a warning is simply to reinforce the American guilt and fear concerning him, it is most forcefully to limit him to that previously mentioned social arena in which he has no human validity, it is simply to condemn him to death. For he has always been a warning, he represents the evil, the sin and suffering which we are compelled to reject. It is useless to say to the courtroom in which this heathen sits on trial that he is their responsibility, their creation, and his crimes are theirs; and that they ought, there-fore, to allow him to live, to make articulate to himself behind the walls of prison the meaning of his existence. The meaning of his existence has already been most adequately expressed, nor does anyone wish, particularly not in the name of democracy, to think of it any more; as for the possibility of articulation, it is this possibility which above all others we most dread. Moreover, the courtroom, judge, jury, witnesses and spectators, recognise immediately that Bigger is their creation and they recognise this not only with hatred and fear and guilt and the resulting fury of self-righteousness but also with that morbid fullness of pride mixed with horror with which one regards the extent and power of one's wicked-ness. They know that death is his portion, that he runs to death; coming from darkness and dwelling in darkness, he must be, as often as he rises, banished, lest the entire planet be engulfed. And they know, finally, that they do not wish to forgive him and that he does not wish to be forgiven; that he dies, hating them, scorning that appeal which they cannot make to that irrecoverable humanity of his which cannot hear it; and that he *wants* to die because he glories in his hatred and prefers, like Lucifer, rather to rule in hell than serve in heaven.

For, bearing in mind the premise on which the life of such a man is based, *i.e.*, that black is the colour of damnation, this is his only possible end. It is the only death which will allow him a kind of dignity of even, however horribly, a kind of beauty. To tell this story, no more than a single aspect of the story of the 'nigger', is inevitably and richly to become involved with the force of life and legend, how each perpetually assumes the guise of the other, creating that dense, many-sided and shifting reality which is the world we live in and the world we make. To tell his story is to begin to liberate us from his image and it is, for the first time, to clothe this phantom with flesh and blood, to deepen, by our understanding of him and his relationship to us, our understanding of ourselves and of all men.

But this is not the story which *Native Son* tells, for we find here merely, repeated in anger, the story which we have told in pride. Nor, since the implications of this anger are evaded, are ever confronted with the actual or potential significance of our pride; which is why we fall, with such a positive glow of recognition, upon Max's long and bitter summing up. It is addressed to those among us of good will and it seems to say that, though there are whites and blacks among us who hate each other, we will not; there are those who are betrayed by greed, by guilt, by blood-lust, but not we; we will set our faces against them and join hands and walk together into that dazzling future when there will be no white or black. This is the dream of all liberal men, a dream not at all dishonourable, but, nevertheless, a dream. For, let us join hands on this mountain as we may, the battle is elsewhere. It proceeds far from us in the heat and horror and pain of life itself where all men are betrayed by greed and guilt and blood-lust and where no one's hands are clean. Our good will, from which we yet expect such power to transform us, is thin, passionless, strident: its roots, examined, lead us back to our forebears, whose assumption it was that the black man, to become truly human and acceptable, must first become like us. This assumption once accepted, the Negro in America can only acquiesce in the obliteration of his own personality, the distortion and debasement of his own experience, surrendering to those forces which reduce the person to anonymity and which make themselves manifest daily all over the darkening world.

**Hazel Rowley,** 'The Shadow of the White Woman:
Richard Wright and the Book-of-the-Month Club'

Until recently, all biographies of Richard Wright were either academic in tone, excessively personalized, or hamstrung by difficulties involved in gaining access to his private correspondence and other unpublished writings. This situation ended with the publication in 2001 of Hazel Rowley's *Richard Wright: The Life and Times*. Rowley's biography uses full access to the writer's archive to paint a portrait of unrivalled detail. It is a valuable resource in its own right.

Yet the clarity that Rowley's longer work brings to personal issues long shrouded in innuendo is also evident in the following article, first published in the Fall 1999 issue of the *Partisan Review*. This article puts flesh on the bones of the commercial censorship referred to at the end of the biographical section, whereby the directors of the Book-of-the-Month Club insisted on adjusting *Native Son* before making it one of their monthly nominations. Rowley, here laying bare the racial and gender assumptions behind this decision, is particularly alert to the impact of the club's censoring of *Native Son*'s more sexually explicit passages. These requested omissions, she argues, 'upset the novel's delicate balance' on a range of wider matters. In particular, Rowley suggests, Wright's original Bigger, as revealed in the original draft, was altogether more anxious and confused about sex than the eventual Bigger revealed in the eventual draft. Instead of encountering the young and damaged sexuality that Wright intended for Bigger, readers must look beyond the rapist for his humanity – must read between the lines to understand how such a man could morph so quickly into a monster.

Rowley also points out that Wright's original draft made Mary Dalton a more sexual figure – made her at once more flirtatious and more open in her desire for Bigger. The Book-of-the-Month Club, Rowley suggests, systematically removed such statements from Mary's mouth, restoring polite society's silence about female lust. On one level, this restoration of silence seems simply a sign of Wright's times. In the early 1940s, American literature certainly spent a good deal less time in the bedroom than it does today. On another level, however, this silence helped make safe the radical racial politics of the book, deleting from it the dangerous *possibility* that a white woman – any white woman – might want 'a black man's hands on her breasts.' Indeed, when reading Rowley's essay, it might be worthwhile thinking once more of 'Many Thousands Gone' and asking whether Baldwin's problems with this novel were at all exacerbated by the effects of this censorship.

Rowley followed *Richard Wright: The Life and Times* with *Tête à Tête: Simone de Beauvoir and Jean-Paul Sartre*, published in 2005. She is currently working on a study of ethnic communities in New York. This article was originally published without footnotes, and those that I have included here are intended to help guide your reading.

## Hazel Rowley (1999) 'The Shadow of the White Woman: Richard Wright and the Book-of-the-Month Club', *Partisan Review* 66(4): pp. 625–34

From the time he first put pen to paper, Richard Wright became a signifier for race. No issue is more emotionally charged. What he wrote about, and what Wright himself symbolizes, generates so much passion that it is scarcely possible to see him or his work through the steam. His art has been consistently reduced to statements. The man himself has been stripped of his ambiguity and complexity.

The surviving drafts of Wright's works in the Beinecke Library at Yale, as well as his unpublished manuscripts and correspondence, reveal the almost impossible context in which he was writing. The conflicting forces were such that the Richard Wright we know is a censored, mediated, packaged Richard Wright. Like a ball of wool, there is a complex tangle of threads wound around Wright's work and its reception. It is not easy to disentangle.

Wright passionately believed in the revolutionary potential of writing; his words were going to "tell" and "march" and "fight". Seeing himself as a mediator between cultures, he aimed to "build a bridge of words" between the black and white worlds he inhabited. And yet, in order to commit words to paper at all, Wright had to shut out the clamor of protesting voices inside his head. As Jean-Paul Sartre pointed out in *"Qu'est-ce que la littérature"* ["What is Literature"] (1947), Richard Wright was writing for a "split public," one black, one white, and this gave his every word, his every phrase, an "incomparable tension." Reminiscent of Virginia Woolf's struggle with "the angel in the house," Richard Wright comments in his essay "How 'Bigger' Was Born": "I felt a mental censor . . . standing over me, draped in white, warning me not to write."[1] There were black censors out there too, not just white, and there were real censors, not just those in the head.

Wright wanted to tell the truth, as he saw it, and he wanted to be critical, like any other good writer, but since he was writing about the charged issue of

---

1   'How "Bigger" was Born', p. 26.

race, these aspirations had repercussions quite outside his control. There was the difficulty of criticizing blacks. In an interview shortly before his death in 1960, he told Georges Charbonnier: "You know, we Negro artists are in a rather difficult position . . . I don't want to provide whites with words to strike at black people. This is a moral trap." And there was the difficulty of criticizing whites. He told himself. "I'd be acting out of *fear* if I let what I thought whites would say constrict and paralyze me." The problem he almost certainly underestimated was that his fighting words had to pass muster in what was then the all-white territory of book publishing.

While Wright was absorbed in the process of creating Bigger Thomas, the angriest, most violent anti-hero ever to have appeared in black American literature, he had to fight his anxiety. He wanted to show that stunting and deforming psychosocial conditions have a stunting deforming effect on the individual—*any* individual, white or black. But since Bigger is a black man, Wright worried that whites would see him as the confirmation of all their prejudices. And he could already hear black voices protesting: "But, Mr. Wright, there are so many of us who are *not* like Bigger! Why don't you portray in your fiction the best traits of our race?"

This has been a common response to Wright among black critics. It is hardly surprising. Bigger played into the stereotype of the semi-socialized black man who threatens the established order of white civilization. His very name, Bigger, deliberately evokes racist terminology. On the surface, *Native Son* appears to confirm the very prejudices with which white supremacy propped itself up: here was a black man ready (it seemed) to rape a white woman, kill her and chop her body into pieces to stuff her into a furnace. Here was a brute prepared to pulverize his black girlfriend with a brick, then pitch her body down an airshaft.

In a 1946 article called "It's About Time," Langston Hughes wrote pointedly: "It's about time some Negro writer wrote a good novel about *good* Negroes who do *not* come to a bad end. . . . With all of the millions of colored people in America who never murder anybody, or rape or get raped or want to rape, who never lust after white bodies, or cringe before white stupidity . . . with all the millions of normal human, lovable colored folks in the United States, it is about time some Negro writer put some of them into a book."

Some thirty years later, the African-American writer David Bradley proclaimed that he hated *Native Son* "with a passion." He too was convinced that the novel "was pandering to white expectations." As he put it: "I myself did not want a nut like Bigger Thomas sitting next to me on a bus or in a schoolroom, and certainly I did not want him moving in next door." In Bradley's view, Richard Wright had "sold his people down the river to make a buck."

In the light of the frequent criticism, particularly among black scholars, that Wright's fiction reinforces white prejudices, it is revealing to know something about the publishing history of Wright's work. The drafts and unpublished manuscripts among Wright's papers at Yale tell a somewhat different story from his published works. In fact, Richard Wright did not write to please white readers any more than he wrote to please black readers. If anything, he rather enjoyed provoking the wrath of both; there was an element in him that liked to shock. Unfortunately for him, it was the white literary establishment that accepted or rejected his manuscripts.

Since *Native Son* and *Black Boy* are the two narratives with which Wright is invariably associated, and since every entry on Richard Wright in directories and anthologies mentions the Book-of-the-Month Club as playing an invaluable part in these spectacular early successes, I will focus on this small aspect of the larger story.

"An interesting development has occurred which promises very exciting possibilities if it comes off. I want to tell you about it, but please don't base any hopes in it yet." It was late August of 1939 when Wright's publisher, Edward Aswell of Harper & Brothers, told Wright that the Book-of-the Month Club judges were excited about *Native Son*. Aswell had asked Wright to make some revisions to his original manuscript, but the book was now set in galley proofs, ready for publication the following month.

It came as a complete surprise to both Aswell and Wright to be told that the Book-of-the-Month Club liked the book. There was, however, a catch: selection was contingent on Wright making some changes—mostly in the form of excisions. Publication of the novel would have to be postponed.

The enticement of being a Book-of-the-Month selection cannot be underestimated. Wright would be the first black writer to be promoted by the Book-of-the-Month Club. It meant sales of a scope that no black writer had ever enjoyed before, a fat check, and considerable prestige. We know where Wright's publishers and his literary agent stood on the matter. The pressure on Wright was immense. He was thirty-one, it was his first novel, and he wanted as many readers as possible. There is no record of his feelings about the changes; what we do know is that he made them.

The judges hesitated for seven more months, holding up publication. They worried that by selecting this "red-hot poker", they were "risking the utter condemnation of the reading subscribers." Eventually, they declared it one of two Books of the Month for March 1940. (Their other choice was *The Trees*, by Conrad Richter.) But the *Native Son* they were now promoting was no longer quite the same book that had crossed their desk the previous summer. The changes they had asked Wright to make appear minor and insignificant, but the overall effect was subtly different. (Only since 1991, when the Library of America published the text that was originally sent to the Book-of-the-Month Club in galley form, have we been able to read the narrative as Wright intended it.)

As Book-of-the-Month for March 1940, *Native Son* appeared to have the best start in life it could possibly hope for. In the first few weeks, it sold faster than any book Harper & Brothers had published in the last twenty years: close to 215,000 copies within three weeks—an astounding figure for a first novel. Renowned playwrights and theatre producers scrambled for the stage rights, and Hollywood put in a bid for the movie rights (with an all-white cast!). With trumpets and heraldry, *Native Son* was hailed as the book of the month, the book of the year, the book of the times. Negative criticism, every bit as passionate as the praise, came later.

Richard Wright's main champion in that period of dazzling triumph seemed to be Dorothy Canfield Fisher. She was a formidable figure. Eleanor Roosevelt considered her one of the ten most influential women in the United States. Robert Frost called her "the great lady of Vermont." A well-known Quaker liberal,

Canfield wrote popular novels. She was also a member (a dominant member, by all accounts) of the Book-of-the Month selection committee.

Canfield Fisher wrote an introduction to the first edition of *Native Son*. She alluded to the Dostoyevskian depths of human experience plumbed by the novel. She added: "I do not at all mean to imply that *Native Son* as literature is comparable to the masterpieces of Dostoevsky."

She declared: "The author shows genuine literary skill." But her starchy introduction made it clear that the value of Wright's novel was as a sociological case study. The situation of Bigger Thomas—and Negro youths generally—was similar, she said, to that of rats in scientific experiments set up to produce psychopathic behavior. "*Native Son* is the first report in fiction we have had from those . . . whose behavior-patterns give evidence of the same bewildered, senseless tangle of abnormal nerve-reactions."

It was unfortunate to reduce a powerful work of fiction to a sociological report. Nevertheless, Canfield Fisher was a worthy name and Wright's publishers thought it "a very good send-off for *Native Son*." Wright himself thanked "Miss Fisher" in a tone that for him was decidedly lukewarm: "I feel that you did present the material in the book in a light that would make it understood by the American reading public." Was there a touch of irony in his phrasing? Generally, writers aspire to communicate with the reading public without mediation. And Canfield Fisher had already done her best to mediate between Wright and the reading public. She would do so again, far more radically, with *Black Boy* in 1945. Canfield Fisher, more than any other of the Book-of-the-Month Club judges, took it upon herself to "improve" *Native Son* and *Black Boy*. What this meant, essentially, was to make them into narratives that were less shocking to white readers.

With *Native Son*, the selection committee asked for some deletions. Nothing major. They wanted some of the flab cut out of the speeches in the trial scene, and since this scene was longwinded and highly didactic, this was on the whole a good thing. But the cuts they asked for in the early expository sections had nothing to do with longwindedness.

The question that looms large in the novel is that of Bigger Thomas's guilt. Just how guilty is he? He inadvertently kills a white woman, and he willfully murders his black girlfriend, Bessie. The episode that sets off this train of disasters is a scene between Bigger and Mary—a scene that burns itself into the reader's imagination because it deliberately hovers around the edges of an issue primordial in race mythology: the alleged rape of a white woman by a black man. It is Bigger's terror at being falsely accused of this crime that causes him to silence the white woman by smothering her with a pillow. But what if the shadowy figure of Mrs. Dalton, Mary's mother, had not hovered in the doorway at that point? What if Bigger had kept his hands on Mary's breasts? Would he have raped her?

If Wright was to challenge this racist stereotype rather than reinforce it, it was crucial that his readers understood that Mary Dalton desired her black chauffeur every bit as much as he desired her—if not more so. The build-up of Mary Dalton's somewhat wanton sexuality is every bit as important as the build-up of Bigger as a highly libidinous young man. By modifying what they called Wright's "savage frankness" when it came to sex, the Book-of-the-Month Club judges upset the novel's delicate balance.

It is true that Wright was testing the boundaries of 1930s literary realism in an early scene (some twenty-five years ahead of its time) which was a graphic portrayal of two boys masturbating. No sooner has Bigger seated himself in the darkened movie theatre than he starts "polishing [his] nightstick." His friend Jack races him to orgasm. In the background the pipe organ is playing; otherwise, Wright leaves little to metaphor. It is a credit to Wright's publisher, Ed Aswell, that he was prepared to leave in this scene, though he found it "a bit on the raw side." There was, admittedly, less at stake for him: he was publishing the book, not promoting it, in his own name, to the one hundred thousand members of the Book-of-the-Month Club.

After Canfield Fisher and her colleagues had gone through the manuscript with their editing pencil, the masturbation scene disappeared completely. So did the newsreel that then came on, which to Bigger's surprise, featured Mary Dalton (the daughter of his future employer) and her boyfriend, barelegged and kissing on a gleaming Florida beach. Bigger and Jack agreed she was "a hot-looking number" and whispered to each other that some wealthy white women would apparently go to bed with anybody. All this disappeared in the published version.

Arnold Rampersad, who edited the unabridged Library of America edition, comments that "the changes in *Native Son* almost emasculated Bigger Thomas."[2] What he does not point out is that Mary also had her sexual drive dramatically curtailed, and though this involved more delicate snipping—a sentence here and there—the effect on the narrative is more significant. For example, the judges rejected this sentence, when Bigger is with Bessie: "He placed his hands on her breasts just as he had placed them on Mary's last night and he was thinking of that while he kissed her." Was it the sexual explicitness that worried them, or was something else involved?

Under the guise of sexual censorship there was undoubtedly another sort of censorship going on. Arnold Rampersad argues that the Book-of-the-Month Club changes were "the result, not entirely but in part, of racism – racism that was seldom conscious of itself, that was expressed in subtle, even benign ways, but racism nonetheless."[3]

If the judges were uncomfortable with a black man thinking about his hands on a white woman's breasts, they were even less willing to stand behind a book in which the white woman *wants* a black man's hands on her breasts. It was Wright's intention to portray Mary Dalton as somewhat *easy*. Her very name, which we associate with innocence and virginity, was chosen with a playful sense of irony.

Wright was asked to tone down the goings-on in the car when Bigger, now employed as the Dalton family chauffeur, drives Mary Dalton and her Communist boyfriend Jan home from their inebriated excursion to the Chicago blackbelt. In the galley version, Bigger glances in the rear-vision mirror and sees Mary lying flat on her back and Jan bending over her, He sees a "faint sweep of white thigh." Then he hears them both sigh. Realizing what they are up to, he

2  Arnold Rampersad, 'A Note on the Texts' in *Richard Wright: Early Works: Lawd Today!, Uncle Tom's Children, Native Son* (New York: Library of America, 1991), pp. 909–14.
3  Rampersad, 'A Note on the Texts', pp. 909–14.

fights off the "stiffening feeling in his loins." In the published version, all that transpires in the back seat is some kissing. Even the word "spooning" was cut. The white woman had been made to sit up and behave. All Bigger now felt was drunk.

Then comes the pivotal scene in which Bigger helps a languorous Mary Dalton up the stairs and into her bedroom. These sentences the judges wanted deleted:

> He tightened his arms as his lips pressed tightly against hers and he felt her body moving strongly. The thought and conviction that Jan had had her a lot flashed through his mind. He kissed her again and felt the sharp bones of her hip move in a hard and veritable grind. Her mouth was open and her breath came slow and deep.

This is a woman who, like her famous fictional predecessor Madame Bovary, has just been carrying on in the back seat of her chauffeured vehicle. She is, we understand, using her drunkenness as a pretext; suddenly she makes movements that are not limp at all. In the same way that Camus, in his novel *L'Étranger* (1942) intended the shafts of sunlight and the glint of the Arab's knife when Meursault kills the Arab, Wright intended every detail of Mary Dalton's thrusts and grinds.

In the censored published version, the white woman's hips have been stilled. She is pure passivity, as limp as a rag doll, scarcely conscious. The whole delicate balance of desire, guilt and responsibility has been altered. Bigger has become the archetypal black beast pawing the sleeping beauty. The white woman, once again, has been completely absolved from responsibility. Seemingly minor changes had made *Native Son* a less provocative, less disturbing novel for white readers.

Four years later, when the galleys of Wright's autobiographical narrative *American Hunger* arrived at the Book-of-the-Month Club, typeset and ready for publication, the selection committee again liked the manuscript. Or so they said. In fact, they liked some of the manuscript. They approved of the first part, called "Southern Night," about Wright's formative years amid Southern racist terror. But the second part of the manuscript (the last third), about Wright's initiation into the white world through communist circles in Chicago, was an indictment of racism in the North. The ending was a passionate call for struggle: "If this country can't find its way to a human path, if it can't inform conduct with a deep sense of life, then all of us, black as well as white, are going down the same drain."

The judges told Wright they would consider the book if he left off the second part. Nor did they approve of the title, *American Hunger*. Their suggestion, thoroughly innocuous, was *First Chapter*. And they wanted Wright to add a few pages to the ending of the first part, "Southern Night," concluding the narrative on a more hopeful note.

The Chicago section served an important function: Richard Wright wanted to show racism in the United States generally, not just the South. His title, *American Hunger*, referred to the physical and spiritual hunger of black people in America. He had no interest in ending his narrative on a false note of resolution. Nevertheless, pressured by his publishers as well by this stage, he consented to ending the book when he left the South. (Harper & Brothers assured him they would publish the Chicago section later. In fact, it was not published in book form until 1977, seventeen years after Wright's death.) Wright had great difficulty thinking up another title he liked as much, but eventually he came up with *Black Boy*. Ed Aswell took the precaution of asking the Book-of-the-Month judges whether they approved. Then there was the question of the new ending. Dorothy Canfield Fisher wrote several letters to Wright about this. Couldn't he, she asked him, use the word "hope" to describe what he surely must have felt when he left the South for the North?

Richard Wright, who once made the remark, "I am willing to die for my country, but I refuse to be forced to lie for it," approached truth-telling with missionary zeal. He used the word "hope" in his new ending, but not in the way Canfield Fisher had in mind. "In the main," he wrote, "my hope was merely a kind of self-defense, a conviction that if I did not leave I would perish."

Canfield Fisher asked Wright to explore the question: "What was it that made me conscious of possibilities?" Wright's answer was books. Canfield Fisher insisted: weren't they, at least partly, *American* books? "Could it be," she wrote to him, "that even from inside the prison of injustice, through the barred windows of that Bastille of racial oppression, Richard Wright had caught a glimpse of the American flag?"

She hoped Wright would listen to "an elderly woman writing to a young man" about a "troublingly delicate matter." Too embarrassed to spell out clearly what she wanted from him, she told him that some white Americans "have done what they could to lighten the dark stain of racial discrimination in our nation."

> To receive in the closing pages of your book, one word of recognition for this aspiration, if it were possible for you to give such recognition honestly, would hearten all who believe in American ideals. We would never dream of asking it—we were told by our parents and have told our children never to ask for it.

Wright could not bring himself to express gratitude to white Americans. Nor did he share Dorothy Canfield Fisher's patriotic fervor. He toyed with some sentences and sent the revised ending back to her. She wrote again. "I gather than you cannot bring yourself to use, even once, the word 'American' in speaking of 'the tinge of warmth which came from an unseen light'." She finished: "I'm dictating this letter in rather a hurry, trying to catch the one mail out from our tiny village and may not be saying exactly what I mean. But I'm sure that with your sensitive ear you can catch the over-tone. I do hope you also catch the over-tone of my unwillingness to say too much about this."

Canfield Fisher's letter was verging on blackmail. Wright was silent for ten days. When he eventually sent yet another revision to his publisher Edward Aswell, he did not conceal his impatience. "I really feel that this ought to do the thing. I don't think that I could relate myself any better—and keep within the facts —to the American scene."

His silence made Canfield Fisher "very uneasy." Understandably. What if it became known that the Book-of-the-Month Club committee of five was not only directing American readers to certain books (this was controversial enough), but also *modifying* these books to conform to a wholesome American template? She wrote him a hurried note: "I'd never forgive myself if (in my own attempt to be honest) I had stepped beyond the line of permissible influence on a younger writer! Don't you put in a single word which is not from your heart!"

Her letter crossed with Wright's, with his final draft enclosed. For the first time, he used the words "American" and "America"—but not at all as the glowing epithets Canfield Fisher intended. He named some American writers—Dreiser, Masters, Mencken, Anderson, and Lewis—whose critical attitude toward "the straitened American environment" provided him with "a tinge of warmth from an unseen light."

He had taken the risk of infuriating Canfield Fisher. But in fact, she was relieved. "The final version of your ending comes in, to give me the greatest satisfaction," she wrote to Wright. "You have not said a word beyond what you really felt and feel—I might have known you'd be incapable of that—the ending is a beautiful piece of writing and deeply full of meaning." In March 1945, the Book-of-the-Month Club made *Black Boy* once again a dual selection, along with Glenway Wescott's wholly forgotten novel *Apartment in Athens*.

Wright had managed, admirably, to keep his integrity—but the fact is, the abridged narrative cushioned white readers from the much more serious challenge of *American Hunger*. Whether or not the removal of the Chicago section was a good idea in aesthetic terms, it distorted the book's message and lessened its punch. The lyrical tone of the new ending was very different from the ferocity and passion of the original ending. Though Wright never actually says so, in the final pages of *Black Boy* the North appears to represent hope and possibility. "With ever-watchful eyes and bearing scars, visible and invisible, I headed North, full of a hazy notion that life could be lived with dignity."

*Black Boy* has always been seen as a story of triumph: a black man who succeeds, despite all the odds. The narrative's status as autobiography encourages readers to see the gap between the tormented protagonist and the famous author he became as evidence that the American Dream is real. This was scarcely the point Wright wanted to make.

Dorothy Canfield Fisher reviewed the book in the February 1945 *Book-of-the-Month Club News*. Richard Wright, she asserted, was "one of the most accomplished and gifted of our younger American authors." It was, she thought, lamentable that Wright felt caution toward *all* whites, many of whom were "trying to open the door of decent opportunity to colored people." In particular, she praised the book's conclusion:

> In the last pages he sweeps his readers out from the concrete and definite, with their crushing weight of literal fact, into a spacious realm of thought, poetry, beauty, and understanding. . . . *He quiets his deeply troubled spirit—ours with his—by drawing a long breath under the open sky of the universal.* [Italics mine.]

The new ending soothed the reader's "deeply troubled spirit." That was the crux of it. Dorothy Canfield Fisher had once again made Richard Wright's narrative more palatable to white readers. The issue remains highly ambivalent. Canfield Fisher adamantly believed that she was helping Richard Wright write a more balanced book. Whether she thought through the implications of this is not clear. Most people would agree with her that the removal of the Chicago section made *Black Boy* a better "work of art." Almost certainly, the abridged version has been more widely read and better appreciated than the complete narrative would have been, with its flatly narrated account of Communist Party machinations in Chicago. Packaged as a Book-of-the-Month Club selection (with a brief introduction, again, by Canfield Fisher), Wright's autobiographical narrative had the stamp of respectability from the literary establishment, along with unprecedented sales for a black writer—twice as many as *Native Son*.

But for these gains, Wright must sometimes have felt he had sold his soul. His message had been softened. His marching, fighting words had been smothered, silenced. Across his two most famous narratives the shadow of a white woman had fallen.

**Anthony Dawahare,** 'From No Man's Land to Mother-Land: Emasculation and Nationalism in Richard Wright's Depression Era Urban Novels'

'From No Man's Land to Mother-Land' is probably the most intellectually formidable of our five essays. But it is also rich and rewarding and a work that opens a window on the world of 1930s American Marxism so important to Wright's novel. In it, the critic of African-American literature Anthony Dawahare assembles together long-dispersed and little-read writings that Wright produced for Communist papers and magazines before *Native Son*'s publication. Salvaging this neglected area of Wright's œuvre, Dawahare then produces an interpretation at once psychological and political. In the process, he unearths a Wright quite unlike the man whom Baldwin sometimes saw as a mere hawker of stereotype. He unearths a Wright, indeed, who remains even now 'avant-garde' because he explores something that few 'contemporary theorists' stop to consider: the 'deep psychology' of black nationalism.

How should we approach this complex but rewarding essay? We certainly need to be familiar with certain key historical points of reference. We need to know that, between the world wars, Georg Lukács pioneered Marxist literary criticism, extolling the realist novel in particular for what he saw as its anti-capitalist potential. We need to know that, whenever Dawahare talks of black nationalism, he is referring to what *The Oxford Companion to United States History* calls an 'important ideology in African-American history ... grounded in the belief that efforts to operate within a political system deemed racist and unresponsive to black needs are doomed to failure' and which therefore agitates 'for the creation of an autonomous nation-state'.[1] And we also need to

1    William L. Van Deburg 'Black Nationalism' in Paul S. Boyer (ed.), *The Oxford Companion to United States History* (Oxford University Press, 2001). *Oxford Reference Online*. Available at <http://www.oxfordreference.com/views/ENTRY.html?entry=t119.e0181&srn=6&ssid=691781357#FIRSTHIT> (accessed 26 April 2006).

know that Melanie Klein was a psychoanalyst who, born in Austria but practising in Britain until her death in 1960, did much to revise and consolidate Freud's theories of child development.

Knowledge of these historical details, however, will only carry us so far. We also need to know more about the general psychoanalytical concepts that stand behind Dawahare's references to impotency and the 'Oedipal'. We need to know that, as another encyclopaedia from the Oxford series puts it, Sigmund Freud's original idea of the Oedipus Complex referred to 'an organized collection of loving and hostile feelings of a child towards its parents'. For Freud, this complex 'manifests itself in its positive form as a sexual desire for the opposite-sex parent and a jealous hatred of the same-sex parent, in its negative (or inverted) form as a desire for the same-sex parent and hatred of the opposite-sex parent.'[2] The fact that Klein developed this Freudian complex by (among other things) considering the infantile personalities of psychotics immediately suggests that Bigger is likely to feel particularly ferocious love for the mother and hate for the father. And the fact that Freud defined neurosis as the 'renunciation of a function whose exercise would give rise to anxiety' furthermore reveals that Bigger is at risk of impotency, that sexuality is for him a neurotic business seething with bad associations.[3]

The importance of Dawahare's scholarly contribution is to take this psycho-analytical model, familiar to theorists, and expand it: to show how it signifies crisis, not in the Thomas family, but in the American state. In Dawahare's reading, psychoanalytical concerns in Wright's fictions map out a struggle with the white father. Such white racist authorities, Wright realizes, like to call black men 'boy' because the nickname helps to shore up their sense of power over the American 'family' as a whole. Black nationalism, in Dawahare's reading of Wright's landmark fictions, in turn seems prone to envision an Oedipal violence: it seems prone to define political struggle as the overthrowing of a white father, to be replaced with a powerful black masculine authority. And the ensuing concern is that this tendency within black struggle shares much with tendencies within contemporary European fascism, echoing the latter's rampant machismo, its cultish violence. When reading Native Son or 'How "Bigger" was Born', you might have wondered why Wright seems so preoccupied with events in faraway Europe. In this stimulating, authoritative essay, Dawahare provides a fascinating answer.

Apart from my own references to the Vintage edition of Native Son, footnotes throughout the following essay are Dawahare's own; these include some to the novel's restored Harper Perennial edition. An amended version of the essay appears in form in Dawahare's book Nationalism, Marxism, and

2   Andrew M. Colman, 'Oedipus complex n.' in A Dictionary of Psychology (Oxford University Press, 2001). Oxford Reference Online. Available at <http://www.oxfordreference.com/views/ENTRY.html?entry=t87.e5715&srn=4&ssid=570320003#FIRSTHIT> (accessed 26 April 2006).
3   Derek Russell Davis, 'neurosis' in Richard L. Gregory (ed.) The Oxford Companion to the Mind (Oxford University Press, 1987). Oxford Reference Online. Available at <http://www.oxfordreference.com/views/ENTRY.html?entry=t159.e629&srn=13&ssid=815314385#FIRSTHIT> (accessed 26 April 2006).

## Anthony Dawahare (1999) 'From No Man's Land to Mother-Land: Emasculation and Nationalism in Richard Wright's Depression-Era Urban Novels', *African-American Review* 33 (3, fall): pp. 451–66

> Not to plunge into the complex jungle of human relationships and ana-
> lyze them is to leave the field to the fascists and I won't and can't do
> that.[5]
>     . . . anything that is felt to give out goodness and beauty, and that calls
> forth pleasure and satisfaction, in the physical or in the wider sense,
> can in the unconscious mind take the place of [the infant's perception of
> the mother's] ever-bountiful breast, and of the whole mother. Thus
> we speak of our own country as the "motherland" because in the
> unconscious mind our country may come to stand for our mother, and
> then it can be loved with feelings which borrow their nature from the
> relation to her.[6]

While serving as Director of the Harlem Bureau of the *Daily Worker* between 1937 and 1938, Richard Wright wrote an article for the newspaper praising the launching of *New Challenge*, a black American literary quarterly that published first-rate black writers such as Ralph Ellison, Margaret Walker, and Langston Hughes. Wright was particularly excited about the quarterly because "for the first time in Negro history problems such as nationalism in literature, perspective, the relation of the Negro to politics and social movements were formulated and discussed".[7] For those familiar with Wright's "A Blueprint for Negro Writing," first published in *New Challenge* in 1937, it is obvious that he was applauding his own planned contribution to the quarterly, as "Blueprint" deals first and fore-most with the problem of nationalism for black writers. Moreover, since the *Daily Worker* article and the *New Challenge* essay were written in the middle of 1937, it is safe to say that Wright, then twenty-eight years old, was beginning to formulate just what sort of contribution to black American writing he would make during the next few years. The literary works Wright wrote between 1937 and 1941 focus explicitly on issues related to nationalism, although scholars have yet to explore this fact in depth.

Remarkably, Wright's literary treatment of nationalism remains avant-garde since he reveals what many contemporary theorists have yet to disclose: a

4   Anthony Dawahare, *Nationalism, Marxism, and African-American Literature between the Wars: A New Pandora's Box* (Jackson, Miss.: University of Mississippi Press, 2003).
5   Richard Wright quoted in Michel Fabre, *The Unfinished Quest of Richard Wright* (Urbana, Ill.: University of Illinois Press, 1993), p. 185.
6   Melanie Klein, 'Love, Guilt and Reparation' in *Love, Hate and Reparation* (New York: Norton, 1964), pp. 57–119 (p. 103).
7   Richard Wright, 'Negro Writers Launch Literary Quarterly', *Daily Worker*, 8 June 1937, p. 7.

complex insight into the deep psychology of nationalism. Like many contemporary theorists, Wright viewed nationalism as an historical phenomenon that constructs what Benedict Anderson has termed "imagined communities" for people who in fact are anonymous to each other but wish for social communion. Wright also perceived nationalism as a divisive political ideology that must be supplanted with a Communist ideology he believed necessary for the emancipation of the working class. But Wright's most significant contribution is his synthesis of Marxist and psychoanalytic concepts in his effort to portray critically the insidious appeal of nationalistic ideas to the infantile desires of working-class men. For Wright, the danger posed by nationalism was its *unconscious* appeal to the psyches of male workers. His Depression Era works suggests that, since all male workers are raised in a patriarchal society, their feelings of powerlessness can evoke feelings of emasculation. Wright shows how these feelings of emasculation can be intensified for black men, since they are extra-oppressed by racism and are symbolically emasculated as "boys" in a racist discourse. In somewhat Oedipal terms, the black man is put in the position of having "to kill" the white man/father in order to cancel his "boy" status. Wright's concern is that black working-class men are apt to heed the call of black nationalists, precisely because they promise a reclamation of manhood and the goal of disposing of the white father—namely, the acquisition of the mother-land.

In *Lawd Today!* (completed in 1938 and posthumously published in 1963) and *Native Son* (1940), Wright represents urban black men in the grip of such a racialized Oedipal struggle. His urban protagonists internalize the racist dynamic of the black boy-white father dialectic and are thus psychologically caught between an impulse to act the black "boy" who submits (in various ways) to whites and a desire to be the "man," which involves behaviors associated with the powerful white father. In other words, his protagonists seek to compensate for their socially conditioned feelings of impotence through fantasies of omnipotence, which are fed and formed by the "logic" of American racism, as well as the nationalistic and fascistic ideologies that flourished internationally in the 1930s. Both social-psychological and political factors contribute to a complex ethnic/nationalistic psychology for his protagonists, who unconsciously associate the attainment of manhood with the possession of a black "motherland." However, while Wright represents the appeal of nationalism, he considers such an ideology incapable of self-reflexively addressing the very precondition for its being—i.e., a racist class society. As the above epigraph suggests, Wright believed it vital to disclose and, therefore, to lessen the subconscious appeal of nationalism in order to make possible progressive political action for working-class men that is not determined by the self-defeating logics of American racism and nationalism.

Before delving into the psychology of nationalism in Wright's Depression Era writings, we must first briefly work through his cultural history of black Americans, since only at the conclusion of a phase of that history do we find the black nationalist "resolution" of the Oedipal crisis alluded to above. It is well known that Wright was influenced by the Communist Party's (CP's) understanding of nationalism, which was largely based on Stalin's popular book *Marxism and the National and Colonial Question* (1912). As Wright asserts in "A Blueprint for Negro Writing," he too believed that blacks had a common "national" culture that originally arose from a "plantation-feudal economy" and persisted in the Jim Crow political system of the South. The foundation of this modern black culture lies in the African-American folk tradition of the blues, spirituals, work songs, and folk tales. Black social institutions, such as the black church, black sports, black business, black schools, and a black press, represent "a Negro way of life in America".[8]

However, Wright implicitly differs from other Communists on an important point: Black cultural nationalism in the U.S. was neither so stable nor so progressive as the CP black nation thesis made out. On the contrary, he views black cultural nationalism as the result of forced common experiences of slavery and segregation that produced an *unwanted* common black culture. Wright argues that

> the Negro people did not ask for [their cultural nationalism], and deep down, though they express themselves through their institutions and adhere to this special way of life, they do not want it now. This special existence was forced upon them from without by lynch rope, bayonet and mob rule.[9]

Such a nationalism is unstable for Wright because, even though he, like the CP, saw the social history of black Americans as an historical process, it was a process with a very different direction: As he writes in *Twelve Million Black Voices* (1941), Wright perceived "a complex movement of *debased* feudal folk toward a twentieth-century urbanization" that has occurred at an historically rapid pace.[10] The more or less homogenous black consciousness and cultural community resulting from provincial, Southern material conditions was in the process of being eroded by modernization. Wright contends that

> it is in industry that we encounter experiences that tend to break down the structure of our folk characters and project us toward the vortex of modem urban life. . . . we are gripped and influenced by the world-wide forces that shape and mold the life of Western civilization.[11]

For Wright, the feudal black peasantry's liberation lay not in preserving or developing a black "national" culture in the South, but in an historical overcoming of "black" identity and cultural nationalism. In other words, Wright only provisionally accepts the unified cultural identity of the post-war "New Negro," since he favors a "multi-cultural" identity in the process of further socialization by modernity. Nowhere in his literary work, or in his more than 200 articles written for the *Daily Worker*, do we find an endorsement for the CP's desire for a black republic in the Southern Black Belt. On the contrary, Wright lauded the historical movement toward modernity wherever he saw it. For example, one of his *Daily Worker* articles written in 1937 celebrates a former slave woman who

---

8  Richard Wright, 'Blueprint for Negro Writing' in *The Norton Anthology of African-American Literature*, pp. 1380–8 (p. 1385).
9  Wright, 'Blueprint for Negro Writing', p. 1383.
10  Wright, *Twelve Million Black Voices*, p. xix. My emphasis.
11  Wright, *Twelve Million Black Voices*, p. 115.

became an active Communist in Harlem. "This woman," he writes, "has seen the face of her country changed more than once during her 71 years, and she has the strength, the courage, and the faith to fight and wait for still another change." He ends this short article by quoting her, saying for a second time, that "I live in the 20th Century", as if to underscore her own recognition that the movement from Southern slave to urban Communist is part and parcel of the progressive movement of history itself.[12]

While Wright identifies a cultural nationalism in decline, he nonetheless believed that writers should acknowledge and *strategically* appropriate the varying degrees of cultural nationalism among black Americans. "Negro writers who seek to mold or influence the consciousness of the Negro people," asserts Wright, "must address their messages to them through the ideologies and attitudes fostered in this warping way of life." It is important to note that "their messages" for Wright were (or should have been) derived from "a Marxist conception of reality."[13] And, in this sense, he was consistent with the dominant thinking by Communist intellectuals of the time on "minority" literature. According to one Soviet intellectual of the period who published an article on Langston Hughes in *International Literature*, minority literature should be "socialist in content and national in form."[14] In short, black writers should represent the cultural nationalism of blacks from a socialist perspective by depicting "national" difference, inter-nationalist identity, and—echoing Georg Lukács's influential essay " 'Tendency' or Partisanship?" published in the *Partisan Review* in the 1930s—"society as something becoming rather than as something fixed and admired."[15] As a reading of *Uncle Tom's Children* (1940) attests, Wright was careful to represent contextually degrees of cultural nationalism in his characters, depicting virtually all of his Southern characters as cultural nationalists.[16]

One therefore finds cultural nationalist identifications most eroded in his male urban protagonists from the 1930s, namely Jake Jackson from *Lawd Today!* and Bigger Thomas from *Native Son*. Jake and Bigger represent Wright's view of what

12 Richard Wright, 'Born A Slave, She Recruits 5 Members for Communist Party', *Daily Worker*, 30 August 1937, p. 3. Another *Daily Worker* article of Wright's particularly notable in this regard is one he wrote about Spanish Harlem women who actively belonged to the La Pasionaria Branch of the Communist Party of the USA (CPUSA). He writes approvingly that 'these women, descendants and relatives of forebears who kept them firmly relegated to the home, have leapt in the span of one short year from the kitchen into the arena of international politics'. Richard Wright, 'Harlem Spanish Women Come out of the Kitchen', *Daily Worker*, 20 September 1937, p. 5.
13 Wright, 'Blueprint for Negro Writing', pp. 1383–4.
14 Lydia Filatova (1933) 'Langston Hughes: American Writer', *International Literature*, 1: pp. 99–107 (p. 107).
15 Wright, 'Blueprint for Negro Writing', p. 1385.
16 Big Boy from 'Big Boy Leaves Home', Mann from 'Down by the Riverside', Silas from 'Long Black Song', and Aunt Sue from 'Bright and Morning Star' are cultural nationalists by definition, although the events surrounding Johnny-Boy's political work and 'arrest' move Aunt Sue Left. Those characters in *Uncle Tom's Children* whose cultural nationalism is weakest are precisely those who have been most influenced by modernity and the ideologies of modernity, such as Marxism. The Communist-influenced Taylor from 'Fire and Cloud' and (of course) Johnny-Boy from 'Bright and Morning Star' are not purely cultural nationalists. Certainly Reverend Taylor and his followers are situated in a highly religious folk tradition, yet Taylor is able to unite and fight with white workers for economic relief. At one point Taylor exclaims, ' "Lawd knows, mabbe them Reds is right!" ' Richard Wright, *Uncle Tom's Children* (New York: Harper Perennial, 1993), p. 157.

happens when a first generation of "debased," male feudal folk are subjected to the modern ideologies and practices prevalent in Northern urban centers (specifically Chicago): They become, as Wright explains of Bigger, "vague" cultural nationalists because, even though they are forced to identify as black, they do not identify with the black culture of their parents;[17] Bigger, Wright tells us, "had become estranged from the religion and the folk culture of his race".[18] Bigger and Jake are "Negro nationalist[s] in a vague sense" only because of their "intense hatred of white people", which serves (in place of a strong folk identity) to strengthen their identification as "black."[19]

Wright refunctions the war-time notion of a "No Man's Land" to designate the experience his urban male characters have of being in the interstice of two cultures or, as Houston Baker argues, of having "black placelessness."[20] Only Wright's male urban protagonists are caught in the "No Man's Land," because they are "granted" by the patriarchal organization of American society more social intercourse with urban culture than his female characters. Most of the representations of Bigger and Jake (both of whom, significantly, grew up in the South) center on their being not at home but on the streets or at work in "civilization", thus alienating them further from their Southern origins.

Interestingly, black nationalism proper is only an issue for Wright's male urban characters: Both Jake and Bigger have visions of a black state that they would like to rule. While undeveloped, their black nationalism equates freedom with national self-determination. Thus, the reflexive, weak cultural nationalism of most of his urban protagonists is supplemented by a black nationalism that imagines the creation of a black national state as a solution to U.S. racism. Ironically, this black nationalism arises in the very place where cultural nationalist "folk" identities have been most dissolved by modern, urban conditions. This in part explains why the black nationalism Wright represents doesn't take root with his characters: The proto-nationalist soil of nationalism proper has been eroded by urban culture and society. The "double-consciousness" these characters possess prevents them from simply identifying as black "nationals" and from being chauvinist. Bigger, for example, so strongly identifies with "white" civilization that he cajoles Gus into "playing white," one of their pastimes.

There are two important causes that explain why Jake and Bigger are attracted to black nationalist visions: the psychological consequences of American racism and the predominance of post-war nationalisms in the 1930s.

In a number of his works, Wright suggests that black men have a particular psychic economy historically conditioned by a complex racist discourse and practice that, as we shall later see, lends itself to nationalists' appeals. He makes perfectly clear that the "Jim Crow education" of blacks in the South and the multiple, somewhat more subtle forms of racism in the North worked together in an attempt to arrest the psychological development of black American men. Black

17  Wright, 'How "Bigger" Was Born', p. 27.
18  Wright, 'How "Bigger" Was Born', p. 8.
19  Wright, 'How "Bigger" Was Born', p. 9.
20  Houston A. Baker, 'On Knowing Our Place' in *Richard Wright: Critical Perspectives Past and Present* (New York: Amistad, 1993), pp. 200–25 (p. 201).

men/"boys" are infantilized by white society, making American racism conterminous with sexism, since the infantilization of black men symbolically aligns them with "women," that other figure long associated with weakness and dependency in patriarchal society.[21] Within the racist, patriarchal logic of American racism, the "father"/"man" is none other than the white male, who exercises authority over the movements of the supposedly helpless, dependent, and ignorant black "boy." The purpose of the psychological arrest is to stop autonomous actions that transgress "place" as defined by the racist structure and ideology of American society. Although indispensable to white oppression, the legal arrest of black men signifies the failure of the ideology of racism.

Furthermore, Wright's texts suggest that the desire male children have to become men (usually like their fathers) is co-opted by white racist ideology in an important way: Black males could become "men" by displacing and/or emulating the white father; the good "boy" obeys the white father's example and becomes like him. The internalization of the racist developmental logic constitutes the unconscious of his male characters and is characterized by a racialized Oedipal struggle against the white "father"/boss. As Abdul JanMohamed writes, "In order for subservience to be automatic it cannot be conscious; it has to become part of one's pre-conscious behavior pattern: precisely at the point where one's behavior is unconsciously controlled by a prevailing ideology, one has succumbed to a cultural hegemony."[22] In other words, the dynamics of psychological development are subconsciously mediated by racist ideology, and the super-ego itself contains the white "father's" judgment. In this way one can say that the "American" part of "double-consciousness" is expressive of the super-white ego that views the black ego as despised and pitiable and yet represents cultural value, here coded as "white male." White folk, as Bigger says, live "right down here in my stomach."

In many ways, Wright's depiction of the psychology of *black* working-class men also applies to *white* working-class men, since both are made to feel helpless under capitalism and can seek modes of escape that are infantile and nationalistic. For example, we can situate the masculinist iconography of a lot of proletarian art and literature within this framework: Those images of hulky white workers underscore how powerless they feel. However, it is essential to theorize the historicity of Wright's psychological understanding of urban black men; that is, how racism *further belittles* the black working class.

The material conditions from which his black male protagonists want to flee are those of racism and wage-labor in a capitalist society. Racist society is the painful, humiliating, and self-negating space that calls forth utopian spaces, including black nationalist ones. Such utopian spaces are shot through with the developmental conflicts of males as mediated by American racism and inter-war

---

21  Of course, the desire to project 'weakness' onto black men truly betrays the white-male working-class racist's own sense of social powerlessness under capitalism; the sense of powerlessness is disowned and often destroyed in an attempt to feel more strong – gendered as 'manly' – than one feels.

22  Abdul JanMohamed, 'Negating the Negation as a Form of Affirmation in Minority Discourse: The Construction of Richard Wright as Subject', in Arnold Rampersad (ed.) *Richard Wright: A Collection of Critical Essays* (Englewood Cliffs, NJ: Prentice, 1995), pp. 107–23 (p. 117).

nationalism. In short, Wright's texts address the question of what happens when black working-class men who subjectively feel socially emasculated or socially disempowered are also assigned a "boy" status within the particular discursive formation of American racism.

The first point to be made here is that Wright's urban black protagonists have internalized the forced "boy" status, and therefore seek ways to take control of their lives, which are likewise mediated by a racist logic. That is, the options to act the "boy" or to become a "man"—certainly a major theme for many of Wright's stories—are not mutually exclusive. We find the twin impulses to be a "boy" and to be a "man" in the character of Jake from *Lawd Today!* [. . .]

. . .

Bigger is a more fully developed character than Jake, and he therefore presents us with a more refined psychological presentation of Wright's urban black male. Like Jake, Bigger is a character on the verge of losing control of his actions. He is about to "snap," and the only thing that keeps him from being torn asunder is his "dogged strength," to use a phrase from Du Bois.[23] The causes of his "tensity" are multiple, the most obvious being the abject racist conditions of his life on the South Side of Chicago, which include the rat-infested room he must call his home and a lack of meaningful employment—in a phrase, a life of ghettoization. Wright's portrayal of Bigger's tension is itself remarkable for the times, since until then blacks had rarely been represented with such psychological depth and complexity.

What is more remarkable, however, is the way Wright portrays Bigger's response to the tension, and it is here that we find a psychological state similar to Jake's. Like Jake, Bigger wants to be immediately free from his emotional tumult, and so his methods are essentially regressive. He, too, seeks forms of escape that are infantile. The conclusive sign of this desire to regress is his masturbatory response to tension. Max, the mouthpiece of Wright's political understanding of Bigger, expresses the fundamental psychological truth of Bigger's character. As he tells the court in "defense" of Bigger's masturbating in a movie theater: " 'Was not Bigger Thomas' relationship to his girl a masturbatory one? Was not his entire relationship to the whole world on the same planet' ".[24] The significance of these two lines should not be underestimated, for they succinctly encapsulate what Wright spent so much time disclosing in his novel. Masturbation, as depicted here, is regressive because it allows for a narcissistic and sadistic way out of painful emotions. That is, instead of working to change the circumstances that gave rise to these emotions, Bigger tries to discharge his emotions in ways that only create momentary relief for himself and pain or death for others. As Max suggests, Bigger sort of "masturbates" through Bessie, thus dehumanizing her by turning her into an object useful only for his satisfaction. Indeed, not much separates sex and murder for Bigger, since both "blot out" the other as a way to escape pain and/or to experience a narcissistic pleasure. " 'All you care about is

23  W. E. B. Du Bois, *The Souls of Black Folk* (New York: Penguin, 1989), p. 5.
24  See restored edition of Richard Wright, 'Fate' in *Native Son* (New York: HarperPerennial, 1993), p. 468.

your own pleasure!'" exclaims his mother ["Fear", p.39]. Thus, when he has sex with Bessie before he kills her, we learn that she tells him not to force her to have sex, but that the "loud demand of the tensity of his own body was a voice that drowned out hers".[25]

Masturbation here also signifies an idealized response to tension, since he fantasizes that he has control of his life where he has virtually none. Of course, his reference to his penis as a "nightstick" – an emblem of violence and power – in the masturbation scene is instructive, but perhaps more instructive is the fact that he also turns Bessie into an idealized mother figure who should exist only for him.[26] Thus, once the "lessening of tension in his muscles" fades after murdering Mary, ["Flight", p. 144] he decides to release the new quantity of tension that had accumulated while he was being questioned by the racist Mrs. Dalton. We read: "To go out now would be the answer to the feeling of strain that had come over him while talking to Mrs. Dalton. He would go and see Bessie. That's it!" ["Flight", p.159]. He immediately thinks of discharging his pain into Bessie, whom he turns into an idealized womb he can occupy:

> He felt two soft palms holding his face tenderly and the thought and image of the whole blind world which had made him ashamed and afraid fell away as he felt her as a fallow field beneath him stretching out under a cloudy sky waiting for rain, and he slept in her body, rising and sinking with the ebb and flow of her blood, being willingly dragged into a warm night sea to rise renewed to the surface to face a world he hated and wanted to blot out of existence.
>
> ['Flight', p. 165]

The passage abounds with images of the womb (fallow field, warm night sea) and images of penetration (the rain, rising and sinking). He wants "a wholeness, a oneness"[27] akin to what Freud refers to as the "oceanic feeling" one experiences as an infant in the womb or at the breast before the ego has learned to differentiate itself from the mother and to relate to people in other ways. Like a fetus, he wants to be "inside" Bessie, "rising and sinking with the ebb and flow of her blood." [. . .] But Bigger can maintain this fantasy of Bessie only by depreciating and ultimately killing the Bessie that resists him and questions his confused thinking and harmful actions:

> He wished he could clench his fist and swing his arm and blot out, kill, sweep away the Bessie on Bessie's face and leave the other helpless and yielding before him. He would then gather her up and put her in his chest, his stomach, some place deep inside him, always keeping her there even when he slept, ate, talked; keeping her there just to feel and know that she was his to have and hold whenever he wanted to.
>
> ['Flight', p. 170]

25 Restored edition of Wright, 'Flight' in *Native Son*, p. 270.
26 Restored edition of Wright, 'Fear' in *Native Son*, p. 32.
27 Restored edition of Wright, 'Fate' in *Native Son*, p. 490.

Like Jake, he wants to cling only to his fantasy of an idealized mother who never frustrates him by always doing what he wishes; i.e., by making the painful emotions of racism go away. This necessarily causes him to split Bessie (in fantasy) into a "good" mother and a "bad" mother (who withholds infantile gratification), and later to kill Bessie since she refuses to conform to his infantile fantasies.[28]

Yet Jake and Bigger are struggling to be in control of their lives, which brings us to the issue of nationalism and, in particular, the second cause in Wright's black male protagonists' attraction to black nationalism—namely, the cultures of nationalism of the 1930s that Wright depicts in his novels. In essence, to quote Eric Hobsbawm, post-World War I nationalism "filled the void left by failure, impotence, and the apparent inabilities of other ideologies, political projects and programmes to realize men's hopes. It was the utopia of those who had lost the old utopias of the age of Enlightenment, the programme of those who had lost faith in other programmes . . .".[29] Of course, we should add that nationalism was also the utopia for those who never were truly included in or believed in "the old utopias of the Enlightenment"! In any case, Hobsbawm's linking of a sense of impotence, ideological confusion, and, in this context, the failure of bourgeois-democratic political ideals in America with an embrace of nationalism is compelling, since Wright's urban male protagonists are caught in a "No Man's Land" of disbelief, somewhere between their parents' Southern "folk" beliefs and urban, mass-cultural ideologies. In particular, it is the patriarchal, nationalistic cultural density of Jake's and Bigger's Chicago that shapes the nationalist fantasies that function to compensate for their sense of emasculation.

In fact, from the intrusive radio program commemorating Lincoln's birthday to newspaper headlines reporting Nazi nationalism and anti-Semitism, *Lawd Today!* is truly a study of cultures of nationalism in America circa 1935 and their effects on identity formation. Mass culture is less an explicit subject in *Native Son* but nonetheless an important one. Bigger, Wright tells us, "was trying to react to and answer the call of the dominant civilization whose glitter came to him through the newspapers, magazines, radios, movies, and the mere imposing sight and sound of daily American life."[30] This dominant civilization in the 1930s, as Hobsbawm notes in *The Age of Extremes*, was becoming increasingly militaristic, fascistic, and nationalistic: "Taking the world as a whole, there had been perhaps thirty-five or more constitutional and elected governments in 1920. . . . Until 1938 there were perhaps seventeen such states, in 1944 perhaps twelve out of the global total of sixty-four. The world trend seemed clear." Moreover, he adds, Hitler's ascension to power in 1933 greatly accelerated the trend of fascism since, "without Hitler's triumph in Germany, the idea of fascism as a universal

---

28  For an extended analysis of the kinds of infantile mental processes found in Bigger, see Melanie Klein, 'Our Adult World and Its Roots in Infancy' in *Envy and Gratitude and Other Works* (New York: Free Press, 1975), pp. 247–63.

29  Eric Hobsbawm, *Nations and Nationalism since 1780: Programme, Myth, Reality* (Cambridge: Cambridge University Press, 1993), p. 144.

30  Wright, 'How "Bigger" was Born', p. 8.

movement . . . would not have developed," nor would it have had "serious impact outside of Europe."[31] Bigger and Jake come of age during this fascisization of "civilization," and both characters are politically reactionary.

[. . .] Bigger is a man who rejects his mother's black folk culture and is dazzled by American popular culture and, like Jake, identifies with the rabid nationalist projects of the 1930s:

> Dimly, he felt that there should be one direction in which he and all other black people could go whole-heartedly. . . . He liked to hear of how Japan was conquering China; of how Hitler was running the Jew to the ground; of how Mussolini was invading Spain. . . . He felt that some day there would be a black man who would whip the black people into a tight band and together they would act and end fear and shame.
>
> ['Flight', pp. 144–5]

Bigger identifies with these supposedly nationalist leaders because they are father figures or führers who "whip" the imagined helpless black masses into shape for their own good. Both Jake and Bigger identify with nationalists precisely because they are authoritarian, supposedly omnipotent, and historically have been patriarchal to the core.

A supreme irony resides here, because Wright's male urban protagonists' displacement from the South (and its white father-black boy dialectic that narrowly defines place) results in the reemergence of the super-white ego in blackface. That is, displacement to a contradictory urban environment that promises all but grants little – and the desires, anxieties, and tensions which accompany it—has produced a counter-desire for placement structurally akin to that from which the characters originally fled. The discourse of American racism has worked so effectively that the original desired usurpation of the (Southern) master and desire for freedom have produced (within the racist wage-slavery of the urban society) a desire for a black master, motivated by the character's infantile "reflex urge towards ecstasy, complete submission, and trust".[32] Wright's texts suggest that the frustrations of the No Man's Land and the appeal of nationalism are symptomatic of the failure of American capitalism to provide political, economic, and psychological stability conducive to his characters' desires for happiness and an enduring fulfillment.

The black master, then, functions as the father figure for these socially emasculated men without fathers. (In *Lawd Today!* there is no mention of Jake's parents, and in *Native Son* we learn that Bigger's father was killed in a riot in the South, the ultimate act of social emasculation for a black man and Jim Crow lesson for a black son.) Bigger, in particular, is represented as a man in search of a father figure; hence, the black führer is a suitable compensatory image, and the various Depression Era fascisms "simply appealed to him as possible avenues of escape" ['Flight', p. 145]. He identifies with Hitler and Mussolini because he

---

31  Eric Hobsbawm, *The Age of Extremes: A History of the World, 1914–1991* (New York: Vintage, 1996), pp. 112–17.
32  Wright, 'How "Bigger" was Born', p. 9.

desires the control and power that have been culturally gendered as masculine. As he tells Max, " 'a guy gets tired of being told what he can do and can't do. You get a little job here and a little job there. . . . You don't know when you going to get fired. . . . *You just keep moving all the time*, doing what other folks say. *You ain't a man no more*' " ['Fate', p. 382]. To be a "man" is finally to be free from the displacement—the "moving all the time."

The fascist father figure is the one who defines place for all. As Slavoj Zizek [*sic*] argues, "The fascist dream is simply to have *capitalism without its 'excess,' without the antagonism that causes its structural imbalance* . . . [which] would enable us to obtain a stable social organism whose parts form a harmonious corporate body, where, in contrast to capitalism's constant social *displacement*, everybody would again occupy his *own place*."[33] Likewise, both Zizek [*sic*] and Wright suggest that the fascist dream of omnipotence appeals to the desire to control what Wright calls "a hot and whirling vortex of undisciplined and unchannelized impulses" produced by modernity.[34] The fascistic, nationalistic projects of Jake and Bigger are another way they imagine a freedom from their emotional tumult. And it is important to note that, in truth, their fantasies of a black master are mediated by a desire to be "white," which they equate with being a desired and powerful object. In essence, as the Garveyite parade and Bigger's and Gus's game of mimicry suggest, to be a political leader is to "play white." The "dual narcissism" about which Franz Fanon [*sic*] writes in *Black Skin, White Masks*—that white is right and black is beautiful—merges here. By indulging their fantasies, the two characters display their ego-ideal of the white man who *looks* black or the black man who *acts* white. Conflated are the concepts of white father-nationalist/fascist man as opposed, in the final analysis, to the concept of "black boy."

The black nation (ruled by the black father) thus functions as a wishful political and psychic economy: The white father is dethroned, and the black "boy" becomes the (white) "father," creating a (home) place that, because the white father is usurped, "end[s] fear and shame."[35] The psychological goal of nationhood in these novels is a type of unity that, based on male fantasies, is infantile, since the object is to reclaim "a wholeness, a oneness" associated with an idealized infantile state that views the nation as a womb mother or an originary site of pleasure.[36] The internal torment and desires these characters display, generated in large part by the super-white ego, is projected out and solved in fantasy as if it were solely an external problem.

A dialogue immediately following the passage from *Lawd Today!* on the necessity of a Hitler or Mussolini for national unification cited earlier establishes the link among nationalism, maternity, and masculinity in the unconscious of the text:

33  Slavoj Žižek, 'Enjoy Your Nation as Yourself!' in *Tarrying with the Negative: Kant, Hegel, and the Critique of Ideology* (Durham, NC: Duke University Press, 1993), pp. 200–37 (p. 210).
34  Wright, 'How "Bigger" was Born', p. 14.
35  Restored edition of Wright, 'Fear' in *Native Son*, p. 145.
36  Restored edition of Wright, 'Fate' in *Native Son*, p. 444.

"Well, I reckon the best thing for a guy to do is get together with a woman."

"State Street Mama!"
*My name is Jim Taylor*
*My John is a whaler*
  *And my balls weigh ninety nine pounds*
*If you know any ladies*
*Who want to have babies*
    *just tell 'em Jim Taylor's in town . . ."*
                    "Hahaha!"
                    "Hohoho!"[37]

The maternal woman or the imagined black state (whose shorthand here reads: black "State [Street] Mama" land) provides an escape from the pain caused by racism to a place without the "fear and shame" of the internalized white father's gaze and a reclaimed (and exaggerated) sense of masculine potency ("balls"). In the imagination of these characters, the mama-land lies the greatest distance from no-*man*'s land. The patriarchal core of the nationalist fantasy is also exposed here, since these characters have recourse to sexist ideas precisely when the nationalist fantasy fails them. And, as with the threatened child in the Oedipal situation who clings desperately to the mother, Wright's urban male protagonists demonstrate a tyrannical possessiveness over the imaginary motherland (recall Lil and Bessie), which is simultaneously expressive of both the desire to regress and a desire to advance to the position of the father (who appears to possess the mother). The black nation is the Oedipal fantasy writ large in political terms, where the infantile desires for a womb/breastlike "oneness" and paternity are simultaneously met.

Clearly, Wright does not advocate such a political and psychic economy. His representation of a highly patriarchal black nationalism as *just one more* illusion of freedom for his characters should make us pause at the unfair criticisms of his work that mistakenly conflate the sexism of Jake and Bigger with Wright's own stance. On the contrary, it is one of Wright's major achievements to write incisively (whether wholly consciously or not) of the social and psychological *disorder* of (black) working-class men, of his own experience as a Southern-raised boy who reaches manhood in Chicago. In this way he was able to explore why the impossible, "childish" politics of the black nationalists appeals to otherwise grown men. Indeed, Wright's Depression Era work shows that there is no going back to a "folk" way of life. More importantly, there is no going forward to a black nation-state for these twentieth-century black men: In spite of socio-psychological neurotic desires created by American racism, black male identities are too complex for any kind of exclusive "black" identity/nation.

The question we are left with is this: Why do the novels not represent Wright's alternative to the neurotic and reactionary protagonists—e.g., black Communists? Instead of assuming some grand anti-Communist narrative that informs his urban fiction years before his actual break with the CP, I think it is more

---

37  Richard Wright, *Lawd Today!* (Boston, Mass.: Northeastern University Press, 1993), p. 184.

instructive to see how Wright's urban fiction (particularly *Native Son*) is concerned with representing the "working through" of infantile desires and black nationalist fantasies. In this sense, Max can be read as a figure for the analyst, who provides the opportunity for Bigger to talk and to think his way through the feelings that he had previously and murderously discharged. Through his exchanges with Max, Bigger comes a long way, for he finally is able to see others as human beings; that is, he projects less by the novel's end. Certainly, by perceiving Max as a father figure (which Max encourages by constantly referring to Bigger as "son"), Bigger's transference continues through to the last page. But even here Max as father figure suggests Bigger's psychological and political development: Unlike the punishing father/führer figure who contributes to his omnipotent fantasies, the nurturing Max teaches Bigger how to think about his feelings and actions; and, more importantly, he teaches the hard lesson of the reality principle concerning the slow process of collective social change. The premature termination of the "therapy" for Bigger—the death sentence—does not affect the social work of the novel, since, in the last analysis, what is at stake is that the reader continues thinking through his own potentially destructive emotions and ideas—presuming that Bigger's psyche is not all that unique, as Wright claimed in "How 'Bigger' Was Born". Or to presume a female reader or one without such psychological issues, the end of the novel would prompt further reflection on how an unresolved social and (racialized) Oedipal struggle for men contributes to sexism and makes working-class men susceptible to the call of nationalism. In either case, the reader comes away with a better sense of the interrelatedness of the oppressive social system and neurosis. Ironically, then, in Wright's urban fiction, the path to socialism involves retracing the hazardous, regressive road that leads to fascism. The novel ends where revolutionary action may begin.

The central place where Wright reserved his depictions of a desirable alternative to Jake and Bigger are the articles he published in the *Daily Worker* between 1937 and 1938. One could cite the many articles he wrote on progressive black leaders such as James Ford, A. Philip Randolph, and Louise Thompson; the unknown black working-class people who fought for better lives in their neighborhoods and communities (most of whom, Wright reports, were women!); or those who fought in Spain with the Loyalists against the fascists. These articles compose part of a larger panorama of black leaders to be emulated in various ways (including Frederick Douglas [*sic*], Nat Turner, and Angelo Herndon) written about by contributors to the *Daily Worker*. *Lawd Today!* and *Native Son* need to be (re)placed next to these articles, for in them we find black men and women who have subjectively beat racism *enough* to struggle for an end to the racist society. Wright reports about black workers and leaders who have overcome the racist "Manichean concept of the world" and do not conceptualize liberation in terms of color: Present struggles and the desired future society of socialism are not driven by the desires to be white, or black slave or boss, or boy or father. For Wright, the thirties' Communists' ideal of socialism, as well as the very struggle for the ideal—social order without sexism, classes, and racism—provides a channel for, and ultimate solution to, the kinds of emotions and desires of Jake and Bigger. He reports of black men and women who, in conjunction with white workers and Communists, *actively worked to change themselves by changing their circumstances*. As many events of the 1930s suggest, through multi-racial praxis, workers were able substantially to defeat the debilitating racist preconceptions that function to keep people separate and unequal.

*Native Son* illustrates this point somewhat, since both Bigger and Jan are forced to give up their faulty perceptions of each other only by struggling together. After having met with Jan and directly after one of his "sessions" with Max, Bigger reflects that, "if that white looming mountain of hate were not a mountain at all, but people, people like himself, and like Jan – then he was faced with a high hope the like of which he had never thought could be ..." ['Fate', p. 390]. The hypothesis about the "white looming mountain" seems borne out, since Bigger's last request in the novel divests Jan of his putative "master" status: " 'Tell Mister ... Tell Jan hello' " ['Fate', p. 454]. Bigger has learned to work through his fantasy only by confronting reality or, rather, by having reality confront him when flight is no longer an option.

In the end it is a young black man named Edward Strong Wright had in mind when he did "fictionally" write of a black Communist in "Bright and Morning Star". Strong, who Wright interviewed for one of his *Daily Worker* articles, was the executive secretary of the Communist-organized Southern Negro Youth Congress, which fought for jobs for black youth and civil rights, and against war and fascism.[38] Both a consequence and a cause of a new progressive and militant subjectivity in the Southern heartland of racism during the Great Depression, Strong beat one of the greatest odds in America, by fighting actively with black and white workers against racist oppression internationally. We know that Wright was so impressed with Strong that not only did he write an article on him, but he also used his words for his epigraph to *Uncle Tom's Children*. "Uncle Tom is dead," declared Strong, precisely because black men and women have taken "their destiny into their own hands" and, more importantly, "are breaking down the wall between the two races."[39] Thus, one of the greatest but least discussed truths of Wright's Depression Era work—a truth perhaps worth more than scores of tracts against racism—is that the dialectical overcoming of racism (and its complex psychological consequences) occurs through the repetition of multi-racial action against the social system founded on racism and slavery.

38  Richard Wright, 'Negro Youth On March, Says Leader', *Daily Worker*, 7 October 1937, p. 3.
39  Richard Wright, *Uncle Tom's Children* (New York: HarperPerennial, 1993), p. 3.

**Clare Eby,** 'Slouching Toward Beastliness: Richard Wright's Anatomy of Thomas Dixon'

Most critics today agree that D. W. Griffiths' epic film *The Birth of a Nation* (1915) stands as the classic document of American racism. During its circulation around the country in the late 1910s, the film – unquestionably, the greatest blockbuster of its day – recounted the aftermath of the Civil War from an explicitly racist point of view (see Chronology, **pp. 46–7**). It held up the Ku Klux Klan as the true heroes of Reconstruction, brought about the rebirth of that movement, crudely animalized black male sexuality, and, in the process, contributed hugely to the dramatic upsurge in lynchings that followed the First World War (see Chronology, **p. 48**). Alert to this dreadful impact, leading African-American writers of the post-1945 period, from James Baldwin to Toni Morrison, can seem almost thankful for the sheer candour of the film. They can seem to consider its bald affirmation of the Ku Klux Klan and attack on racial miscegenation useful, as though finding it to be one of those rare instances when racism has dispensed with its customary euphemisms and exposed itself to the full glare of public scrutiny.

Perhaps because he alone was directly endangered by the violence that *The Birth of a Nation* unleashed, Wright never discussed the film in such strategic or open terms. Griffiths, however, can seem present by his absence from *Native Son*. First, his ghost can seem to haunt Bigger's entry into the cinema in Chicago, shadowing the filmed images which lay bare the lowly view American culture holds of African people. Griffiths' status as the chief architect of Hollywood racism also seems present in the more cinematic passages of the novel, in moments such as the very visual account of Bigger, stealing into Mary Dalton's bedroom, which not only echo the conventions of film melodrama and filmed violence but do so in such a way as to expose their racial import. And third – as the following article by the literary critic Clare Eby suggests – Griffiths can also seem present because *Native Son* and *The Birth of a Nation* share a preoccupation with the racist myth of the black rapist.

In this fascinating study Eby argues that this myth, or stereotype, achieved a kind of perfection in the source of *The Birth of a Nation*: the novels of Thomas Dixon. Eby asserts that, if this notorious film can seem curiously 'useful' to Baldwin and Morrison, then Dixon's novels provided a similar service to Wright and *Native Son*. Eby here is not saying that Wright was necessarily an avid reader of Dixon's unpleasant novels. Rather, she is suggesting that these disturbingly popular works were what familiarized American culture with the image of the black rapist, and that it is this familiar image against which Wright then draws Bigger Thomas's character. The texture and detail of Eby's argument flow from this important proposition. By closely reading Dixon's œuvre, Eby not only spares us from what sounds a dull task but in the process uncovers parallels that show how – contrary to Baldwin's accusations – *Native Son* knowingly played upon and satirized existing racial stereotypes. As Eby puts it, in Dixon's racist novels *eros* and *thanatos* collide: the Greek god of love crashes into the Greek word for death, feelings of interracial ambivalence 'fuse sex with fear' and we duly confront the white nightmare of the black sexual predator. This racist myth is for Eby the catalyst for Bigger Thomas.

This essay first appeared in the fall 2001 edition of the *African-American Review* and is reproduced here by kind permission of its publishers. Professor of English at the University of Connecticut, Clare Eby is the author of *Dreiser and Veblen, Saboteurs of the Status Quo*, editor of the Norton Critical Edition of *The Jungle* and co-editor of *The Cambridge Companion to Theodore Dreiser*. Her current projects include an essay on Ann Petry's *The Street* and a book on progressive-era marriages. Again, footnotes are Eby's own, apart from those that I have adapted to refer to the Vintage edition of *Native Son*.

## Clare Eby (2001) 'Slouching Towards Beastliness', African-American Review, 35 (3, fall): pp. 439–58

"Like Nemesis of Greek tragedy," writes W. E. B. Du Bois in *Black Reconstruction*, "the central problem of America after the Civil War, as before, was the black man."[1] U.S. literature has both tried to resolve that problem and contributed to it. Two of the most influential fictional portrayals of African-American men, Uncle Tom and Bigger Thomas, illustrate polarized responses. These protagonists, one notoriously passive and the other violently aggressive, are linked in more than name. Indeed, James Baldwin's complaints in "Everybody's Protest Novel" have made the most important precursor of Richard Wright's character appear to be Harriet Beecher Stowe's Uncle Tom. But I would like to direct attention to an equally important depiction of the "problem" of African-American masculinity against which Wright defined the protagonist of *Native Son*: the black male "beast" of Thomas Dixon's novels.

The North Carolinian novelist did not, to be sure, invent this degrading representation of black men. While historians debate how far back the stereotype goes,

---

1    W. E. B. Du Bois, *Black Reconstruction 1860–1880* (New York: Atheneum, 1969), p. 237.

the "beast" exploded in notoriety in the 1890s, a time of massive black dis-
enfranchisement and the rise of legalized Jim Crow. Whites touted this construct
as proof of the supposed "degeneration" of blacks and used it to justify their own
increasing acts of brutality during this period.[2] Critical race studies boasts an
extensive bibliography on the D. W. Griffith blockbuster, *The Birth of a Nation*
(1915), but few treatments of the Dixon novels that inspired the racial stereotypes
so widely disseminated in that film. As consolidated in these novels, especially
*The Leopard's Spots* (1902) and *The Clansman* (1905), the "beast" stereotype
delineates a particular linking of eros and thanatos: the rape of a white woman as
prelude to her death and/or to the lynching of her accused rapist. I do not propose
a study of Dixon's direct influence on Wright here but rather an examination of
*Native Son*'s complex relation to a pervasive myth, a myth that finds its most
complete articulation in Dixon's novels. Convinced that radical Reconstruction –
which marked the first attempt in the U.S. to incorporate blacks into the body
politic – had unleashed the "beast," Dixon crystallized the anxieties of many
whites of his time. Wright interrogates the white fantasy about black "beasts"
through a plot centering on a legal lynching in response to a presumed rape that in
fact never occurred. Wright so closely examines Dixon's assumptions about black
masculinity that *Native Son* needs to be seen as parodying the white supremacist
vision. In anatomizing the "beast," Wright both follows and makes strategic
revisions in the stereotype. Much as Dixon sought, by his own admission, to
correct Stowe's influential representation of African-Americans, providing what
he described as the "true story" of the South [. . .] so did Wright seek to amend the
consequential image of the black male "beast" and, with that, the portrait of
the nation.[3]

In preparation for writing his so-called Reconstruction Trilogy, Dixon organized over a 1000 pages of historical notes [. . .], and his perspective can quickly
be captured by reviewing his historical assumptions.[4] According to Dixonian
history, after the Civil War white Southerners were perfectly happy to accept
their defeat and rejoin the Union. But unscrupulous whites such as Simon
Legree (Stowe's villain reappears in *The Leopard's Spots* as "master artificer of
Reconstruction policy", Wall Street millionaire, and evil industrialist)[5] engineered
policies that created interracial strife. For instance, *The Leopard's Spots* depicts
the short-lived Freedman's Bureau—created in 1865 to oversee education and
free labor while providing provisions and shelter to the destitute—as forcing
whites to pay blacks for work they hadn't done, thus precipitating innocent and
hard-working whites into bankruptcy. Most ominously, freedom has unleashed
the Negro male's lust for the white woman, and the white man's response is
lynching. As Dixon sums up his view, "since the Negroes under Legree's head had
drawn the color line in politics, the races had been drifting steadily apart," and
lynching—a practice he claims to regret—emerged in response.[6] Dixon glorifies

2   George M. Fredrickson, *The Black Image in the White Mind: The Debate on Afro-American
    Character and Destiny, 1817–1914* (New York: Harper & Row, 1971), pp. 98, 258, 282.
3   Quoted in Raymond A. Cook, *Thomas Dixon* (New York: Twayne, 1974), p. 51.
4   Cook, *Thomas Dixon*, p. 65.
5   Thomas Dixon, Jr., *The Leopard's Spots* (Newport Beach, CA: Noontide, 1994), p. 103.
6   Dixon, *The Leopard's Spots*, p. 197.

the original Ku Klux Klan as a heroic response to the unleashing of the black "beast" by Reconstruction policies.

Dixon claims never to have forgotten his childhood Reconstruction experiences. In what obviously served as a primal scene that would determine much of his subsequent character, Dixon describes his first contact with the Klan, while his family lived in Shelby, North Carolina. The widow of a Confederate soldier arrived at the Dixon home in tears, claiming that an escaped black convict had raped her daughter. That night, the young Dixon awoke to the sound of horses galloping. Creeping to the doorway, he looked out to see the Klan hanging a black man and riddling the body with bullets.[7] This defining moment in Dixon's childhood fuses sex, race, and violence in a way that he would never forget, and it is not difficult to see in it the germ of the future novelist. "My object," Dixon once explained, "is to teach the north . . . the awful suffering of white men during the dreadful reconstruction period."[8]

Wright, growing up in the Jim Crow South two generations after Dixon and on the other side of the color line, had a childhood memory that provided an alternative primal scene. The components are the same—race, sex, and violence—though rather than Dixon's fusion into a scene of traumatic heroism, Wright depicts a youthful revelation that others view his essential nature as depraved and criminal. At age fifteen, Wright took a job doing chores for a white family, the Walls, which provided him with money to pay for books and incidentals. One day he entered Mrs. Wall's bedroom without knocking, his arms filled with wood. She was in the process of dressing, and his generally liberal employers reprimanded him. As Michel Fabre describes the significance of the event, Wright "had . . . inadvertently broken the barrier protecting white women from black men. . . . The sin of being a potential . . . ravisher only reinforced the guilt" that the youth had already accumulated concerning sexuality.[9] Wright's and Dixon's traumatic primal scenes helped to shape their decisions to write such differently positioned protest novels.

Given the role that *The Birth of a Nation* played in disseminating Dixon's ideas, it is appropriate that the first sure sign of Bigger Thomas's "beastliness" occurs in a movie house. The passage as originally published in 1940 juxtaposes a newsreel featuring glorified images of rich white women with *Trader Horn*, a film depicting "naked black men and women whirling in wild dances and . . . drums beating" in Africa. The juxtaposition illustrates the interlocking assumptions determining the white fantasy of the "beast": the desirability of white women and the essentially "primitive" nature of people of African descent.[10] The scene as it appears in the restored Library of America text makes the anatomy of the "beast" yet clearer, superimposing on the celluloid images of desirable white femininity and uncivilized Africans the sight of Bigger and company engaging in what Jonathan

7  Cook, *Thomas Dixon*, p. 23.
8  Raymond A. Cook, *Fire from the Flint: The Amazing Careers of Thomas Dixon* (Winston-Salem, NC: John F. Blair, 1968), p. 140.
9  Fabre, *The Unfinished Quest of Richard Wright*, p. 47.
10  Restored edition of Wright, 'Fear' in *Native Son*, p. 36.

Elmer calls competitive masturbation.[11] Lying at the center of the "beast" stereo-type is the assumption of the black male's uncontrollable sexual appetite, believed to crystallize in the lust for white women. Thus the disturbing juxtapositions in the scene as restored illustrate the process of young black males watching widely disseminated images of blackness and whiteness while confirming stereotypes about black masculinity.

While commentators have noted Bigger's resemblance to the black "beast," little attention has been paid to the location of the alleged rape: the Daltons' home. As becomes clear in Dixon's novels, multiple meanings of the home structure and indeed rationalize the white fantasy of black "beasts." *The Clansman* addresses the problem of a nation fragmented, as Dixon sees it, by Reconstruction policies, and he figures the political issues as domestic problems. Dixon's concern with the political implications of domestic arrangements becomes especially clear in his depiction of the radical Republican Congressional leader Austin Stoneman (Dixon's fictionalized version of Thaddeus Stevens), whose real deformity is not the clubfoot the narrator obsessively mentions, but rather his position at the head of a miscegenous household. Or more precisely, Stoneman's housekeeper Lydia Brown, described as "a mulatto, a woman of extraordinary animal beauty and the fiery temper of a leopardess," presides over his home.[12] What scandalizes Dixon is that Lydia exercises unnatural power over Stoneman, who in turn exer-cises ungodly power over the nation, and thus "the seat of Empire had moved from the White House to a little dark house on the Capital hill, where dwelt an old clubfooted man, alone, attended by a strange brown woman of sinister animal beauty."[13] The torn nation resembles nothing so much as a miscegenous house-hold, and the "first lady of the land" has become "the strange brown woman," Lydia.[14]

Dixon is a terrible writer, but he knows enough to pose the solution in the same terms he employed to define the problem: through images of purified homes and consecrated marriages. Although later novels such as *The Sins of the Father* (1912) show him to be surprisingly critical of slavery, in the Reconstruction Trilogy Dixon posits the peculiar institution as a happy family of whites and blacks destroyed by the Civil War. The horror of Reconstruction lies in its having exchanged slavery, which Dixon paternalistically casts as "the old familiar trust of domestic life," for the "complete alienation of the white and black races."[15] As Dixon presents President Lincoln's position early in *The Clansman*, " 'There is no room for two distinct races of white men in America, much less for two distinct races of whites and blacks. . . . We must assimilate or expel. . . . I can conceive of no greater calamity than the assimilation of the Negro into our social and political life as our equal'."[16] What is interesting is the positing of two *white* "races," though Dixon clearly finds the separation of Northern from Southern white man horrific. His narrative means of rectifying this problem is through two unlikely

11  Jonathan Elmer (1998) 'Spectacle and Event in *Native Son*', *American Literature* 70 (4): pp. 767–98 (p. 779).
12  Thomas Dixon, Jr., *The Clansman* (Lexington, ky.: University Press of Kentucky, 1970), p. 57.
13  Dixon, *The Clansman*, p. 79.
14  Dixon, *The Clansman*, p. 91.
15  Dixon, *The Leopard's Spots*, p. 103.
16  Dixon, *The Clansman*, p. 46.

marriages: Stoneman's son Phil and daughter Elsie marry the daughter and son of an ex-Confederate. When Phil Stoneman declares his love to the Southern belle Margaret Cameron, significantly telling her how "'homelike'" he finds her accent, she asks if he "'won't be disappointed in my simple ideal that finds its all within a home?'."[17] Of course he won't, for "home" is everything in *The Clansman*. Sex among siblings within the home sounds suspiciously like incest, but the unseemly connotation Dixon's narrative generates by spotlighting marriages of sisters and brothers—in fact two such marriages—fails to trouble him. In fact, something very close to incest among whites seems to be Dixon's solution to the threat of miscegenation. That is because consolidating white energies by inter-breeding would address the second problem Dixon has Lincoln identify: the impossible coexistence of blacks and whites. The President explains that "'God never meant that the Negro should leave his habitat or the white man invade his home. . . . And the tragedy will not be closed until the black man is restored to his home'."[18] Here "home" patently means country and becomes part of the argument for colonization of blacks to Africa. To sum up Dixon's argument: whiten "races" must intermarry, just as much as blacks and whites must not.

In *Native Son*, the second dictum voiced by Dixon's Lincoln—that blacks and whites should maintain separate homes—has been accomplished, not by coloniza-tion but by Chicago's segregated neighborhoods. Blacks cross the color line only when whites invite them to do so (as servants or other menial workers), or as presumed criminals. No wonder that Bigger, whose crossing of the color line illustrates both propositions, finds his choices so limited. *Native Son* demon-strates the problem of the nation to be precisely the demarcation of separate "homes" that Dixon hoped to achieve. Wright's hypocritical white capitalist, Mr. Dalton, owns the South Side Real Estate Company, an institution outrageous enough to force African-Americans to pay to maintain the color line. Thus Dixon's solution becomes the problem Wright exposes: black and white "homes" are fully segregated. Bigger's defense attorney articulates the problem: "'Taken collectively, [Negroes] are not simply twelve million people; in reality they consti-tute a separate nation, stunted, stripped, and held captive within this nation'" ['Fate', p. 423]. Through segregation and black ghettos, America has achieved the colonization of blacks that Dixon desired, only colonizing them *within* the nation.

Lying behind the white construct of the black "beast" is the fear that political rights would lead to social contact. This fear motivated the U.S. Supreme Court's regressive interpretation of the Fourteenth Amendment, intended to secure black citizenship, in *Plessy* vs. *Fergusson* (1896). Guaranteeing black citizenship could not, the court majority worried, possibly have meant "abolish[ing] distinctions based upon color, or . . . enforc[ing] social, as distinguished from political equality".[19] Dixon captures the white concern that Reconstruction era gains in civil rights for blacks had abolished race distinctions and threatened to result in egalitarian interracial relations. Dixon is so trapped in the logic of dominance

---

17  Dixon, *The Clansman*, p. 282.
18  Dixon, *The Clansman*, p. 47.
19  Quoted in Lee D. Baker, *From Savage to Negro: Anthropology and the Construction of Race, 1896 to 1954* (Berkeley, Calif.: University of California Press, 1998), pp. 23–4.

and submission that he can only read "the equal rights of man, [to] mea[n], of course, the right of the Negro race to rule the white man of the South, the former slave to rule his master."[20]

*The Clansman*, again, is particularly explicit in illustrating white anxieties concerning the link between political rights for and personal contact with blacks. In this novel Dixon depicts Washington, prior to the Civil War, as ruled "by an aristocracy founded on brains, culture, and blood," but after Reconstruction, "Now a Negro electorate" reigned. Drunken, armed, and disrespectful, this newly empowered black citizenry, with its "onion-laden breath, mixed with perspiring African odour, became the symbol of American Democracy".[21] Dixon's revulsion at black male bodies grows hysterical when he imagines them touching the deformed white body of Stoneman, as "two gigantic negroes" carry in the congressman, "his big club foot hanging pathetically from those black arms". In one of the most reprehensible passages of *The Clansman*, Dixon belabors this point, describing "kinky heads, black skin, thick lips, white teeth, and flat noses ma[king] for the moment a curious symbolic frame for the chalk-white passion of the old Commoner's [i.e., Stoneman's] face." He continues,

> No sculptor ever dreamed a more sinister emblem of the corruption of a race of empire-builders than this group. Its black figures, wrapped in the night of four thousand years of barbarism, squatted there the "equal" of their master, grinning at his forms of Justice, the evolution of forty centuries of Aryan genius.[22]

A later scene depicts the Capitol in Columbia, South Carolina overtaken by blacks (101 blacks and 23 whites in congress) in similar terms.[23]

This image of a partly white, partly black body entering the Senate Chamber—the occasion, appropriately, the impeachment of Dixon's fellow Southerner, Andrew Johnson—reveals Dixon's real terror at the prospect of what we might call a mulatto nation. A character in *Leopard's Spots* voices this fear: "Shall the future American be an Anglo-Saxon or a mulatto?"[24] To Dixon the mulatto nation signifies "barbarism strangling civilisation by brute force."[25] Not only does he see "Democracy" (touted by Stoneman) as in conflict with "Civilisation" (the ideal of the Southerner, Cameron), but Dixon finds it easy to choose between them. A democratic mulatto nation is anathema, for as Dixon says through his Southern character, the very idea of "assimilat[ing]" blacks is "pollution".[26] In a 1964 article, Maxwell Bloomfield rightly observes that Dixon was the first novelist to dramatize the Negro "problem" as a matter of national, not merely sectional, concern.[27] As Walter Benn Michaels succinctly puts it, for Dixon, "the

---

20  Thomas Dixon, Jr., *The Traitor* (Newport Beach, Calif.: Noontide, 1994), p. 453.
21  Dixon, *The Clansman*, p. 155.
22  Dixon, *The Clansman*, pp. 170–1.
23  Dixon, *The Clansman*, pp. 264–5.
24  Dixon, *The Leopard's Spots*, p. 82.
25  Dixon, *The Clansman*, p. 267.
26  Dixon, *The Clansman*, p. 291.
27  Maxwell Bloomfield (1964) 'Dixon's *The Leopard's Spots*: A Study in Popular Racism', *American Quarterly*, 6: pp. 387–401 (p. 400).

legitimacy of the state . . . was guaranteed by its whiteness."[28] It was, after all, Dixon who came up with *The Birth of a Nation* as the title for Griffith's blockbuster.

As Cameron's talk of assimilation suggests, while the white reaction against black equality is often expressed in horror at the prospect of interracial contact between men, it is centered on fears of miscegenation. One of Dixon's most devious Negroes, the disturbingly named Silas Lynch, demands " 'the privilege of going to see [any white man] in his house or his hotel, eating with him and sleeping with him, and when I see fit, to take his daughter in marriage!' "[29] Here lies the emotional center of Dixon: As a white character succinctly puts it in *The Leopard's Spots*, " 'If a man really believes in equality, let him prove it by giving his daughter to a Negro in marriage. That is the test' ".[30] The bizarre slippery-slope reasoning, by which political and social equality translates necessarily and inevitably into sexual contact of black men with white women, takes us to the core of the white fantasy of the black beast. In *Leopard's Spots* Dixon depicts the fancyman mulatto Tim Shelby (Stowe's Kentucky Shelbys' free slave resurrected as a Negro organizer) as eager for a " 'fair white bride'." Shelby seems likely to get what he wants, for the Supreme Court passes a law that not only allows intermarriage but actually " 'command[s] its enforcement on every military post'. "[31] The children resulting from this "amalgamation" of races, according to Dixon, "simply meant Africanization. The big nostrils, flat nose, massive jaw, protruding lip and kinky hair will register their animal marks over the proudest intellect and the rarest beauty of any other race. The rule that had no exception was that one drop of Negro blood makes a Negro." In other words, one drop turns a white man into a "beast." Simply put, according to the Dixonian slippery slope, political and social equality leads inexorably to miscegenation, which leads to the "Africanization" of white Americans, extending the reign of the beast.[32] Martha Hodes explains the reaction: "white southern politicians beg[a]n during the Civil War to conflate the possibility of freedom . . . for black men with a fear of widespread sex." After the war, "because it was the men of the free black population who now gained formal political power and began to achieve economic independence, it was they who had enormous power to deny the South's racial caste system." Hodes sums up: "Political power, economic success, and sex with a white woman – all such actions on the part of the black man confounded the lines of racial categories . . . and therefore became unforgivable transgressions."[33]

Dixon's novels demonstrate that what John Hope Franklin calls "the mythical threat of 'Negro rule' as excuse for [white] lawlessness"—what I am terming the threat of the mulatto nation—expresses itself fundamentally in terms of sexual

28  Walter Benn Michaels, *Our America: Nativism, Modernism, and Pluralism* (Durham, NC: Duke University Press, 1995), p. 18.

29  Dixon, *The Clansman*, p. 275.

30  Dixon, *The Clansman*, p. 237.

31  Dixon, *The Clansman*, pp. 74–5.

32  Dixon, *The Clansman*, p. 197.

33  Martha Hodes, *White Women, Black Men: Illicit Sex in the Nineteenth Century South* (New Haven, Conn.: Yale University Press, 1997), pp. 145–57.

anxieties.[34] But like other white supremacists of his time, Dixon painstakingly maintains a double standard. Shockingly, rather than condemn or even ignore the extensive history of couplings of white men and black women—extending back through slavery and the much more common sort of miscegenous relationship in American history—Dixon rationalizes it. When in *The Leopard's Spots* a deacon from Boston inquires about the offspring of white men and black women, he is informed, " 'This mixture . . . has no social significance. . . . It is all the result of the surviving polygamous and lawless instincts of the white male.' " Somehow a matter of instinct but not of race, "Racial integrity remains intact" as long as no black man can choose a white woman for a mate.[35]

The "mixture" that alarms Dixon, like other white supremacists, is the sexual contact of black men and white women. He can not imagine such liaisons as consensual, and so rape scenes, and scenes of sexual violation narrowly averted, lie at the heart of his novels. Dixon presents rape, in fact, as the inevitable consequence of allowing black men to share power with whites. In *The Leopard's Spots*, for instance, the poor white family of Tom Camp is twice violated. In the first instance, the "winsome" and "plump" sixteen-year-old daughter Annie is engaged to be married to Hose Norman, until a "black shadow" is cast over the Camp home the day of the wedding. A "big Negro" accompanied by six of his "scoundrel" friends break into the Camp home, carrying the white virgin off to the woods. The enraged father manages to knock down one of the Negroes, using his own wooden leg as a weapon. (One of the few rewards of Dixon's style is such moments of unintentional comedy.) When the bridegroom quails at the father's cry to fire, worrying they might inadvertently injure Annie, Camp commands, " 'Shoot, men! . . . there are things worse than death'." When they bring the mortally wounded (but still virginal) woman back to the house, the father tells the grieving mother not to cry, for they should be " 'thank[ing] God she was saved from them brutes'."[36] Saved, that is, from rape.

The actual rape in *Leopard's Spots* occurs years later, when Tom Camp's younger daughter, Flora, refuses to display the aversion toward and fear of blacks that Dixon considers normal and self-protective in white women. When this virgin turns out to be missing, the preacher's prophecy comes true: The white "race" unifies against the threat, "fus[ing] into a homogeneous mass of love, sympathy, hate, and revenge. The rich and the poor, the learned and the ignorant, the banker and the blacksmith, the great and the small, they were all one now." When the now-unified whites discover the girl, she lies on the brink of death:

> Flora lay on the ground with her clothes torn to shreds and stained with blood. Her beautiful yellow curls were matted across her forehead in a

34 John Hope Franklin, 'Introduction' in *Three Negro Classics* (New York: Avon, 1965), p. vii.
35 Dixon, *The Leopard's Spots*, p. 172. Dixon devotes an entire novel to rationalizing the problem of white male lust for black women, *The Sins of the Father* (1912). This reprehensible work aims at explaining why the best white men have fornicated with black women. Again Dixon uses the rhetoric of the 'beast,' assigning the degenerate attribute to white males – while making its appearance the fault of the 'black' woman. Dixon's astounding attempt at rationalizing white male lust for black women reconnoiters the ideological boundaries of the 'home' and the related demarcation of public and private 'spheres' so important in his earlier novels.
36 Dixon, *The Leopard's Spots*, pp. 62–4.

dark red lump beside a wound where her skull had been crushed. The stone lay at her side, the crimson mark of her life showing on its jagged edges.

With that stone the brute had tried to strike the death blow. She was lying on the edge of the hill with her head up the incline. It was too plain, the terrible crime that had been committed.[37]

While Dixon is lavish with the violent details, most of them point to murder, few to rape. The only indicator of rape here is Flora's torn clothes. Nevertheless, "the terrible crime"—by which Dixon means rape, not murder—is clearly legible to the entire party. The girl's imminent death comes as something of an anticlimax after the rape.

*The Clansman*'s rape scene is infamous, its shelf life extended by *The Birth of a Nation*. In this novel, white women uniformly show the fear and aversion toward black males that Dixon finds natural, healthy, and self-protective, and those who don't suffer for their folly. Marion Lenoir, a sixteen-year-old specimen of "the full tropic splendour of Southern girlhood", is torn from her home by "four black brutes."[38] Having experimented with several rape scenes already, in this one Dixon can now evoke the "beast" with more precision:

"We ain't atter money!" [cries one of the black intruders.]
The girl uttered a cry, long, tremulous, heart-rending, piteous. A single tiger-spring, and the black claws of the beast sank into the soft white throat and she was still.[39]

Ben Cameron's prediction—" 'The next step [following Reconstruction] will be a black hand on a white woman's throat' "—has proven true.[40] The rape of Marion provides Dixon's most ideologically loaded account of the activity of the "beast," particularly because she survives it only to commit suicide in horror at her violation.

Wright anatomizes all of Dixon's premises when Bigger crosses the color line and enters the Daltons' white house. Mary Dalton and Jan Erlone's fumbling attempts to treat Bigger as equal, not chauffeur, in the car and at Ernie's Kitchen Shack do lead inexorably to the black man's entering the white woman's bedroom, to his becoming a criminal, and to her death. But particularly in his treatment of what Dixon considers decisive proof of black male bestiality— insatiable lust for white women—Wright carefully examines every proposition while providing alternative explanations.

Prior to meeting Mary, Bigger had found all white women "cold [. . .] and reserve[d]; they stood their distance and spoke to him from afar. But this girl waded right in and hit him between the eyes" ['Fear', p. 90]. Physical proximity soon follows. Once her boyfriend insists on driving the Dalton car himself, Bigger finds himself wedged in tightly between two white people and realizes, "Never . . .

37 Dixon, *The Leopard's Spots*, pp. 188–92.
38 Dixon, *The Clansman*, pp. 284, 303.
39 Dixon, *The Clansman*, p. 304.
40 Dixon, *The Clansman*, p. 262.

had he been so close to a white woman. He smelt the odor of her hair and felt the soft pressure of her thigh against his own" ['Fear', p. 99]. The restored passages in *Native Son* make clear that Mary is not Dixon's chaste pillar of virtue but a sexually active woman. While getting drunk and making out with Jan in the back seat, she inadvertently flashes Bigger "a faint sweep of white thigh," causing him to fight off an erection. After Jan leaves, Mary slumps down, "her legs sprawled wide apart." She starts telling Bigger how much she likes him. Back at the house, she tells Bigger several times to help her out of the car. When Bigger has to help Mary upstairs because she is too drunk to walk on her own, appropriately "he felt strange . . . as if he were acting upon a stage in front of a crowd of people."[41] He might as well be on stage, for this scene was scripted decades earlier. However much Wright changes the characterization of the main players, Bigger has entered a white-authored script here, the ending of which is overdetermined.

The harrowing scene that follows—with Bigger fondling Mary while her face comes up to kiss him, when he responds with a kiss, and, swaying and grinding her pelvis against him—unmasks the Dixonian norm of white female purity as yet another white male fantasy. In attributing fear to certain characters and not to others, Wright further shifts the scene away from the "beast" script. Rather than assigning terror to the white woman, Wright makes Mary too drunk to fear anything. Instead he locates terror in the black man, which intensifies to a fevered pitch once a second white woman enters the room. In Wright's version of the "beast" plot, the black male kills neither because lust has led him to rape nor in retaliation for the terror he inspires in his victim, but because of his own fear. Wright also revises the reaction of white women to the crime. In the climactic rape in *The Clansman*, Mrs. Lenoir witnesses her daughter's violation and the women decide to " 'hide quickly every trace of crime' "—which necessitates a joint suicide.[42] In *Native Son*, the daughter is not violated, nor does the mother witness the murder (even though she is present when it occurs) because she is blind. In a brilliantly compressed passage immediately after his accidental killing of Mary, Bigger rehearses the essential plot components and how they will be interpreted: "She was dead; she was white; she was a woman; he had killed her; he was black; he might be caught; he did not want to be caught; if he were they would kill him" ['Fear', p. 121].

In a nightmare version of Dixon's worst fears, Bigger Thomas experiences a revelation of his power as a direct consequence of passing through the threshold of Mary's bedroom. He comes to feel, after killing Mary, both "power" and "security" as a direct result of his crime. This response bears comparison with that of the stereotypical "beast": "The knowledge that he had killed a white girl they [white people] loved and regarded as their symbol of beauty made him feel the equal of them" ['Flight', p. 194]. Yet for a black man to defy the color line will be read as not merely as an individual action, but rather in racially represen- tative terms, as a "symbolic challenge" to white supremacy, and be dealt with accordingly.

---

41  Restored edition of Wright, 'Fear' in *Native Son*, pp. 89–95.
42  Dixon, *Clansman*, p. 305.

Beyond the trepidation felt by blacks toward the prospect of committing crimes against whites lies Wright's more fundamental revision of the "beast" stereotype. He depicts the fear blacks have of whites—the inverse of the white fear of blacks that Dixon considers natural and healthy—as sexualized. Early in Book Two, as Bigger recalls carrying Mary to her bedroom, he realizes that "each time he had come in contact with her . . . [fear and shame] had arisen hot and hard." This passage comes right before the memorable description that "to Bigger and his kind white people . . . were a sort of great natural force" ['Flight', p. 144]. Thus Wright does depict the interaction of black men and white women as strongly charged erotically, but the erotic component comes from the fear and shame instilled *in* blacks *by* whites. Like the erection he fought off when Jan and Mary made out in the back seat, Bigger's fear is a response to whites' actions.

Wright's revision of the "beast" plot so as to show how whites fuse sex with fear in the consciousness of black males helps account for the logic of one of the most disturbing passages in *Native Son*. When Bessie, who comprehends what whites think about black "beasts," warns Bigger that . . . " 'they'll say you raped her [Mary],' " Wright follows with a disturbing redefinition. Confronting for the first time the inevitability of the accusation to follow, Bigger asks himself,

> Had he raped her? Yes, he had raped her. Every time he felt as he had felt that night, he raped. But rape was not what one did to women. Rape was what one felt when one's back was against a wall and one had to strike out, whether one wanted to or not, to keep the pack from killing one. He committed rape every time he looked into a white face. He was a long, taut piece of rubber which a thousand white hands had stretched to the snapping point, and when he snapped it was rape. But it was rape when he cried out in hate deep in his heart as he felt the strain of living day by day. That, too, was rape.
>
> ['Flight', pp. 257–8]

By this account, rape is not an act of aggression but of retaliation, with Bigger its initial victim. The black man in America, far from being a "beast"/rapist, is raped by white society—gang raped, actually. "To keep the pack from killing one" clearly alludes to lynching. Wright's redefinition of rape makes perfect sense given the white stereotype of the "beast," according to which black men are ex post facto rapists of white women. As Wright puts it in "How 'Bigger' Was Born", "the reason for the lynching is usually called 'rape.' "[43]

But what remains profoundly disturbing in Wright's redefinition of rape is his erasure of violence against women—especially the long history of sexual violence against black women. No matter how often Bigger may be figuratively raped by white society, he does of course rape a woman in this novel, though his victim is his black girlfriend, not the white socialite. Hazel Carby explains that "the institutionalized rape of black women has never been [seen] as [so] powerful a symbol of black oppression as the spectacle of lynching," and Wright's blind spot,

43 Wright, 'How "Bigger" was Born', p. 7.

unfortunately, confirms this generalization.[44] Yet Wright deserves some credit for restoring in *Native Son* the real historical victim of rape – the black, not the white woman. With chilling accuracy, Wright has Bessie function after her death merely as evidence on the slab to convict Bigger of the miscegenous rape he never committed.

Simultaneously extending and revising Dixon's assumptions, *Native Son* demonstrates the legal, and supposedly civilized, methods that have taken lynch law out of the closet. Three centers of white power articulate Bigger's status as "beast" and contribute to his lynching: the press, the legal system, and the mob.

*Black Boy* discloses the formative role of the press in disseminating racist stereotypes. Wright describes one of his earliest exposures to racism coming through newspapers that he, ironically, delivered as a youth living in Jackson, Mississippi. He was horrified to find in these papers such statements as, " 'The only dream of a nigger is to be president and to sleep with a white woman.' "[45] That shocking sentence illustrates again the pathological linking of white anxieties about black bestiality with fears of a mulatto nation. *Native Son* elaborates on how newspapers disseminate these fears under the guise of objective reportage. One of the reporters in the novel quickly stakes out the tack all the papers will take in reporting the killing of Mary Dalton: " 'Say, I'm slanting this to the primitive Negro who doesn't want to be disturbed by white civilization' " ['Flight', p. 244]. Initially casting Bigger as "Negro rapist and murderer," the fuller account from the Chicago *Tribune* as given in Book Three rehashes all the usual assumptions ['Flight', p. 276]. Referring directly or by innuendo to Bigger's race about thirty times in fewer than three pages, the report features him as apelike "jungle beast" and "sex-slayer." The reporter sees only two options for black masculinity, and since Bigger is no Uncle Tom—"lack[ing] the charm of the average, harmless, genial, grinning southern darky so beloved by the American people"—he must be part of the problem, a "missing link. . . . out of place in a white man's civilization". An interview with a newspaper editor in Jackson, Mississippi instructs the Northerners in how to proceed: " 'Our experience here in Dixie with such depraved types of Negroes has shown that only the death penalty, inflicted in a public and dramatic manner, has any influence' " ['Fate', p. 310]. Simply put, the Mississippian recommends a lynching.

Making the *Tribune's* account even more destructive is a crucial (and unverified) assumption the paper disseminates concerning Bigger's racial ancestry. Through this assumption Wright shows how the North follows rather than revises Southern stereotypes about black men. Again quoting the Mississippi editor, the *Tribune* reports that, although the fugitive is " 'dead-black, . . . [he] may have a minor portion of white blood in his veins, a mixture which generally makes for a criminal and intractable nature.' " The fear of miscegenation—evoking the threat of the mulatto nation—is embedded in this account of Bigger's ancestry. Once again recycling the basic problem as the solution, the Southern editor recommends extending Jim Crow: " 'Crimes such as the Bigger Thomas murders could be lessened by segregating all Negroes in parks, playgrounds, cafés,

---

44  Hazel Carby, *Reconstructing Womanhood: The Emergence of the Afro-American Woman Novelist* (New York: Oxford University Press, 1987), p. 39.
45  Wright, *Black Boy*, p. 153.

theatres, and street cars. Residential segregation is imperative.'" Given his sources and his assumptions, no wonder the *Tribune* writer finds it "'easy to imagine how this man [Bigger], in the grip of a brain-numbing sex passion, over-powered little Mary Dalton, raped her, murdered her, beheaded her,'" for "'All in all, he seems a beast. . . . [a] brutish Negro'" ['Fate', p. 311]. Easy to imagine, indeed: This is all the product of a diseased white imagination.

Wright's depiction of the press not only reflects the assumptions current in his time but also alludes to the newspaper's historical treatment of lynching, in which the white press in general and the *Tribune* in particular played significant roles. As anti-lynching activists such as Ida Wells-Barnett make clear, newspapers contributed to the lynching furor by biased reporting, by inaccurate accounts, even by suggestive omissions. As Wells-Barnett points out, "Those who commit the murders write the reports," but when the Negro seeks to publish an alternative account, the bias of the white-dominated press stops him: "The columns of the powerful dailies, religious periodicals and thoughtful magazines have printed these charges wholesale until the civilized world has accepted them, but," she reports, "few wish to consider the refutation of them or give space for the possible other side".[46] In several pamphlets, she reprints lynching statistics published by the Chicago *Tribune*—the same paper that recommends lynching Bigger Thomas —which demonstrate a scant one-third of people lynched had even been charged with rape (and there was rarely any factual foundation that for those so charged). White apologists did not let the absence of facts stop them. For instance, Thomas Nelson Page set forth in a 1904 article that, notwithstanding the *Tribune*'s statistics, the cause for lynching is the unprintable activities of black beasts: "The death of the victim of the ravisher was generally the least of the attendant horrors. In Texas, in Mississippi, in Georgia, in Kentucky, in Colorado, as later in Delaware, the facts in the case were so unspeakable that they have never been put in print. It is these unnamable horrors which have outraged the minds" of lynchers.[47] Page's comment inadvertently provides a revealing glimpse into the role of the white imagination in manufacturing "unspeakable" horrors. As Jacquelyn Dowd Hall eloquently puts it, "the fear of rape, like the practice of lynching, was embedded far beyond the reach of factual refutation—in the heart not only of American racism, but of American attitudes toward women as well."[48]

The District Attorney's performance in *Native Son* continues this process of manufacturing unspeakable horrors. To District Attorney Buckley, Bigger is simply a "'human fiend,'" and he whips the audience into a frenzy with the image of "'some half-human black ape . . . climbing through the windows of our homes to rape, murder, and burn our daughters.'" Convinced that Bigger has committed a "'bestial monstrosity,'" Buckley intones, "'Your Honor, the central crime here is rape!'" ['Fate', pp. 432–7]. The D.A. then whips himself into a frenzy, painting a picture that could come straight out of Thomas Dixon:

46  Mildred I. Thompson (ed.) *Ida B. Wells-Barnett: An Exploratory Study of an American Black Woman, 1893–1930* (New York: Carlson, 1990), p. 239, p. 180.
47  Thomas Nelson Page (1904) 'The Lynching of Negroes: Its Cause and Prevention', *North American Review*, 178: pp. 33–48 (p. 38).
48  Jacquelyn Dowd Hall, *Revolt against Chivalry: Jessie Daniel Ames and the Women's Campaign against Lynching* (New York: Columbia University Press, 1993), p. 149.

"My God, what bloody scenes must have taken place! How swift and unexpected must have been that lustful and murderous attack! How that poor child must have struggled to escape that maddened ape! How she must have pled on bended knee, with tears in her eyes, to be spared the vile touch of his horrible person! Your Honor, must not this infernal monster have burned her body to destroy evidence of offenses *worse* than rape? That treacherous beast must have known that if the marks of his teeth were ever seen on the innocent white flesh of her breasts . . ."

['Fate', p. 436]

In *Native Son*, the legal system and its representatives remain unable to imagine alternative narratives featuring a black male and a dead white woman.

What is perhaps most depressing (and accurate) of all is that, as Wright paints the legal lynching system, not even reasoned eloquence such as defense attorney Boris Max's will have any effect. Declaring the entire legal system negated when a person can be tried by a jury that has prejudged him guilty, Max says, " 'An outright lynching would be more honest than a "mock trial" ' " ['Fate', p. 405]. Showing no tolerance for a critical view of America, Buckley revealingly paints Max's competing explanation as " 'cynically assail[ing] our sacred customs.' " As if an appeal to capitalist patriotism and racist fear were not enough, Buckley's coup de grace is an appeal to white male solidarity: " 'Every decent white man in America ought to swoon with joy for the opportunity to crush with his heel the woolly head of this black lizard' " ['Fate', p. 433]. Countering Dixon's fantasy about politics and the legal system as controlled by blacks, Wright demonstrates the reverse to be true.

Wright appropriately uses Max as the defense lawyer, for in 1930s America, communism provided the most convenient target for anxieties about the mulatto nation aided and abetted by whites who betrayed their "race." Even before Bigger becomes a suspect, Dalton's private detective, Britten, asks twice if Jan had lured him to the left by enticing him with white women. Later during his cross-examination, the coroner inquires if the communist pamphlets Jan gave Bigger included " 'a plea for "unity of whites and blacks." ' " The predictable follow-up question is whether Jan told the chauffeur " 'it was all right for him to have sexual relations with white women' " ['Fate', p. 350]. Thus the conflation of political equality with miscegenation—Dixon's slippery slope—remains alive and well, with communism assuming the role of white race betrayers previously occupied by radical Republicans during Reconstruction. Otherwise the assumptions remain identical, as Bigger's response manifests: " 'I didn't know nothing about that woman,' " he tells Max. " 'All I knew was that they kill us for women like her.' " The accused "beast" is correct that it doesn't matter if he raped her since it will be assumed he did; charges of rapes of women he never even encountered have been accumulating at Bigger's feet ['Fate', p. 380].

While it may be difficult to believe the crudeness of these insinuations about luring black men into the Communist Party with promises of white women, Wright is not exaggerating or veering from the documentary record. In his last published novel, *The Flaming Sword*, appearing one year before *Native Son*, Thomas Dixon confirms the merger in the white supremacist mind of fears about communism and anxieties about black male-white female couplings. After disposing of the requisite murder and rape by the inevitably burly black male in Part 1 of this lengthy novel, Dixon turns to what he considers an even more insidious form of miscegenation. When his heroine, Angela (daughter of *The Clansman*'s Ben Cameron and Elsie Stoneman) moves to Manhattan, she discovers consensual relationships across the color line. As another character soon points out, this "'catering to the black man's lust for white women'" probably has an underlying "'political significance.'"[49] Part 3 discloses this political import, examining a "'subtle scheme'" by which white women volunteer themselves as sexual partners for black men so as to recruit them to the Communist Party.[50] Thus for Thomas Dixon, 1930s radicalism illustrates the follies of the Reconstruction period all over again.

Anti-Communist sentiment dooms Bigger's defense attorney in the courtroom; Max can no more defend the accused against the mob than against insinuations of political defection. While the legal system joins forces with the press to condemn Bigger, the mob prepares a quicker conviction of the "beast". Book Two ends with cries of "'Lynch 'im'" and "'Kill that black ape!'" as Bigger is captured ['Flight', p. 301]. When the "beast" is brought back to the scene of his alleged crime, the white man's house, and asked to reconstruct the murder/rape, a burning cross awaits him. Bigger responds by tearing off the cross suspended from his neck.[51] The notorious symbology of burning crosses was not in fact practiced by the original Klan; the ritual apparently originated in Dixon's novels.[52] In *The Traitor*, which sharply distinguishes between the original Klan (heroic in Dixon's eyes) and the second-generation Klan that he thought had deteriorated into "an engine of personal vengeance and criminal folly," Dixon explains that "The reign of terror inaugurated by the Black Union League had made necessary the Ku Klux Klan." Although the "new Klan had inaugurated a reign of folly and terror,"[53] Dixon maintains the purity of the original organization, "the sole guardians of white civilization . . . [and] the last resort of desperation."[54] Thus "the masses of the people knew the necessity which had called this dreaded order [the original Klan] into existence—the black threat of Negro dominion."[55]

Wright shows the endurance of this mob mentality when Bigger is brought into the Cook County Morgue and finds himself surrounded by a "compact array of white faces." He senses something ominous,

> a silent mockery that challenged him. It was not their hate he felt; it was something deeper than that. He sensed that in their attitude toward him they had gone beyond hate. . . . he felt that not only had they resolved to put him to death, but that they were determined to make his death mean more than a mere punishment; that they regarded him as a figment of

49  Thomas Dixon, Jr., *The Flaming Sword* (Atlanta, Ga.: Monarch, 1939), p. 397.
50  Dixon, *The Flaming Sword*, p. 404.
51  Dixon, *The Flaming Sword*, p. 390.
52  Allen W. Trelease, 'Ku Klux Klan' in Eric Foner and John A. Garraty (eds) *The Reader's Companion to American History* (Boston: Houghton Mifflin, 1991), pp. 625–6.
53  William Dixon, Jr., *The Traitor* (Newport Beach, Calif.: Noontide, 1994), p. 457.
54  Dixon, *The Traitor*, p. 51.
55  Dixon, *The Traitor*, p. 473.

that black world which they feared and were anxious to keep under control. The atmosphere of the crowd told him that they were going to use his death as a bloody symbol of fear to wave before the eyes of that black world.

['Fate', p. 306]

In this extraordinary passage, Wright anatomizes the lynch mentality: collective hysteria as a matter of symbolic racial representation. Too cool in their attitude for so muddy an emotion as hatred, the white mob does not content itself with putting Bigger to death. Projecting onto Bigger, the "beast" in their midst, all their fears about blacks, the mob achieves a ritual self-purification. In the process they also transform the public identity of Bigger, previously a symbol that all whites could read (the black "beast") into a "bloody symbol" of the lynch victim all too legible for blacks. Trudier Harris's explanation of the psychology of the lynch mob describes this section of the novel well: "Symbolic punishment becomes communal because the entire society has been threatened; thus the entire society must act to put down the victor."[56] Joel Williamson also explains the lynch mentality: "Symbolically, the lynching was often seen as an act against the whole black community and not merely the execution of one or more criminals."[57]

As Boris Max will soon put it, " 'every Negro in America's on trial out there' " ['Fate', p. 397]. Disclosing Bigger's true "crime," as Wright so memorably puts it, to be simply "the crime of being black," he depicts the "beast" as the ultimate form of racial profiling ['Fate', p. 306]. Although to Bigger "his crime seemed natural," it is in fact totally constructed out of white supremacist anxieties. Extending Dixon's proposition that the Klan emerged in response to the unleashing of the black "beast" by misguided Reconstruction policies, Wright shows how white men keep recreating the beast.

For the underlying reasons that this version of the "problem," the black male "beast," had to be constructed as a psychosexual criminal, we need to take up not only sexual anxieties but also economic realities. *Native Son* reveals that Wright understood what has become a central premise of the recent wave of "whiteness studies": that perceptions of race in the U.S. are intertwined with perceptions of social class. As Eric Lott puts it, "It was through 'blackness' that class was staged."[58] Lynchings, so often overtly sexual in their sadism, also betray profound economic anxieties. As Walter White noted in his 1929 study, *Rope and Faggot*, "The deeper one inquires into the subject, the more one must regard lynching as being of only minor importance in itself; it is as a symptom of a malodorous economic and social condition that it is chiefly significant."[59] In Bigger's case, as in the majority of historical lynchings, the actual crime whites sought to punish

---

56  Trudier Harris, *Exorcising Blackness: Historical and Literary Lynching and Burning Rituals* (Bloomington, Ind.: Indiana University Press, 1984), p. 12.
57  Joel Williamson, *The Crucible of Race: Black-White Relations in the American South Since Emancipation* (New York: Oxford University Press, 1984), p. 187.
58  Eric Lott, *Love and Theft: Blackface Minstrelsy and the American Working Class* (New York: Oxford University Press, 1993), p. 64.
59  Quoted in Marlene Park (1993) 'Lynching and Antilynching: Art and Politics in the 1930s', *Prospects*, 18: pp. 311–65.

was not usually rape, even though rape retained its status as the assumed reason because of its effectiveness in mobilizing angry whites. In a penetrating study of the South after Reconstruction, Edward L. Ayers analyzes the pattern of lynchings during its peak, the 1880s and 1890s, and finds the highest concentration in two regions that shared low rural population density, a fairly high proportion of blacks, and considerable migrancy among black and white populations. In such areas, whites could imagine themselves surrounded by what they considered " 'strange niggers,' " mobile and frequently unattached African-Americans who had neither local blacks nor whites to vouch for them.[60] Ayers's study provides an example of how much modern research has confirmed what Ida Wells-Barnett and other activists insisted: Lynchings, while cast as responses to black male bestiality, typically covered for white anxiety about black mobility (hence the "strange nigger" syndrome) and black successes (however modest). However important the sexual anxieties, white men feared economic rivalry from black men at least as much as they did sexual competition. It is far easier brutally to destroy a new and unwelcome economic competitor when you can cast him as a sexually pathological monster. Lynching, therefore, while rationalized by charges of rape, in fact reaffirms the social and economic place of all actors—male and female, black and white—in the hierarchy as dictated by white men.

In *Native Son* this racial hierarchy, enforced and protected by the color line, is so tangible as to achieve spatial form. As Bigger accurately remarks from prison, " 'They draw a line and say for you to stay on your side of the line. . . . And then they say things like that about you [that black men want to rape white women] and when you try to come from behind your line they kill you' " ['Fate', p. 381]. Whites create the fantasy of the black beast so they can read any attempt of an African-American to cross the color line symbolically as miscegenation. That is the reason that, immediately after killing Mary, Bigger feels "the reality of the room fell from him; the vast city of white people that sprawled outside took its place" ['Fear', p. 119]. As Mary's death makes clear, the supposition of black male bestiality does nothing to protect white women. What it protects is property – white male control of economic resources. [. . .]

[. . .]

In *Native Son* shame becomes, along with criminality, a defining feature of being black. In the much-discussed scene during Book Three in which whites and blacks crowd into his prison cell, Bigger internalizes the white view of blacks: "He felt that all of the white people . . . were measuring every inch of his weakness. He identified himself with his family and felt their naked shame under the eyes of white folks" ['Fate', p. 326]. When Mrs. Thomas throws herself at Mrs. Dalton's feet, begging mercy for her son, Bigger feels doubly exposed, "paralyzed with shame . . . violated" ['Fate', p. 331]. The language of "violation" again positions the black male as rape victim. As Max presses Bigger, trying to find out if he had intended to rape Mary, the accused man explains how much he had hated the white girl for her invasive questions. Suddenly he has what the narrator calls an "associative memory":

---

60  Edward L. Ayers, *The Promise of the New South: Life after Reconstruction* (New York: Oxford University Press, 1992), pp. 154–7.

He saw an image of his little sister, Vera, sitting on the edge of a chair crying because he had shamed her by "looking" at her . . . He shook his head, confused. "Aw, Mr. Max, she [Mary] wanted me to tell her how Negroes live. She got into the front seat of the car where I was. . . .

['Fate', p. 379]

Mary's questions, however well-intentioned, combined with her physical proximity made Bigger Thomas feel as exposed, as violated, as his little sister when he peeped under her dress. Thus in one of his most important revisions of the "beast" stereotype, Wright reveals that Bigger was emasculated by contact with Mary far more than he was aroused. While emphasizing the claustrophobia, lack of privacy, and enforced shame of Bigger and other blacks on one side of the color line, Wright anatomizes the sacrosanct white "home," which functions as a site of unparalleled value in Dixon's novels, on the other side of that line.

[. . .]

As historical myths obscure the past, so stereotypes are believed to be opposed to "real" human beings. And so when James Baldwin, like many others, criticized *Native Son*, it was because he found Bigger too much a stereotype. That is the reason that Baldwin perceived Wright as too close to Harriet Beecher Stowe: "The contemporary Negro novelist and the dead New England woman are locked together in a deadly, timeless battle," he charged.[61] I would suggest that *Native Son* shows white America locked into a deadly battle, rather, with a stereotype it had created, and that Wright's triumph lies in his anatomy of the reasons for Bigger's truncated humanity. Whites, particularly white males, *make* the black beast, and that beast makes for white solidarity. "How could the black race build a nation within a nation and keep the peace?" asks Dixon in his last novel.[62] *Native Son* raises the same question—but with an entirely different intent.

*Native Son*, which so closely follows the Dixonian logic while turning it inside out—logic that remains, sadly, a prominent and enduring strand in American culture—anatomizes this interlocking of whites and their "beasts." Bigger is made into a stereotype by economic exploitation and residential segregation practiced by the likes of Dalton well before that status is confirmed by the white media, legal system, and mob. Wright shows the real crime to be not any actions committed by the "beast" but the ideology that made the black man kill. Yes, Wright would agree with Dixon, the "position of the Negro in America" is an "impossible" one.[63] Showing Bigger Thomas made into the black beast, Wright depicts one of America's native products. As he once remarked, "There isn't any Negro problem; there is only a white problem."[64]

61  Baldwin, 'Everybody's Protest Novel', p. 22.
62  Dixon, *The Flaming Sword*, p. 90.
63  Dixon, *The Leopard's Spots*, p. 197.
64  Quoted in Keneth Kinnamon and Michel Fabre, *Conversations with Richard Wright*, Jackson, Miss.: University of Mississippi Press, 1993), p 99.

**James Smethurst,** 'Invented by Horror: The Gothic
and African-American Literary Ideology in *Native Son*'

Gothic literature – an imaginative form exemplified by the scientific apocalypse
of Mary Shelley's *Frankenstein* (1818), by the barbarism that surfaces in Horace
Walpole's *The Castle of Otranto* (1764) and by the sexual panics of Bram Stoker's
*Dracula* (1897) – exerts a powerful influence over African-American culture.
From Frederick Douglass's account of the horrifying punishments of slavery to
the white capitalist vampires of Ishmael Reed's *Mumbo Jumbo* (1972) – and
indeed, from the zombified crack addicts of Public Enemy's 'Night of the Living
Baseheads' (1988) to the S & M fantasies of the Wu-Tang Clan – Gothic tropes
saturate black culture high and low. Black Gothicism, however, remains critically
neglected. Perhaps because this literary style is associated with decadence and
Europe, or perhaps because African-American literature is often reduced to its
political element, the influence of someone such as Edgar Allen Poe – the white
writer of the antebellum (pre-Civil War) South, whose works stand as
the fullest expression of the American Gothic – is altogether overlooked. Yet
this influence is there, in black and white, in the work of Richard Wright
among others. Indeed, nearing the end of 'How "Bigger" was Born', seeking to
encapsulate the alienations and intimidations of technological America, Wright
states: '[I]f Poe were alive, he would not have to invent horror; horror would
invent him.' Wright could hardly be more explicit. Bigger, in his mind if not his
critics', is a Gothic creation.

In this essay, James Smethurst suggests that Bigger has not been seen as such
for two main reasons: because critics have categorized *Native Son* as a realist
novel – a work of black political protest – and because they have assumed that
this is a polemical, political genre too straightforward to accommodate the
emotional excesses and allegoric tendencies associated with Gothic fiction.
Smethurst seeks to correct this critical bias – this partiality that, effectively,
ignores Wright's own acknowledgement of his debt to Poe. His essay does this
by pointing out that *Native Son* is in fact crowded with 'Gothic' symbols – with

what he calls 'premonitions, curses, prophecies, spells, the subterranean, paintings, veils, trapdoors, demonic possession, graves, returns from the dead, skeletons, hauntings, ghosts, confinement, doubles, gothic mansions, visions, conspiracies, premature burial, and so on.' But the essay also raises key questions, asking: how do these Gothic elements function within *Native Son*? How do they relate to the blues and other elements that Wright inherits from the African-American folk culture of the rural South? How do they relate to the new mass media and technological cultures that dominate the urban North? In the course of providing answers to these questions, Smethurst opens further avenues of potential interpretation, raising fascinating parallels with all manner of cultural texts with which Wright was well acquainted: not only the short stories of Poe, but also *Frankenstein*, the American romances of Nathaniel Hawthorne, the prose of Karl Marx, and the horror films of the 1930s.

Students interested in this area will benefit greatly from exploring Smethurst's other writings. Smethurst looks much more closely at the influence of 1930s horror films on *Native Son* in a new essay, entitled 'You Reckon Folks Really Act Like That', which will appear in Susan Watkins and Jago Morrison's collection *Scandalous Fictions: The Twentieth-Century Novel in the Public Sphere* (forthcoming). Smethurst's other works are also relevant to the study of *Native Son*: students can gain much from *The New Red Negro: The Literary Left and African-American Poetry, 1930–1946* (1999) and *The Black Arts Movement: Literary Nationalism in the 1960s and 1970s* (2005); and from the co-edited volumes *Left of the Color Line: Race, Radicalism and Twentieth-Century Literature of the United States* (2003, with Bill V. Mullen) and *Radicalism in the South since Reconstruction* (forthcoming, with Chris Green and Rachel Lee Rubin). James Smethurst teaches in the W. E. B. Du Bois Department of Afro-American Studies at the University of Massachusetts-Amherst. This article originally appeared in the spring 2001 edition of the *African-American Review*, and is here reprinted with kind permission of its publishers. Again, footnotes are Smethurst's own, except for those in the text itself that refer to the Vintage edition of *Native Son*.

## James Smethurst (2001) 'Invented by Horror: The Gothic and African-American Literary Ideology in *Native Son*', African-American Review 35 (1, spring): pp. 29–40

Richard Wright's *Native Son* is still usually taken as one of the foremost examples of late American naturalism, and much is made of the impact of modern sociology, particularly what became known as the Chicago School of Sociology, on the conception and shape of the novel. Yet numerous scholars, at least in passing, have remarked on the influence of the gothic tradition on Wright's novel, arguing to one degree or another whether his usage of the gothic undermines or supports the sociological "realism" of the work.[1] However, the crucial

---

1   Scholars have connected gothic literature in the United States to slavery and the subsequent ideologies and practices that descended from slavery since, at least, Leslie Fielder's 1960 book *Love and Death in the American Novel* (though Fielder's work is almost entirely concerned with white writers, other than a brief mention of Ralph Ellison at the expense of Wright).

importance of gothic literature and what might be thought of as the gothic sensibility to the representation of political consciousness and political development (and the relation of the gothic to contemporary mass culture) in *Native Son* has not received much sustained scholarly attention. The primary question here is not whether *Native Son* is a gothic novel, but how the gothic functions within the novel and how it relates to the African-American folk culture of the South as well as the mass culture associated with the urban North. In fact, *Native Son* is not a gothic novel, but an anti-gothic in which the gothic figures an American consciousness, particularly the consciousness of black Americans, which is the product of the particular social relations of American capitalism and hence something to be transcended. Wright's use of the gothic is also implicitly a critique of the African-American writers who preceded him, and their handling of the actual and symbolic journeys from and to the African-American folk and constructions of the folk inheritance. Wright's use of the gothic is not in conflict with his ideological stance as a black male Communist writer of the mid-twentieth century, but in fact follows from this stance.

As Teresa Goddu points out, it is not hard to see why black writers (and such white writers as Herman Melville and Theodore Weld) in the nineteenth century, particularly during the antebellum era, would find such works attractive literary models for the representation of slavery and American race relations.[2] Generally speaking, classic European gothics, such as Walpole's *Castle of Otranto* or Radcliffe's *Mysteries of Udolpho*—not to mention such later American gothic-influenced texts as Hawthorne's *The House of the Seven Gables* and the short fiction of Poe—contain a past event involving an unrightful and violent usurpation which constrains the actions of succeeding generations. This familial original sin is often passed down through the bloodlines of both the sinners and the sinned against. There is a strange doubling in which the two families strangely come to resemble each other. One also sees in the classic gothic novel patriarchal tyranny, transgressive sexuality which generally accompanies relations of power, and an instability of markers of social identity, such as family, class, race, gender, and nationality.

Slavery also involved a moment of usurpation in which the birthright of the enslaved individual was stolen. As in the gothic, the results of this usurpation are transmitted through the bloodlines of the enslaved. One finds in the novels and fugitive slave narratives by such nineteenth-century black writers as William Wells Brown, Frederick Douglass, Frances Harper, and Harriet Jacobs a patriarchal tyranny and a concomitant transgressive sexuality in which the slave master coerces or attempts to coerce female slaves into unwanted sexual relations. One also often sees a flight from tyranny on the part of the female slaves which resembles that of the typical gothic heroine from the typical gothic villain. There is a foregrounding of the instability of the normative markers of social identity such as those of nationality, family, class, citizenship, and so on, insofar as such markers exist, at the sufferance of the slave master. Finally, there is within many

---

2    Teresa A. Goddu, *Gothic America: Narrative, History, and Nation* (New York: Columbia University Press, 1997), pp. 133–40.

of these texts a strange doubling of the slave and the enslaver. Perhaps the most ubiquitous figure of nineteenth-century black literature is that of the "mulatto," a person of equal African and European ancestry. This "mulatto" is almost always the offspring of the female slave and the slave master and, though legally a slave, stands as a sort of double of the slave owner's white offspring. In fact, this figure, often female, is typically paired explicitly with the slave owner's wife and/or the slave owner's white daughter.

The point here is not to claim that the gothic is the most important single influence on African-American literature or to attempt to show every shared concern and trope, but simply to suggest that the gothic, along with other genres such as the spiritual autobiography, the captivity narrative, and the sentimental novel, was extremely important in the development of a rhetoric that allowed black authors who preceded Wright to reach an essentially white audience while figuring their particular social and aesthetic concerns. This use of a gothic rhetoric and a gothic sensibility obviously did not end with slavery. For example, much of the terminology of W. E. B. Du Bois could be said to be gothic, particularly his use of the term *veil* as that which hides the black world from the white world and vice versa—or perhaps more accurately that by which the white ruling class of America conceals the black subject as human, much like a concealed skeleton in a classic gothic novel. Similarly, Du Bois's notion of "double-consciousness," which was largely drawn from the work of William James, proposes a version of Spencer Brydon's split consciousness in Henry James's gothic-influenced short story "The Jolly Corner" as a more or less permanent condition for African-Americans. Some prominent uses of the gothic in African American fiction of the early twentieth century would include Jean Toomer's *Cane* (particularly in the concluding "Kabnis" section which opens with the wind whispering ominously to Ralph Kabnis) and, to a lesser extent, Nella Larsen's *Quicksand* (especially in the section set in Chicago when Helga Crane confronts her "white" family).

As strange as it seems, the Marxism with which Wright became engaged in the 1930s also drew on the gothic tradition—though, as with Wright, this tradition was invoked in order to critique and transcend it. This Marxism was the "Marxist-Leninist" version propounded by the Communist Party of the United States (CPUSA) and the Communist International, or as some might say, a Stalinist model. This is not to demonize Wright's ideology, but only to remind us that Wright's Marxism is quite different from that of his contemporary and friend C. L. R. James, a black Trotskyist, or from that of the various neo-Marxists of contemporary literary studies, and is based on the particular practices of certain political organizations of that time. The Communist International and the CPUSA made an argument, more or less unique among radicals of the 1930s and 1940s (and their immediate socialist and anarchist predecessors), that the struggle for Negro Liberation was at the heart of the possibility for the revolutionary transformation of the United States.

A crucial text for the Communists of the 1930s was Marx's *The Eighteenth Brumaire of Louis Bonaparte*. *The Eighteenth Brumaire* was considered a key text because it was taken to most clearly and concretely apply to actual historical events the methods of "dialectical materialism," the Marxist "science" which was supposed to allow the scientist to analyze historical events and determine the general historical laws underlying those events. In that book Marx wrote:

> Men make their own history, but they do not make it under circumstances chosen by themselves, but under circumstances directly encountered, given and transmitted from the past. The tradition of all the dead generations weighs like a nightmare on the brain of the living. And just when they seem engaged in revolutionizing themselves and things, in creating something that has never yet existed, precisely in such periods of revolutionary crisis they anxiously conjure up the spirits of the past to their service.[3]

Marx here of course is referring to the tendency of all politicians, and not just revolutionaries, to invoke the past to justify their present political positions. As Marx says, such claims to the past are usually more than a little ludicrous and never adequate to the needs of the present moment. Marx goes on to write later in the *Eighteenth Brumaire* that "the social revolution of the nineteenth century cannot draw its poetry from the past but only from the future. It cannot begin with itself before it has stripped off all superstition in regard to the past."[4]

While one can debate the truth of Marx's words, particularly the second quote, which sounds like a cross between Ralph Waldo Emerson and a French surrealist manifesto, the problem of the revolutionary in the first quote is remarkably similar to that of a character in a gothic novel in which "the dead generations" also "weigh like a nightmare on the brain of the living." And the solution proposed in the second quote, the stripping off of all superstition in regard to the past, can also be seen as a solution to the problems of the gothic character. Without such a solution, both gothic characters and social revolutionaries are doomed to replay the dramas of the past over and over without any fully satisfactory resolution. This solution is fundamentally one of consciousness in which the subject refuses to obsessively, and one might say gothicly, interpret the present through a narrative of the past—a narrative which distorts both past and present, and instead constructs a new and forward-looking narrative.

For the Marxist Wright, the gothic represents the old consciousness of capitalism, particularly of capitalism in the crisis of the Great Depression, which is retailed to the masses through mass culture. Like most gothic texts, *Native Son* is obsessively intertextual. One sees allusions to and revisions of the works of Dostoevsky, Stowe, Flaubert, Zola, Poe, James, Hawthorne, Dreiser, and, despite Wright's disclaimers about the value of earlier black writers, such writers of fugitive slave narratives as Douglass, to name a few. Though many of these works are not thought of as gothic per se, virtually all of them draw on the gothic, especially those of Poe, James, and Hawthorne. For instance, a number of critics have noted the obvious invocation and revision of Poe's "The Black Cat" in Bigger's supervision by the Daltons' white cat as he tries to dispose of the body of Mary Dalton.[5] Many of the invoked texts, particularly those of James,

3   Karl Marx, *The Eighteenth Brumaire of Louis Bonaparte* (New York: International, 1963), p. 15.
4   Marx, *The Eighteenth Brumaire*, p. 18.
5   For the most extended treatment of Poe's considerable influence on Wright, see Fabre, *The Unfinished Quest of Richard Wright*, pp. 27–33.

Hawthorne, Flaubert, and Poe, connect the gothic to the popular and, as in *Native Son*, regard the beginnings of mass culture with considerable ambivalence, if not hostility.

While Poe, with some justification, is most frequently cited as the primary model for the gothic moments of *Native Son*, Hawthorne is even more important in terms of the larger design of *Native Son*, since the gothic in *The House of the Seven Gables* and *The Scarlet Letter* represents a certain social consciousness or mode of social relations which is ultimately transcended, allowing a reintegration of what had previously been intractably conflicting elements. Despite Wright's obvious differences with the essentially conservative politics of Hawthorne, that underlying Hawthorne's gothic conflicts was a sectional antagonism left over from chattel slavery based on race that threatened to tear the nation apart no doubt contributed to his attractiveness as a literary model for Wright.

Beyond such "high" literary ancestors for *Native Son* as the works of Poe, Hawthorne, and James, mass culture is also a crucial conduit for the gothic in Wright's novel. After all, most Americans were familiar with gothic conventions and sensibilities through mass culture at the time Wright wrote *Native Son*. Though British, Daphne Du Maurier's *Rebecca* (1938) established the model for the modern American popular gothic romance sold in drug stores and the emerging institution of the supermarket. Perhaps more importantly for Wright, the 1930s saw the blossoming of the American horror film, often based on such classic gothic works as Bram Stoker's *Dracula*, Mary Shelley's *Frankenstein*, and Poe's "The Black Cat" and "Murders in the Rue Morgue"—though the movies allegedly based on the Poe stories retained little of the originals beyond the titles.

In fact, while *Native Son* is most often connected to melodrama, the first two sections of the book resemble a typical horror movie of the 1930s. The 1931 film version of *Frankenstein*, which underwent a major revival in a double-bill with *Dracula* (also first released in 1931) as Wright was working on his novel in 1938, is a particularly important subtext. The thousands of police officers with flashlights and searchlights who pursue Bigger through an urban gothic landscape of abandoned tenements on the South Side at the end of the second section of *Native Son* closely resemble the villagers with torches who chase Frankenstein's monster through an expressionist landscape. The final fight scene at an old windmill between Frankenstein and the cornered monster also resembles the battle between Bigger and the policeman he knocks unconscious. During the last struggle in the film one of the villagers looks up and, seeing the monster with Frankenstein on the windmill, shouts, "There he is, the murderer." Particularly significant for Wright's novel is this moment where the line between the monster and the man who created him is blurred. Bigger, then, is a monster created by a murderous society, initially marked not by an "unnatural" origin so much as by his physical appearance.

Wright's novel is also filled with allusions to what might be called the topoi or landmarks of the gothic: premonitions, curses, prophecies, spells, the subterranean, paintings, veils, trapdoors, demonic possession, graves, returns from the dead, skeletons, hauntings, ghosts, confinement, doubles, gothic mansions, visions, conspiracies, premature burial, and so on. Yet despite this use of the terminology of the supernatural and the uncanny, there is nothing supernatural in

*Native Son*.[6] What these terms represent is both an instinctual understanding of the results of the capitalist system in the United States and a mystification of the laws of that system. For example, Mrs. Thomas foretells her son's future:

> "Well, I'm telling you agin! And mark my word, some of these days you going to set down and *cry*. Some of these days you going to wish you had made something out of yourself, instead of just a tramp. But it will be too late then."
> "Stop prophesying about me," he said.

['Fear', p. 39]

Mrs. Thomas's prophecy turns out to be correct in the extreme—just as Bigger's own premonitions about his tragic ending come true. However, there is nothing magical in these predictions; rather, they are realistic, if instinctual, assessments of what the results of straining against the limits of life set for someone like Bigger will be. However, because these predictions are expressed in supernatural terms, they offer no understanding of why these limits are set or, once understood, how these limits might be changed. It is worth noting that this incomprehension is not limited to the black characters of the novel. Mrs. Dalton is described as a "blind" and ineffectual, though well-meaning, "ghost" because she is a sort of ghost of good intentions, unable to understand the real causes of poverty and degradation in the ghetto and unwilling to undertake the sort of actions to change society fundamentally so that such conditions are no longer possible.

The gothic also mystifies the social system in other ways, most notably through a type of transference. Thus we see a sort of doubling in which an African-American character, generally Bigger, becomes a double or stand-in for a white character, allowing the black character unconsciously to reenact and control a formerly uncontrollable situation. For example, Bigger, psychologically unable to rob the white storekeeper Blum, recasts his fellow gang member Gus as Blum and beats up, and symbolically rapes, Gus. Likewise, Bessie becomes a double of Mary Dalton in that her rape by Bigger is actual and her murder intentional, whereas the rape of Mary was a half-formed desire and her murder accidental. Other moments of black-white doubling include the pairing of Bigger's brother Buddy with the young white Communist Jan Erlone, Mrs. Thomas with the Daltons' [*sic*] Irish servant Peggy, and in a very telling scene the doubling lifestyles of the rich and famous in the film *The Gay Woman* with a stereotypically savage Africa in *Trader Horn*, which Jack and Bigger watch in a double feature. And, of course, there is the opening moment of terrifying and uncanny doubling in which Bigger kills a version of himself: a monstrous black rat filled with rage and fear.

A similar sort of doubling also takes place in which Bigger posits two Biggers—one who is in control of himself and one who is controlled by gothic terror: "There were two Biggers: one was determined to get rest and sleep at any cost;

---

6    This ultimate appearance of a 'rational' explanation for an apparently supernatural phenomenon is often true of the classic gothic romance, also. However, in the classic gothic, both European and American, the supernatural or 'unnatural' often remains a possibility even when a 'rational' explanation is offered – as in James's 'Turn of the Screw', for example. However, in Wright's novel the supernatural is rigorously exposed and rejected even as the language of the supernatural is employed.

and the other shrank from images charged with terror" ['Flight', p. 174]. In much the same way Bigger also sees two bizarrely dissociated Bessies—a corporeal Bessie entirely under his control and a consciousness who contests that control and demands things of him: "As he walked beside her he felt that there were two Bessies: one a body that he had just had and wanted badly again; and the other was in Bessie's face; it asked questions; it bargained and sold the other to best advantage" ['Flight', p. 170].

Both of these doublings—the pairing of black and white and the bifurcation of the individual—are aspects of a sort of gothic vision by which Bigger attempts to interpret and control his environment. Or at least these doublings allow Bigger to control himself enough to be able to act in some manner which validates him as a person—at least in his own view—within that environment. Needless to say, this vision is severely distorted, not to say psychotic.

Though this doubling or identification between apparently disparate people and things allows Bigger at least an imagined control of his situation, there is another side to this projection. This side is the further mystification of the social system when uncontrollable or inescapable elements of that system are projected onto various objects. There is a constant reference to the whiteness of things that Bigger sees: walls, smoke, clouds, snow, cigarettes, hair, and so on. This white hems Bigger in just as violence, real estate covenants, gentlemen's agreements, and so on hem in Chicago's African-Americans behind the veil of the South Side "Black Belt."

Perhaps the most notable example of this projection is onto the Dalton's [*sic*] white cat, an obvious intertextual allusion to Poe's "The Black Cat," in which the Dalton's [*sic*] cat embodies the white supervision of the black subject. This sense of being watched might be displaced onto a weird object by Bigger, but it could hardly be called paranoid since the reader gets to see the whole machinery of supervision—the police, the press, the State's Attorney, the detective, and various other witnesses and experts as well as the self-supervision which has been ideologically induced largely by mass culture in Bigger—in some detail. (In this regard, the projection of white supervision onto the cat is the flip side, so to speak, of the projection of a certain black self-policing onto the black rat from the novel's opening.) But to say that Bigger's vision, or narrative if you will, is not paranoid does not mean that this projection, though emotionally or psycho-logically powerful, helps him understand how the system works. Quite the contrary, it makes such an understanding impossible. In short, while the virtual blizzard of whiteness is a powerful metaphor for a system of supervision and control and its effect on the black subject, what is required is the examination and understanding of that system through some scientific method, say dialectical materialism, not simply a representation of that system.

Again, it should be noted that such mystification and misunderstanding are not restricted to Bigger. They are characteristic of virtually everyone the reader encounters in *Native Son*. Once again Wright utilizes a central gothic convention, a terror of incomprehension. This is the terror that the world one inhabits is guided by rules other than those one is able to see, or that within one's world or very close to it are contained secrets—deeds, other selves, sisters, explanations—of crucial importance to us if only one could find them.

In *Native Son*, particularly in the first two sections, nearly all the major characters look for a certain meaning in the other characters which they are sure is there, but which they are unable to understand or which they misconstrue. Bigger is constantly saying that he is unable to make out what various white characters, particularly the Daltons and Jan Erlone, are talking about. Mary Dalton says that she wants to *know* black people and that she knows so little despite the fact that her family's house in Hyde Park is an easy walk from the South Side black community. In this regard, perhaps the most painful moment of an extremely gruesome book for the reader is not either the grisly murder of Bessie or that of Mary, but when Mary sings "Swing Low, Sweet Chariot" to what Bigger recognizes as the wrong tune. Jan Erlone's demand that Bigger take Jan and Mary to an "authentic" black restaurant on the South Side rates a close second. For that matter, the mystery of the Daltons is not solved when the skeleton in their basement is revealed, leading eventually to Bigger Thomas, because it is clear that they will never understand the secret behind the veil of the black belt where people live in houses the Daltons own. Thus, like the gothic dance of the Maules and the Pyncheons in *The House of the Seven Gables* before they give up their twin obsessions of property and revenge, *Native Son* intimates that the Daltons of the world will continue to encounter the Biggers. And neither will be able to understand the other because the rules which guide their world are hidden in a web of gothic figuration. In fact, that both the Biggers and the Daltons perceive each of their worlds as largely disjunct from that of the other is actually another form of mystification which will hinder them from objectively apprehending the nature of their social order.

The fundamental reason that none of the characters that we see in the first two sections of the novel understands the underlying rules of society is that they are caught up in various narratives the function of which is to perpetuate the power relations of American society and, again, to mystify the true nature of those relations. Some of these narratives are basically ghosts of a past era of American society. These narratives are not simply accounts of the past which make sense of the present and offer a guide to conduct—this is implicitly or explicitly true of all the narratives in the text—but are holdovers from the past. This category of ghosts would include both Mrs. Thomas's stoic and accommodationist Christianity, which has its ultimate origin in the slave South, as well as the older Daltons' paternalistic narrative of philanthropy. Both of these older narratives no longer have the desired impact on a new generation of uprooted and marginalized young people represented by Bigger and his gang: They have no desire to defer desire until the next world or go to night school in order to become better educated servants. Of course, the Daltons have an interest in not demystifying these narratives despite the death of their daughter.

Wright sees virtually all black literature before *Native Son* as essentially part of these mirroring narratives of stoic deference and paternalism. It is also interesting, though disturbing, to see how Wright, like Claude McKay in the novels *Home to Harlem* (1928) and *Banjo* (1929), assigns gender to these narratives so that the conservatism of the black folk culture and its accommodation to white paternalism are seen as feminine, as opposed to an implicit masculine narrative of rebellion and liberation. Even in the case of the equally uprooted and marginalized Bessie, her response to her confinement in the face of extravagant mass culture narratives of desire is basically passive, whereas Bigger's is active. It is also notable that Bigger's greatest sense of validation comes from acts of extreme misogyny which are not fully repudiated by the novel.

Bigger and his gang are alienated from the folk culture that his mother represents, from the black politicians of the South Side who hold their positions through accommodation with the white power structure, and from the white power structure itself, whether in its more blatantly corrupt and hostile form, as represented by State's Attorney Buckley, or in the more apparently benign and unconscious form represented by the Daltons. Bigger and his peers are caught in narratives of mass culture and the hungers and fears inculcated by those narratives which glamorize the lifestyles of the rich and famous while demonizing the poor, particularly African-Americans, and the politically radical, especially the Communists. For example, the first of the two movies that Bigger and Jack see, *The Gay Woman*, titillates them with the possibility of a chaotic modern world of unlimited gratification, represented as threatening in the figure of a Communist assassin, which ultimately is repelled with a return to a mythic past of "family values." The second movie, *Trader Horn*, is an equally eroticized narrative of a mythic Africa in which Africans, and by extension African-Americans, are shown to be "savage" and therefore terrifying as well as "natural" and therefore desirable. In both cases, what is seen is ultimately a justification of the present social order through narratives of the past which are literally projections of the present. The problem for society is that the desire that these mass culture products incite to attract consumers is not so easily sated or repressed.

Practically all Bigger's knowledge of the world, particularly outside the ghetto, and of how to conduct oneself in that world whether as a lover or as the writer of a ransom note, comes from mass culture—tabloids, newsreels, movies, detective stories, and so on. Like Emma Bovary, and in a less tragic manner Catherine Morland in Jane Austen's *Northanger Abbey*, Bigger is the victim of these mass culture narratives. As models of how to act, they cannot help but lead him to disaster.

And as models of normative desire, desire that he can never satisfy, they are equally disastrous. Of course, African-Americans are not the only ones caught in such narratives. The posse of the 8,000 racist white police and the racist mob screaming for Bigger's blood outside the courthouse in the third section are clearly inflamed by a narrative of black bestiality retailed by the popular press. Ironically, this mob is comprised largely of people who might be categorized as white Biggers, other uprooted and marginalized people whom—along with marginalized blacks such as Bigger—Wright sees as the potential basis for a mass fascist movement in America.

One could argue that what makes Bigger's existence truly gothic is the wild terror and the extravagant desire that are produced when these narratives of mass culture act on an individual for whom the normative markers of identity—markers of class, race, gender, sexuality—have broken down and who is confined within the rigid and narrow limits of the ghetto. It is this intersection of fear, desire, and confinement that produces the doubling, the projection, the transference, the transgressive sexuality—which includes rape—both real and imagined, followed by murder, real and imagined miscegenation, symbolic homosexual coupling and the possibility of incest, the anxiety about who one is and how one should act, the apprehension and misapprehension of possible meanings, and the sense of an inescapable past which is also the future so common to the gothic genre.

Perhaps the most telling moment of *Native Son* is the book's opening. First, an alarm clock goes off. The alarm clock ostensibly is a reminder of linear time. But in fact the alarm clock is a symbol of cyclical time marking the beginning of a day, a journey that will be almost exactly like yesterday and tomorrow. Immediately after the bell goes off, we are introduced to themes of confinement and transgressive sexuality. This transgressive sexuality is present explicitly in the shame that Bigger and his family feel about having to dress and undress in such close quarters. It is also present implicitly in the difference in skin color between the "black" Buddy and Bigger and the "brown-skinned" Vera, reminding the reader that repressed behind the hysterical fear of "miscegenation" between black men and white women is a massive number of often coercive sexual couplings between white slave masters and black slave women. Then a black rat appears, both terrified and terrifying. In the first moment of doubling in the text, Bigger kills his rat double, who attacks Bigger in a fit of terror, hunger, and defiance. Bigger goes on to terrify his sister with the dead rat, enjoying her fear. Bigger's mother prophesies a tragic end for him. End of story. But not really. There will be more rats. The slum buildings of the ghetto produce an endless stream of hungry and fearful rats. Bigger and his mother foresee Bigger's ending even if they don't grasp why such an ending is inevitable. But there will be more Biggers. (This is made even clearer in Wright's essay "How 'Bigger' Was Born", appended to the novel by Harper and Brothers in 1942, in which Wright describes five different Biggers who represent many other Biggers he knew.) There will also be more Bessies, more Mary Daltons, more Mr. and Mrs. Daltons, more State's Attorney Buckleys, and so on. In essence the past is destiny. Again, what we see is some notion of a cyclical journey in which no destination is really reached, a migration which brings no real material or spiritual improvement.

*Native Son*, then, would seem to be a gothic text in which history is destined to repeat itself as both tragedy and farce. In fact, if the book ended with Bigger's capture and the signing of the confession the State's Attorney gives him, then it would be a sort of gothic. Why is it an anti-gothic? Bigger, primarily through his interaction with the Communist lawyer Boris Max and the particular Marxist-Leninist ideology that Max embodies, attains a genuine self-consciousness or at least recognizes his ability to attain some sort of true self-consciousness, even if his execution will cut the process short. [. . .] This willingness to act on his stated ideals, as well as to expound them directly and clearly, are at least as important in distinguishing Max from the other white speakers who either disassociate their acts from their ideals (as in the case of the slumlord Mr. Dalton) or conceal the real significance of their acts with appeals to allegedly commonly held ideals (as does the corrupt State's Attorney Buckley, who invokes God and civilization in his opening statement at Bigger's trial).

Bigger begins to understand the motivations for his actions and the social laws which have shaped his actions, or at least he sees that such an understanding may be possible. The way Wright represents the process is not as a simple linear progression—and how far the process has moved by the end is ambiguous. Rather it is a process that moves in fits and starts. Neither is it a process by which the Communist Party simply gives Bigger the truth: The white Communists Boris

Max and Jan Erlone learn at least as much from Bigger as Bigger learns from them. In fact, Bigger's vision of himself at the end may well be clearer than Max's own self-knowledge. Ultimately, Bigger rejects the various narratives which have shaped his life and his self-perception and takes responsibility for his actions. He no longer feels terror, even about his impending execution. In essence, he takes control of his own narrative, basing it on himself rather than trying to conform himself to the various narratives of mass culture.

This of course is still a moment of tragedy. Bigger is still going to die. And what he has accepted about himself is his identity as a murderer. [. . . As his concluding speech indicates,] Bigger has a clearer sense of why he killed, but this does not comfort us (or Boris Max) very much. Nonetheless, we can see in the last section of the book the possibility of an escape from the gothic consciousness or gothic vision that characterizes the first two sections of the book. Wright posits the possibility of a more fully developed consciousness as to self and society on the part of the marginalized black subject. He raises the possibility of an alliance of the oppressed across racial lines. Moreover, the author proposes the possibility of the black subject's control of his or her own voice, of producing his or her own narrative which draws not, as Marx puts it, "on the poetry of the past," but the poetry of the future. In this respect, it is important to remember the congruence of the trajectory of much of Wright's early life with that of Bigger Thomas's. Wright was also a product of the migration of African-Americans to the urban North – though we are also reminded of the disjunctures between the fictional character and the figure of the author in "How 'Bigger' Was Born," since the author lived to tell the tale and since the author claims that he was even more a prisoner of fear than Bigger Thomas. We are shown that such a narrative control is possible because we are holding the product in our hands. It is worth noting here that, despite the dismissal of earlier black literature in both Wright's introduction and in the court speech he has Boris Max give, this emphasis on the importance of control of voice by the black speaking and writing subject has been, as many scholars have shown, a hallmark of African American literature since the eighteenth century.

The gothic then is crucial to Wright's project because it is the perfect literary analogue to what Wright sees as the ideology and psychology guiding the relations between black and white Americans under what he viewed as late capitalism. The highly developed gothic rhetoric of extreme social anxiety or terror on the part of the individual subject with respect to social identity as well as the repression of that anxiety by the subject with the concomitant return of the repressed as the uncanny allowed Wright graphically to represent the pathology of American racism. Yet as in the Communist critique of Freudianism which gothic literature prefigured and influenced, it is in part rejected because of its focus on individual terror rather than broader social forces—a limitation that remains even when the gothic is used to figure social conflict and anxieties. Also, because of the relation of black literature to the gothic genre, the representation of the gothic and its limitations can be seen as a critique of black expressive culture, particularly literature, and a statement of the need for a new type of African-American literature of which Native Son was to be the forerunner. As Wright concluded the essay "How 'Bigger' Was Born" (sounding much like Jean Toomer and Claude McKay): "We have only a money-grubbing industrial civilization. But we do have in the Negro the embodiment of a past tragic enough to appease the spiritual hunger of even a James; and we have in the oppression of the Negro a shadow athwart our national life dense and heavy enough to satisfy even the gloomy broodings of a Hawthorne. And if Poe were alive, he would not have to invent horror; horror would invent him."[7] The problem for Wright, however, was not simply to represent the world, but to change it.

7   Wright, 'How "Bigger" was Born', p. 31.

# 4

# Further reading and Web resources

## Further reading

Footnotes used throughout this book can be effectively used as an extensive guide to the leading scholarship on Richard Wright and *Native Son*. Below, following the structure of the Texts and contexts and Critical history sections of this book, I make particular recommendations, identifying between two and four texts that should prove most useful to given areas of research.

## Richard Wright: a brief biography

Bone, Robert (1986) 'Richard Wright and the Chicago Renaissance', *Callaloo 9* (3): pp. 446–68.

Michel Fabre, *The Unfinished Quest of Richard Wright* (Urbana, Ill.: University of Illinois Press, 1993), trans. Isabel Barzun.

Hazel Rowley, *Richard Wright: The Life and Times* (New York: Henry Holt, 2001).

Keneth Kinnamon and Michel Fabre (eds) *Conversations with Richard Wright* (Jackson, Miss.: University of Mississippi Press, 1993).

## The voices of *Native Son*

Henry Louis Gates, Jr., 'Introduction: Talking Books' in Henry Louis Gates, Jr., and Nellie Y. McKay (eds) *The Norton Anthology of African-American Literature* (New York and London: Norton, 2004), pp. xxxvii–xlvii.

Henry Louis Gates, Jr., *The Signifying Monkey: A Theory of African-American Literary Criticism* (New York and Oxford: Oxford University Press, 1988).

Dale E. Peterson, 'Response and Call: The African-American Dialogue with Bakhtin and What It Signifies' in Amy Mandelker (ed.) *Bakhtin in Contexts: Across the Disciplines* (Evanston, Ill.: Northwestern University Press, 1995), pp. 89–98.

Richard Wright, *Twelve Million Black Voices* (New York: Thunder's Mouth, 1995).

Henry Louis Gates, Jr. and Kwame Anthony Appiah (eds) *Richard Wright: Critical Perspectives Past and Present* (New York: Amistad, 1993).

## The Dostoevskian voice

Michel Fabre (1997) 'Richard Wright's Critical Reception in France: Censors Right and Left, Négritude Intellectuals, the Literary Set, and the General Public', *Mississippi Quarterly: The Journal of Southern Cultures*, 50 (2): pp. 307–25.

Michael Lynch, *Creative Revolt: A Study of Wright, Ellison and Dostoevsky* (New York: Peter Lang, 1990).

Dale E. Peterson (1994) 'Richard Wright's Long Journey from Gorky to Dostoevsky', *African-American Review*, 28 (3): pp. 375–87.

## The transplantation of the blues

Houston A. Baker, *Blues, Ideology and Afro-American Literature: A Vernacular Theory* (Chicago, Ill. and London: University of Chicago Press, 1984).

Angela Y. Davis, *Blues Legacies and Black Feminism: Gertrude 'Ma' Rainey, Bessie Smith, and Billie Holiday* (New York: Vintage, 1999).

Leon F. Litwack, *Trouble in Mind: Black Southerners in the Age of Jim Crow* (New York: Vintage, 1999).

Richard Wright, 'Foreword' in *Blues Fell this Morning: Meaning in the Blues* (Cambridge: Cambridge University Press, 1990).

## Bigger's vernacular voice

'African-American Vernacular English' in *The Concise Oxford Companion to the English Language*, ed. Tom McArthur (Oxford: Oxford University Press, 1998). Available online at <http://www.oxfordreference.com/views/ENTRY.html?subview=Main&entry=t29.e36>. Accessed 3 September 2004.

John Baugh, *Beyond Ebonics: Linguistic Pride and Racial Prejudice* (Oxford: Oxford University Press, 2002).

Geneva Smitherman (1971) 'Black Idiom', *Negro American Literature Forum*, 5 (3): 88–91, 115–17.

Richard Wright, 'Blueprint for Negro Writing' in Henry Louis Gates Jr. and Nellie Y. McKay (eds) *The Norton Anthology of African-American Literature* (New York and London: Norton, 1997), pp. 1380–8. This essay can be found in several other collections of Richard Wright's writing and of African-American literary criticism.

## Social determinism: an anti-American accent?

Horace R. Cayton and St Clair Drake, *Black Metropolis* (London: Jonathan Cape, 1946).

Richard Wright, 'How "Bigger" was Born' in *Native Son* (London: Vintage,

2000), pp. 1–31. This seminal essay also features in many other anthologies or collections about African-American literature or Richard Wright.

## Bigger: silenced by whiteness?

Richard Dyer, *White* (London and New York: Routledge, 1997).
Ralph Ellison, 'Twentieth-Century Fiction and the Black Mask of Humanity', in *Shadow and Act* (London: Secker & Warburg, 1967), pp. 24–44.
Toni Morrison, *Playing in the Dark: Whiteness and the Literary Imagination* (New York: Vintage, 1992).
Richard Wright, *The Color Curtain: A Report on the Bandung Conference* (Jackson, Miss.: Banner Books, 1994).

## First responses: James Baldwin, Ralph Ellison

James Baldwin, *Notes of a Native Son* (London: Penguin, 1995).
James Baldwin, *Nobody Knows My Name: More Notes of a Native Son* (New York: Dell, 1961).
Ralph Ellison, 'Remembering Richard Wright' in *Going to the Territory* (New York: Vintage, 1995), pp. 198–216.

## Feminist readings

Angela Y. Davis, 'Rape, Racism and the Myth of the Black Rapist' in *Women, Race and Class* (London: The Women's Press, 1982), pp. 172–201.
Miriam DeCosta-Willis (1986) 'Avenging Angels and Mute Mothers: Black Southern Women in Wright's Fictional World', *Callaloo*, 28: pp. 540–51.
Barbara Johnson's more nuanced and literary minded response, 'The Re(a)d and the Black: Richard Wright's Blueprint' is collected in *Richard Wright: Critical Perspectives Past and Present* (New York: Amistad 1993), eds. Henry Louis Gates, Jr. and Kwame Anthony Appiah, pp. 149–56.
Sylvia H. Keady (1976) 'Richard Wright's Women Characters and Inequality', *Black American Literature Forum*, 10 (4): pp. 124–8.
Claudia Tate, *Psychoanalysis and Black Novels: Desire and the Protocols of Race* (New York and Oxford: Oxford University Press, 1998).

## The black Atlantic and beyond

Paul Gilroy, *Black Atlantic: Modernity and Double Consciousness* (London and New York: Verso, 1993).
Paul Gilroy, *Between Camps: Nations, Cultures and the Allure of Race* (Harmondsworth: Penguin, 2001).
Ezekiel Mphahlele, *The African Image* (London: Faber & Faber, 1974).

Caryl Phillips, '*Native Son* by Richard Wright' in *A New World Order: Selected Essays* (London: Vintage, 2002), pp. 18–27. A reprint of this article can also be found at the start of the 2000 Vintage edition of the novel.

# Web Resources

There is a happy medium, a balance to be struck, between those 'desk-bound' bibliographies that feature nothing but URLs and those dusty professors whose response to such work is to embargo the Internet altogether. Books are alive and well, and remain by far our best literary medium, but the Internet features some brilliant resources for the study of Richard Wright and the African-American novel in general. Some of these depend upon the franchises individual institutions hold, but those who can access any of the leading online catalogues of academic journals (Ingenta, JSTOR, Literature Online) that offer particularly relevant titles for the study of *Native Son* should do so. Journals and periodicals available via these sites, such as *American Quarterly*, *African-American Review*, *Callaloo* and *Mississippi Quarterly*, are constantly publishing refereed scholarship in the field, and you can of course search them with targeted keyword searches quickly, easily and effectively. More general web sites are listed below in alphabetical order.

## American Memory at the Library of Congress

<http://memory.loc.gov/ammem>
Online exhibitions available at the official site of the Library Congress include *African-American Odyssey*, a useful guide to those encountering black US history for the first time, and *The Frederick Douglass Papers*, a definitive collection of the speeches, writings and correspondences of the 'father' of the black auto-biography. The photographs used elsewhere in this book are taken from this web site's fascinating archive of 1930s New Deal photographs documenting black life in the rural south and the Chicago ghetto.

## The C. L. R. James Institute

<http://www.clrjamesinstitute.org/wright.html>
Still under development, this exciting web site, being dedicated to the legacy of the great Trinidadian intellectual C. L. R. James, naturally also offers interesting materials on Wright, James's great friend. Illuminating correspondence between the men is the highlight of this site, which features links to other Wright web sites that are of varying quality.

## Documenting the South

<http://docsouth.unc.edu/about>
Although it focuses primarily on materials dating from before 1900, the University of North Carolina's definitive archive Documenting the South is indispensable to those researching the social conditions of Wright's childhood.

It features unparalleled archives on such subjects as: the emergence of the black church in the American South, the literature of the South, American slave narratives and Civil War correspondence.

## The Hurston-Wright Foundation

<http://www.hurston-wright.org/home.html>
This link is of most use to those young, aspiring writers of African descent whom the foundation was established to assist. To those researching literature rather than writing it, however, the web site offers some useful links to sites devoted to exploring aspects of African-American literature.

## Richard Wright Papers, Yale University Library

<http://webtext.library.yale.edu/xml2html/beinecke.WRIGHT.nav.html>
The definitive catalogue of Richard Wright's œuvre as well as of his unpublished writings is held at Yale University Library. This web site is of greatest use to those planning a visit to the library, but also features some online summaries and original texts of interest to other researchers.

## Schomburg Center for Research into Black Culture

<http://www.nypl.org/research/sc/sc.html>
Long established as the leading scholarly resource for researchers into African-American literature and culture, the Schomburg Center's web site offers only a taste of the Harlem institution's activities. But it is a good taste, and one which is under continual expansion and development. Currently the Schomburg web site houses online exhibitions concerned with such pertinent topics as 'In Motion: The African-American Migration Experience', 'The African Presence in the Americas, 1492–1992' and 'Harlem 1900–1940: An African-American Community'.

## W. E. B. Du Bois Institute for African and African-American Research, Harvard University

<http://www.fas.harvard.edu/~du_bois>
This web site is, perhaps, of primary interest to postgraduates and other researchers: it is rich in interesting links, recent academic news and information for scholarships and other funding schemes. Of more general interest, however, is the fact that the web site also plays host to occasional online exhibitions on various aspects of African-American culture.

# Index

# Related titles from Routledge

## The Post-Colonial Studies Reader
## Second edition
Edited by Bill Ashcroft, Gareth Griffiths & Helen Tiffin

*The Post-Colonial Studies Reader* is the essential introduction to the most important texts in post-colonial theory and criticism. Updating and expanding the coverage of the highly successful first edition, this second edition now offers 121 extracts from key works in the field, arranged in clearly introduced sections on:

Issues and Debates, Universality and Difference, Representation and Resistance, Nationalism, Hybridity, Indigeneity, Ethnicity, Race, Feminism, Language, The Body and Performance, History, Place, Education, Production and Consumption, Diaspora, Globalization, Environment, The Sacred

Leading figures in the areas of post-colonial writing, theory and criticism are represented, as are critics who are as yet less well known. As in the first edition, the Reader ranges as widely as possible in order to reflect the remarkable diversity of work in the discipline and the vibrancy of anti-imperialist writing both within and without the metropolitan centres. Covering more debates, topics and critics than any comparable book in its field, *The Postcolonial Studies Reader* provides the ideal starting point for students and issues a potent challenge to the ways in which we think and write about literature and culture.

ISBN10: 0–415–34564–2 (hb)
ISBN10: 0–415–34565–0 (pb)

ISBN13: 978–0–415–34564–4 (hb)
ISBN13: 978–0–415–34565–1 (pb)

Available at all good bookshops
For ordering and further information please visit:
## www.routledge.com

# Related titles from Routledge

## THE NEW CRITICAL IDIOM

Series Editor: John Drakakis, University of Stirling

*The New Critical Idiom* is an invaluable series of introductory guides to today's critical terminology. Each book:

- provides a handy, explanatory guide to the use (and abuse) of the term
- offers an original and distinctive overview by a leading literary and cultural critic
- relates the term to the larger field of cultural representation

With a strong emphasis on clarity, lively debate and the widest possible breadth of examples, The New Critical Idiom is an indispensable approach to key topics in literary studies.

'The New Critical Idiom is a constant resource – essential reading for all students.' – *Tom Paulin, University of Oxford*

'Easily the most informative and wide-ranging series of its kind, so packed with bright ideas that it has become an indispensable resource for students of literature.' – *Terry Eagleton, University of Manchester*

**Available in this series:**

For further information on individual books in the series, visit:
www.routledge.com/literature/nci